VICTORIAN LIFE
AT THE CAPE 1870~1900

Catherine Knox

VICTORIAN LIFE
AT THE CAPE 1870~1900
ILLUSTRATIONS BY CORA COETZEE

FERNWOOD PRESS

FERNWOOD PRESS
PO BOX 15344
8018 VLAEBERG

REGISTRATION NO. 90/04463/07

FIRST PUBLISHED 1992
COPYRIGHT © TEXT CATHERINE KNOX 1992
COPYRIGHT © ILLUSTRATIONS CORA COETZEE 1992

EDITED BY: TESSA KENNEDY, CAPE TOWN
DESIGN BY: ABDUL AMIEN, CAPE TOWN
PRODUCTION CONTROLLER: ABDUL LATIEF (BUNNY) GALLIE
TYPESETTING BY DIATYPE SETTING CC, CAPE TOWN
REPRODUCTION BY UNIFOTO (PTY) LTD, CAPE TOWN
PRINTED AND BOUND BY TIEN WAH PRESS (PTE), SINGAPORE

ISBN 0-9583154-1-8

☐ A NOTE ON THE CURRENCY

British sterling was the legal currency of the Cape during the period under discussion. There were 12 pennies in a shilling and 20 shillings in a pound. A farthing was a quarter-penny, a florin was two shillings and a half-crown two shillings and sixpence. A guinea was one pound and one shilling.

In the book we have used an abbreviated style to denote sums of money, for example, for pounds, shillings and pence: £5/7/6; for shillings and pence: 5/8. When only shillings are involved we have spelt them out for the sake of clarity − five shillings is an example.

An exact conversion rate to the South African currency of the early 1990s would be tricky to compute, but a few random comparisons give some indication of the buying power of the pound in late Victorian Cape Town.

The medical superintendent of the New Somerset Hospital earned a salary of £300 a year with fringe benefits which included free lodging, generous rations and stabling for one horse; from July 1991 the chief medical superintendent of an important Cape hospital would be earning between R85 and R90 000 per annum. A comfortable double-storey villa in the Gardens cost £27 a month to rent in 1899; in 1992 it would be in the region of R2 500. A pair of luxurious sheets for a double bed cost £1/5/9 then; now about R300. A grand sewing machine cost £5 in the 1890s; more than R4 000 in the 1990s. A live-in housemaid was paid £1/10/- a month; a fair wage for an experienced live-in domestic worker today is in the region of R450. Beef cost sixpence a pound late last century, now the equivalent amount would cost about R7. An imported spider (small horse-drawn vehicle) and horse would have cost less than £100 late last century; equivalent transport, a very small locally made new car, costs in the region of R25 000 in 1992.

☐ A NOTE ON THE ILLUSTRATIONS

Historical photographs have been used as source material for all the illustrations, and where appropriate, the names of people shown in the photographs are mentioned. Because our intention has been to capture the flavour of late Victorian Cape Town, we have taken several liberties with precise dating. The illustrations, like the text, stray over the boundaries of our period − 1870 to 1900 − when it has served our expressionistic purpose to do so. For example, the Tivoli Theatre which is shown in the illustration on page 27 was only erected after the turn of the century, but it was very much in the mood of our period. Similarly, the University building in Queen Victoria Street (shown on page 153) was designed during the period under discussion but its erection was delayed until 1906.

The maps to be found in the pouch at the back of the book are facsimile reproductions. The Cape Town city map was originally published by W.A. Richards & Sons, Castle Street, Cape Town c. 1891. The map of Cape Town and the immediate environs is a detail from a map entitled 'Portion of Cape District' from the One Inch Series published by the Mapping Section, R.E.F.I.D. Cape Town, February 1902.

CONTENTS

MAPS:
Cape Town circa 1891
Cape Town and Immediate Environs circa 1902
(In the pouch at the back of the book)

PUBLISHER'S PREFACE

Sometimes great ideas for books spring fully-formed to the mind of a publisher or author, but more often than not they are conceived less dramatically, after much thinking and after a long time. *Victorian Life at the Cape* has proved to be just such a book; it is difficult now to pinpoint the moment of conception. Perhaps the seed of the idea was planted some 30 years ago when my father, the late Cornelis Struik, published *Life At The Cape A Hundred Years Ago . . . by a Lady.* The book was constructed around the friendly, informal and very personal 'letters from a lady' written to a friend and was a wonderful and fascinating insight into life in Cape Town in the mid nineteenth century. It was a resounding success and made an indelible impression on me in my early teenage years when my interest in publishing was just beginning to form.

It seems apt, therefore, that just as *Life At The Cape* was one of my father's first ventures into general publishing, so *Victorian Life at the Cape* (which could just as well have been entitled *Life At The Cape A Hundred Years Ago*) should be one of mine under my new and independent imprint of Fernwood Press. This book, too, presents an informal and highly personal view of Cape Town in the nineteenth century, but this time with the benefit of hindsight and the perceptive intellect of two ladies rather than one.

Another signpost in the journey towards the book was *Eikestad* which was published by Struik Publishers in 1976. In the course of producing that book, which also enjoyed considerable success, the illustrator Cora Coetzee and I became good friends and during the intervening years we have had many conversations about doing another book, similar in feel to *Eikestad*, but on Cape Town. The book had a warmth about it that was obviously the result of Cora's own deep feeling for the subject and it was that warmth that we were eager to recapture in a new venture.

It was some five years ago that the other major piece of the jigsaw fell into place as it was then that the writer, Catherine Knox, became involved in the project. She brought new ideas with her and gradually our discussions became focused as we settled on what we believe to be the perfect vehicle for what we, collectively, wanted to say and do. We had the generous help of numerous historical experts; they injected fresh, exciting perspectives and ensured us of authenticity and accuracy, but while their counsel undeniably helped to shape the book, we never deviated from our central idea of three people's love for their city and its history.

Pictures often tell a story louder and more clearly than words and this caused Catherine's role to become far broader as she was responsible for picture research, rooting out material to inspire Cora's brilliant reconstructions of those bygone times. The thrill of discovery – the perfect lithograph of the inside of the House of Assembly (page 89), a team of four women cyclists being 'driven' by a 'coachman' at a cycle gymkhana (page 163) – was always the spur and no new find was marginalised as too personal or too eccentric. On the contrary, none of us can resist quirky stories about people and in the long hours of dedication and sweat we discovered a shared sense of humour – a waggishness that belongs quite happily in the late nineteenth century. Thus for us, the picture of the top-hat-and-umbrella swimming race held in the dry dock (page 35) has its own very special historical significance and takes precedence over the familiar image of some established landmark.

Now that the book is going to print, its coming together (skilfully orchestrated by production controller Bunny Gallie) has to be seen as a labour of love rather than a calculated publishing exercise. *Victorian Life at the Cape* is a result of a lengthy and almost organic process that has engrossed three imaginations (and an enormous amount of time). Calligrapher Abdul Amien spent many hours painstakingly hand-lettering cover text and chapter headings as an extra design feature to ensure that the overall appearance of the book enhances the mood of words and illustrations. Publisher, writer, artist and designer have all been involved in creating this book far more completely than would make sense in the hard, commercial world of general publishing. This has been so different an exercise that it does not end for any of us with the publication of the book.

Pieter Struik

PIETER STRUIK

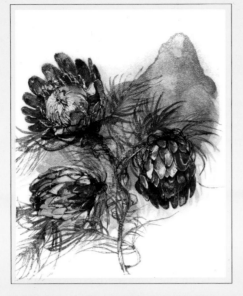

*C*ape Town, an unimposing city nestled in an extravagantly splendid natural amphitheatre of mountains and sea . . . Remotely situated near the furthest extremity of the African continent, it exerted a magnetic attraction on a spectrum of people from millionaires to missionaries, adventurers and black sheep, refugees from Europe's pogroms, families left homeless by war. For some, this was the gateway to the hinterland and its mineral wealth, for others the city seemed to offer fertile ground in which they could establish new roots. Yearning for a better life and spurred on by the prospect of earning a few extra shillings to send home, some walked to Cape Town from as far away as Mozambique. Some came as prisoners and exiles, but for most the Mother City was a beacon of hope promising a home, health and (with a little luck) wealth.

ACKNOWLEDGEMENTS

A work of this scope is made possible by the primary research of others. Every effort has been made to acknowledge these sources in the bibliography and notes and any omission is inadvertant and sincerely regretted; our appreciation is boundless.

For new thinking on the period as well as hitherto inaccessible information, a particular debt of gratitude is owed to the University of Cape Town's History Department for theses as well as papers published in the department's *Studies in the History of Cape Town*. Very special thanks are due to Dr Vivian Bickford-Smith who read an early draft of the manuscript and made helpful comments.

At the South African Library, librarian Arlene Fanaroff and Karel Schoeman of the photographic archives and their colleagues were tireless in their enthusiasm and help. Thanks, too, go the staff of the State Archives and the African Studies section of the University of Cape Town Library. Sport historian Paul Dobson lent his expert assistance as did Dr Dan Sleigh at the Cape Education Museum in Wynberg. Ulrich Fobian at the Cape of Good Hope Bank opened his company's archives to us. Barbara Clarke, Phillida Brooke Simons and Tessa Kennedy provided invaluable help and guidance with the shaping and checking of the manuscript.

CATHERINE KNOX

INTRODUCTION

As the twentieth century draws to a close, Cape Town, the Mother City, stands on the threshold of an uncertain future, where old mores and existing social structures are challenged by a new order. Exciting and frightening forces beckon the city's people and institutions into yet uncharted territory. But perhaps history does repeat itself: the situation on the Peninsula a hundred years ago was very much the same. Social and financial standards had been turned on their heads, the stink of violence lingered in the air, to be only partially dispelled by the heady bouquet of technological progress.

Victorian Life at the Cape is designed to recapture the ambient essence of life during this somewhat forgotten period from Cape Town's yesterdays. Our approach is personal and impressionistic rather than academic; our purpose to convey flavour and mood rather than every last exegetical fact. We have strayed back in time for irresistible details that enhance the contemporary scene and we have pre-empted one or two snippets from the first years of the twentieth century. But, to preserve the spell of immediacy cast by words and pictures, no direct references are made to Cape Town now.

It has been demonstrated that life speeds up and becomes more vivid at the turn of each century and from the perspective of the 1990s, the reader will inevitably find parallels with experience at the Cape a hundred years ago that are both nostalgic and enriching.

In the last decades of the nineteenth century life in the Mother City was just as full of surprises, novelty and challenges as it is today. The heterogeneous community was never more ebullient. In spite of a building boom, the eye and the imagination still had space to roam. Much of the Peninsula was still used as agricultural land, but that was changing rapidly.

Since the dawn of time, man's own history had been written into the landscape – cave paintings and stone tools left by the earliest residents; a star-shaped fort built by the first European colonisers; blockhouses and redoubts proclaiming the defensive will of Dutch, French and then British; a scattered ring of lighthouses passing a warning to mariners along the treacherous coastline; the excavations of miners; drift-sands created by fuel-gatherers; tracks and rails; roofs, walls and hedges; the spires of Christian churches; the series of sacred Muslim kramats protectively encircling

The main gateway to the Castle of Good Hope, a staunch reminder of the enduring past in the face of an uncertain future.

9

Rolling up Victoria Road, Clifton, with the peaks of the Twelve Apostles providing an awesome backdrop to the scene.

the community of Islam's faithful; and, later, the tower on the great synagogue near the old Company's Garden.

A hundred years ago the natural beauties of sea and mountains and the glorious climate helped to make up for what many people lacked materially. Sport was a communal obsession – even in the dingiest of alleys where paraffin-tin wickets fell with as resounding an effect as the willow poles at an international test. Cricket was a craze throughout the British Empire, and a new game developed from football had started to emerge from the so-called 'carrying codes' of British schools like Winchester and Rugby. By the end of the century, football, played with a round ball, was regarded as recreation for the proletariat – 'a gentleman's game played by ruffians' as one snob has described it. Rugby football, played with an oval ball, had become 'a ruffian's game played by gentlemen'. Tennis and golf were played with enthusiasm by the well heeled and athletic. Croquet continued to be a great social standby in genteel circles taking their leisure on manicured lawns rather than gravelly backstreets.

A gateway to the newly discovered mineral wealth of the interior, Cape Town emerged from relative obscurity to become one of the most interesting ports of call in the world. History was in the making at a breathtaking pace: along with the community's political, commercial and industrial coming of age, each day seemed to present something new – motor cars, telephones, electricity, flying machines.

Between 1870 and 1900 the charm, grace and eccentricity of Victorian style coloured life at the Cape but at the same time social, political and technological innovations added pace, excitement and risk to the everyday scene. Lifestyles bore witness to the new *laissez faire* attitude of society. Cape premier and Rand millionaire Cecil Rhodes was photographed in a sloppy bushwhacker's hat playing chess on board ship with an officer who had no shoes on. The owner of the White House Hotel near Mrs Koopmans-De Wet's House in Strand Street kept a young hippo in a menagerie in his courtyard. Rich and reclusive Michiel Hiddingh periodically lashed out with dinner parties so excessive each guest would be presented with an entire roast capon – as just one of the courses.

The new riches of the mineral revolution affected every aspect of life: speculation was rife and fortunes were made and lost again overnight. The wealth of Cape Town was mercantile rather than mineral but 'windfall' fortunes that could be won on the stock exchange by apparent chance caused a shift in values. The old rule of prosperity through sobriety, thrift and hard work was cast in the shade by the excitement of wild ventures and instant wealth. The men of principal seemed dull in comparison with the men of expedience.

Responsible government came into being greatly reinforcing a sense of

English visitors, Lady Edward Cecil and
Lady Charles Bentinck, in the gardens of Cecil Rhodes'
Groote Schuur Estate.

local identity and destiny among the dominant class. It also provided those men of expedience with an extra tool for the manipulation of history and fortune to their advantage. The Cape as the seat of colonial government thus drew the new magnates who made their millions upcountry. Social

The hansom cab was the ubiquitous form of transport for Capetonians who could afford to move one step up from shank's pony.

Darwinism was a fashionable subject of discourse and contributed to the entrenchment of racial prejudice even in otherwise 'freethinkers' like the writer Olive Schreiner. Political awareness was astir amongst other classes too. The Coloured People's Association was formed in 1892 and the African Political Organisation in 1902. These movements emerged organically from 'coloured' social organisations like church, benevolent and sports clubs.

Modern transport and communications roused the Cape from its slumbering isolation bringing the promises of the hinterland and the big businesses of the British Empire much closer. The harbour was transformed from a hazardous roadstead into a commercial facility, though there was never quite enough moorage for the busy traffic in intercontinental steamers and local coasters. A hundred labourers and two hundred convicts were retained at the harbour for maintenance and stevedoring work.

The railway network joined first the once-remote villages of the Peninsula with the city and then the rest of South Africa and eventually Rhodesia (Zimbabwe). Between 1873 and 1883 more than 1 000 miles of railway and 7 000 miles of telegraph were constructed.

The city's streets, already thronged with pedestrians, mule- and ox-drawn wagons and carts, cabs and carriages, saw the advent of horse-drawn omnibuses, electric trams, cumbersome steam traction engines and then the revolutionary motor carriage.

Telegraph links with Europe and the hinterland were introduced. The telephone was quickly put into use at the harbour and by more progressive businesses, but by the end of the century had not really caught on as a domestic and social convenience. Electronic communication radically changed the world view of the average Capetonian; newspapers carried instantaneous reports of events from all over the Empire and immediacy rapidly overtook any aspirations to literary qualities that some of these journals may have cherished.

Health care and nursing services lurched from medieval practices into the twentieth century but uncontrollable epidemics of smallpox, cholera, tuberculosis and (at the turn of the century) bubonic plague threatened to decimate the citizenry very much as Aids does now.

Education became more freely available – infant schools proliferated for poverty-stricken youngsters, Canon Lightfoot ran night schools for adults, Professor Langham Dale brought in the exam system and proper training for teachers, Professor Daniel Hahn successfully integrated young women into his classes for university degrees at the South African College.

The city's skyline altered dramatically as the value of land in the central business district soared and the new barons of commerce strove to outdo one another with the scale and grandness of their business premises. The introduction of steel-frames and reinforced concrete meant that taller and taller buildings became feasible. Electric, gas or hand-driven elevators carried people up higher than the five floors that were regarded as the limit for an average man to ascend by stair. Corrugated iron became *the* roofing material, ideal for the violent weather conditions and temperature changes of the colony.

Electric lighting slowly but steadily replaced gas. Street lighting was slow in coming, but in business premises, places of entertainment and the houses of the wealthy, electric lights meant an extension of the hours in the day and a reduction of the fire hazard that had caused so much destruction in the era of gas and oil lamps.

The abolition of slavery in the Cape in 1834 had appeared to signal a new life for the working class, but little further progress was made until the 1880s and 1890s. Now, increased political awareness whispered the hope of a better future through the prison where convict labour was housed and the slum tenement where the 'free' citizen eked out a wretched existence. Workers held protest meetings on the Grand Parade and struck in the harbour works for better conditions.

Along with the labourers imported from Europe and 'upcountry', came refugees like those from the pogroms and a flood of 'freelance' immigrants each with his or her dream of finding a personal Eldorado. Many of these never got any further than Cape Town, which meant that there was a chronic shortage of housing for the poor. In 1875 a conservative estimate put the population of the municipality of Cape Town at 33 000 souls and there were a mere 4 000 houses, many of them consisting of three rooms or less. The entire population of Cape Town at that date was set at 45 000, Muslims accounting for a large portion of the black community.

Many speculative builders made a quick fortune by whipping up economic housing in 'lower class' suburbs. Architects and the more ambitious contractors devoted their energies to the more profitable business of creating splendid villas and mansions for the rich on verdant suburban estates. This phenomenon was given added impetus by the mining millionaires from the north: every 'Randlord' simply had to have his own Cape palace. The old Cape Dutch farmsteads suddenly acquired new cachet and found themselves in demand again. Groot Constantia was one that just missed the boom and had it fallen under the auctioneer's hammer a few years later, it would most probably have been renovated as a status symbol rather than inspanned as a government experimental station.

For the privileged classes, travel was highly fashionable. South Africa's new millionaires were fêted wherever they went and everyone who was Anyone in the 'civilised' world made his or her way to the Cape at some time or another.

Very much members of the wider community of Empire, rich Cape residents indulged in the Victorian pleasures of globe-trotting too. Henry Arderne, who had been given a good start in life by his diligent and thrifty father, Ralph, shared his father's passion for gardening and travelled widely in search of new botanic specimens to add to the collection at the family estate, The Hill, in Claremont. By stagecoach and on horseback, he travelled to the Niagara Falls then on to Yosemite where fields of white azaleas had him nearly swooning with ecstasy. He climbed to the peak of Mount Washington in the White Mountains. In trains, coaches, rickshaws, hammocks and sedan chairs, he toured Japan, China, Hong Kong, Malaya, Ceylon and India. He combed Europe and Scandinavia and the highlight of his Russian trip was a close encounter with a South African strelitzia in the mile-long glasshouses on Apothecary's Island.

The outbreak of the Anglo-Boer War only served to heighten the attractions of the Cape as a modish destination. For some, the war was a diversion, 'history in the making', to be viewed from an elegant *chaise longue* on the Mount Nelson Hotel terrace. For others, it was a bloody ritual of passage, the ending of an era.

Modest residences in Dorp Street where less privileged Capetonians eked out an existence.

13

Profile of the Peninsula

Gateway to a new Eldorado, the Cape of the last three decades of the nineteenth century enjoyed a very special status in the British Empire. In early times, the Cape was at worst a hazard, at best an inconvenience – the extremity of a continent bothersomely placed in the way of maritime traffic to the East. But where once it had barred the route to the riches of India and China, from 1870 the Cape was the open sesame to southern Africa's treasure chest of minerals.

Down the centuries, the legend of Prester John – a Christian king who was said to have amassed and hidden a fabulous treasure in Africa – had fired the imagination of many a fortune-seeker. But as one after another failed to penetrate far enough into the interior to discover the cache, the story lost some of its lustre. Then the discovery of diamonds and gold vindicated the passions that had driven those old adventurers, so that by 1870, the once impoverished outpost called the Cape of Good Hope was at last living up to its name, poised on the threshold of transformation into a jewel in Britannia's financial and strategic crown.

But the passage of Cape Town through the last three decades of the century was a stormy one. Euphoric years of boom and prosperity were followed by shattering depression and terrible epidemics of fever. Fortunes were made by some and lost by others and throughout the period the threat – and sometimes the actuality – of war hung over the colonies of the Cape and Natal. When the worst fears were realised with the outbreak of the second Anglo-Boer War in 1899 the Mother City was filled with refugees, with troops and, later, with prisoners. However, by then the euphoria and the agony had forced the community into a new maturity: economically and politically the Cape came of age. Responsible government was introduced in 1872. The first phase of a commercial harbour system, begun in the previous decade, was put into use. Road, rail and telegraphic communications improved steadily.

In some of the darker days many would have agreed with the war correspondent G.W. Steevens who said he did not think the city's presiding mountain looked like a table. To him it resembled a coffin. To others it might well have symbolised the Pandora's Box of Africa with its wonderful temptations and terrible dangers.

The view of the massif from the Bay was known to many westerners long before the area was explored by their countrymen. Table Mountain, one of the most famous maritime landmarks on the globe, facing north-north-west and ending the range that begins at Cape Point many miles distant, could be spied from a good way off on clear days – but often with its threatening 'tablecloth' of cloud. The northern edge of the Roaring Forties blew many an ancient mariner clear round this beautiful but hazardous promontory.

Bartolomeu Dias was swept past in a storm in 1488, and it was not until his return journey that he was able to land and plant a *padrão* at the point he aptly named *Cabo Tormentoso*. Vasco da Gama saw the Cape on 18 November 1497 before a gale drove his ships out to sea. Some expeditions (like the French one of 1529) were compelled by the foul weather at the Cape to abandon their plans and turn tail for home.

Above *A Cape cart with the new safety step.*
Right *A Milnerton drover views Table Mountain, affectionately known as the Grand Old Man, or G.O.M.*

Sir Francis Drake, who successfully completed the second circumnavigation of the globe, did not stop at the Cape but saw it on 15 June 1580 and wrote: 'This cape is the most stately thing, and the fairest cape we saw in the whole circumference of the earth . . ' But it was not until 1652 that the Dutch, a major world power at the time, sent a minor official called Johan van Riebeeck to the Cape with instructions to set up a victualling station and halfway house to their Eastern possessions. He was to grow vegetables, arrange easy access to fresh water and meat for passing ships and build a rudimentary fort for the protection of his men and of any sick mariners who might be put ashore in his care.

By the late 1800s, the jetties he had constructed at the ends of what were later Plein and Buitenkant streets had been replaced by larger, more

*The Roman Rock Lighthouse in Simon's Bay saved
many a mariner from going down to Davy Jones's locker.*

sophisticated ones. His old turf fort lay long-forgotten under the hard-trodden surface of the Grand Parade and his modest redoubt, Duijnhoop, near the Salt River mouth, had long been superseded by the more imposing Craig's Battery. Heaven knows what late Victorian Capetonians would have made of these primitive structures – as it was, they regarded the stone Castle of Good Hope (initiated by Van Riebeeck's successor) as enough of a quaint, anachronistic oddity.

But the Castle stood staunch as a reminder of the past – as did the old Supreme Court building near the bottom gate of the Avenue, and with them some of the old manors, most notably the Koopmans-De Wet House in Strand Street. This was no mean feat in a community intent on rushing headlong into the future.

The built-up environment of the city told the story of the lives lived there and of progress and its ravages. At the dark end of the spectrum were the prisons – the great block of the Breakwater Gaol on its eminence above the

harbour works and the Roeland Street Gaol, slightly out of town on the lower slopes of the mountain. The military hospital near the shoreline at Woodstock and the Somerset Hospital had been all but dwarfed by the crenellated bastion of the New Somerset Hospital facing out to sea almost directly above the breakwater that had been the first stage in the harbour works.

The trade in commodities had marked the landscape most importantly with the harbour, its heavy stone-faced warehouses, time ball tower and clock tower, and the basins and dry dock. Spreading back from here were the other buildings to do with maritime traffic: the Harbour Board offices at the foot of Adderley Street, the warehouses of chandlers and forwarding agents in lower St George's Street. And, huddling in their shadows, a labyrinth of wretched wooden shacks where dock workers and sailors on shore leave caroused on long summer evenings.

The growing importance of inland transport and trade was symbolised by the way the new goods railway line cut across the bottom of Adderley Street, seeming to separate the city from her shoreline. The imposing new railways terminal with a grand curved iron-girdered roof over the platforms dominated the lower end of the city.

The open spaces of the Grand Parade Ground and the Company's Garden had been reduced but were still major landmarks. Probably most dominant of all the mid-town buildings were the military barracks — a huge complex of buildings whose lengthy, unornamented frontages compared starkly with smaller, prettier civilian quarters.

Up until the last years of the century, the eternal in the form of churches and mosques had held sway over the temporal in the city centre. But by the turn of the century the pinnacles and spires atop commercial palaces had all but cast the city's ecclesiastical centres in the shade. The Lutheran Church in Strand Street and the Groote Kerk at the top of Adderley Street claimed seniority over other Christian buildings. They, with the spire of St George's Cathedral at the top of St George's Street and the Gothic splendours of St Mary's Roman Catholic Cathedral, had been the city's most impressive landmarks until Mansion House reared its colossal headpiece of cast-iron lacework into the sky in open competition with the grand Stuttafords building opposite. The Standard Bank represented the mighty interests of banking and the renaissance palace of a new General Post Office proclaimed the sovereignty of the Civil Service. Behind it, the Opera House and the Tivoli Theatre spoke of an increasing appetite for entertainment, in counterpoint to the heavy, multistoreyed, steel-framed warehouse of J. W. Jagger, man of property.

In spite of great activity on the part of Cape Town's builders and developers, the tracery of the settlement's overlaid chapters of history could still be made out by anyone with a few moments for quiet contemplation.

Connie Beard and her brother Bert with a harvest of amaryllis gathered at Miller's Point.

When darkness fell, the Cape was ringed with tiny watchful pinpoints of light from a series of lighthouses. The fixed light near the landing place on Robben Island marked the northerly limits of the entrance to Table Bay. This was where Van Riebeeck had his lookout light a fire to guide shipping 'safely between the Lion Mountain and the island, avoiding whale rock'. Robben Island, the extreme seaward limit of Table Bay, lies about five miles west of north of Green Point. Two other lights marked the southerly limit of the entrance: one fixed at Mouille Point and a flashing light at Green Point warning mariners of the hazards of coming too close to the rocky shores. Mouille Point was named after the mole Governor Swellengrebel had vainly tried to construct there in 1743 as a breakwater.

Tiny house lights twinkled around the coast as far as Sea Point but from there on the coast was dark, unless there was a bright lamp at the window of the lonely old gabled farmhouse at Oude Kraal. The canny navigator kept well clear of the shore right down to the jagged spine of Cape Point where another lighthouse flashed a warning. The first was erected in 1860 on the more southerly of the two peaks of Cape Point but, alas, it was situated so high it was often shrouded in fog. Two miles south of Cape Point rises the sharp pinnacle of Bellows Rock. It protrudes about five feet at low water but is submerged at high tide and the waves that break on it cannot be seen at night or during a storm. Having cleared this hazard, the navigator would cautiously nose his vessel in a north-easterly curve. Anvil Rock, only charted once a number of ships had fallen foul of it, is one and a quarter miles south-east of Cape Point. Whittle Rock, another hidden hazard, was marked by fixed beacons at Buffels Bay. One last warning from the lighthouse on Roman Rock was to be heeded before one reached the safe winter anchorage of Simon's Bay, named in honour of Governor Simon van der Stel who first inspected it in 1687.

By the 1890s Simon's Town was linked to the city of Cape Town by road, rail, telephone and telegraph, but it would still have been possible to send a message to the Castle walls by semaphore via the same chain of vantage points used by the Dutch to signal the arrival of nine British ships under Rear-Admiral Elphinstone on 11 June 1795. The flagmen relayed a warning from Simon's Bay to Vlagge Hoek and thence to Muizenberg corner, Wynberg Hill and the Castle.

When Major-General Craig and his columns marched on Cape Town, they were anxious to maintain the illusion that this was not an invasion, so they heeded the protocol of the old French line of defence which had been set up in 1781 when England declared war on the Netherlands and the Dutch entered into an alliance with France. The fortified line stretched from Fort Knokke (which lay between the Castle and Salt River) to halfway up Devil's Peak. New batteries were erected between Fort Knokke and Salt River and another was built at Mouille Point. After the French left in 1784, the Dutch built the Amsterdam Battery (completed in 1787), making the anchorage a tricky target for enemy raiders. Thus the wily British chose to put ashore at Simon's Bay and, having entered Cape Town through the back door, prevailed through negotiation.

Once the English flag had been hoisted at the Castle, General Craig set about reinforcing his own line of defences, the remains of which were still very much part of the local landscape in the latter decades of the nineteenth century. Old and new fortifications created the contemporary military map of the area. Fort Wynyard was established in 1862 between the Mouille Point lighthouse and the site of that grand bastion, the New Somerset Hospital. The Chavonnes Battery eventually disappeared under the new harbour works. The Amsterdam Battery lay between the docks and the north wharf; then there was the Castle itself, and Fort Knokke, just beyond the military hospital. Craig's Tower with its impressive artillery guns stood hard by on the beach virtually at the mouth of the Salt River. This was near the site from which, in 1773, Wolraad Woltemade had ridden out through the surf to rescue seamen on the stricken *Jonge Thomas*. On his eighth trip, when his horse was tiring and panic finally overcame the men aboard, six souls jumped for the succour he offered, pulling themselves, the hero and his horse down to a watery grave.

Further testament to troubled times, an old redoubt still stood in Trafalgar Park, Woodstock, and a second just below the Main Road where the toll gate was once in operation. High on the flanks of Devil's Peak the King's Blockhouse kept guard, with two smaller blockhouses strategically placed to give maximum visibility of the sea approach to Table Bay.

Craig had raised a fourth blockhouse on Kloof Nek and, by the latter decades of the nineteenth century, this was used as a convict station. The inmates were 'inspanned' as labourers for road building and for the extensive replanting of the mountain slopes with shrubs and trees.

Serious concern was felt about the conservation of vegetation on the ancient pile. Gone forever were the days when Lion's Head was so thickly grown with silver trees, it seemed to shimmer like a white flame in the heat of afternoon. For centuries, slaves in search of firewood had created hundreds of crisscrossing paths over the mountain, some dangerously exposed, but runaway fires had done more damage than these foragers.

Table Mountain, 3 500 feet high with a flat top almost two miles long, was a magnificent work of nature very much to late Victorian taste. Its grandeur and scale — work of the Great Architect at his mightiest — served as a constant reminder of Higher Things to which it was every man's duty to strive. The flanking peaks, Lion's Head and Devil's Peak (or Windberg as it was once known), were both acknowledged as splendid natural phenomena in their own right, but completely outclassed by the 'Grand Old Man', or 'G.O.M.', as Victorian Cape Town affectionately dubbed its mountain.

An ascent of Table Mountain by one of the easier routes (Platteklip Gorge being the most favoured) was considered an essential experience for visitors and residents alike. It was, alas, popular with society's outcasts too. Countless dark and secret krantzes had always provided safe bolt holes for runaway slaves and desperadoes, one of the longest stays being made by Joshua Penny in 1799. He was an American who had been press-ganged into service on the *Sceptre*. He feigned sick, escaped *en route* to hospital and survived on the mountain for 14 months.

The northerly aspects of the Mountain were never as verdant as the more sheltered sides and around the spur of Devil's Peak, above Mowbray, the growth became much thicker. Groves of fir trees and oaks swept down like leafy skirts as far as the railway line which followed the course of the Liesbeek River until Newlands Station and then veered south towards Muizenberg.

Village life tended to cluster closer to the line. West of it, on the mountainside, a hovering bird might make out the roofs, gables and whitewashed walls of grand manors buried in the sylvan glories of their estates: Welgelegen, Groote Schuur and Westbrooke, Newlands House, the Grove, Stellenberg, the old Boschheuwel (renamed Protea by Sir Lowry Cole and Bishopscourt by Bishop Gray), Groot Constantia and the vinelands, then back to the trees with the quaint old Tokai Manor House and its exotic arboretum.

Large ponds on Rondebosch Common and near the Newlands cricket grounds reflected the sky like placid mirrors and further down Muizenberg way, brackish vleis gave sanctuary to flamingoes, pelicans and cormorants. In the rainy season, the rivers that meandered towards the Salt River mouth often overflowed their banks, until it seemed that the Valkenburg homestead with the lunatic asylum, Porter Reformatory and the nearby Royal Observatory were adrift on an island between the Liesbeek and Black rivers. In the spring, seas of arum lilies covered the wetlands in entrancing beauty. These extravagant floral displays were favourite subjects for postcards and, later, for scrapbook snapshots.

To the east of the marshy lowlands lay territory that had once been more difficult to cross than the sea. Before nineteenth century road- and rail-building skills had conquered them, acres of drifting sands had ruled the way between Cape Town and the easterly settlements. A desert interspersed by brackish bogs had formed when natural vegetation had been stripped from the flats to fuel early limekilns. In the nineteenth century a variety of solutions to the problem had been mooted. One suggestion had been to deposit refuse on the treacherous dunes and thus hold them down, but wind played havoc with the scheme. The more complicated and ultimately more effective way had been to settle farmers on the wastes. They were equipped with bags of Port Jackson Willow seeds imported from Australia. But maps of the latter part of the century are still smudged with vast

areas running for the most part from north to south marked simply 'Drift Sands'. The Cape Hunt in pursuit of a jackal might race through this wilderness but otherwise few members of polite society would be familiar with it. Certainly no visitors – not even those with a penchant for rural seclusion – would venture here.

And there was no shortage of visitors. Apart from the busy trafficking between South Africa, Europe and the rest of the Empire of those on colonial or military business, the Cape attracted an extraordinary number of private travellers. In the second half of the century, a stay at the Cape was almost as essential a part of a gentleman's experience as the Grand Tour of Europe. Baron Ferdinand de Rothschild, who made a reconnaissance of the territories south of the Limpopo in 1894, wrote in his diary:

❝South Africa had long haunted my dreams, my friendship with some of the "adventurers" of our era, the explorers of unknown realms and founders of a vast Empire, their accounts of the diamond mines of Kimberley and the gold mines of Johannesburg, the prospect of seeing a new country, a new people, a new flora and fauna, no less than the general interest, both political and financial, created by the expansion of the Cape Colony, worked so long on my mind, that I resolved to pay it a visit, and I accordingly booked my passage on the *Dunottar Castle*.❞

Many shared his conviction that history was in the making here and were determined to secure grandstand seats. A few sought the healthy climate but the majority were lured by the promise of wealth.

Looking back towards Green Point from Sea Point over an expanse of sunny beaches and salubrious sea air.

THE CITY CENTRE

'If you are absent for even half a decade you will find Cape Town changed almost beyond recognition. Adderley Street, St George's Street and Strand Street, not to mention less important thoroughfares have been so altered and improved by the erection of imposing-looking buildings and by the removal of the hideous stoeps that were once an obstruction and an eyesore,' commented the 1897 *Cape Town Guide*, clearly in favour of the modernising spirit of up-to-dateness that had fired the Peninsula for three decades.

Even the blissful torpor of those who preferred to doze down Wynberg way behind hedges of dog rose and the indigenous blue plumbago felt the ripples of progress that money brought — it was vain to pine for the days when there were 'no telegrams, no railways, no steamboats ... when the Standard Bank was not, the Commercial Exchange was not, the railway and its electric-lighted station was not, nor did that "jewel in a swine's snout", the Cape Town docks exist ... no weekly mails, no cablegrams, no hurry and scurry of modern commercial express-speed business'. Those days were gone for ever. In fact, there was hardly time even for nostalgia in the new Cape Town.

But let man do what he might, the sea in front and the Mountain behind dominated the bustling metropolis and gave it a special character. However diligently Cape builders tried to raise their works high enough to obstruct the view, one was seldom more than a block away from sight of the sea with its inevitable population of ships riding at anchor under empty rigging, or of the mighty sandstone crags of Table Mountain.

As the century proceeded, less of the traffic in the city streets was directly concerned with the harbour and more with the day-to-day business of commercial life in the colony. Powerful sooty locomotives ferried heavy cargoes out to the hinterland and back to the Mother City. The great white puffs of steam from the Sea Point-bound trains which passed along the shoreline below Garlicks' department store were a feature of everyday life from 1892. In the heart of town a startling variety of horse- and ox-drawn conveyances carried people, goods and produce from point of sale to customer to office to warehouse. Hurrying pedestrians darted in and out

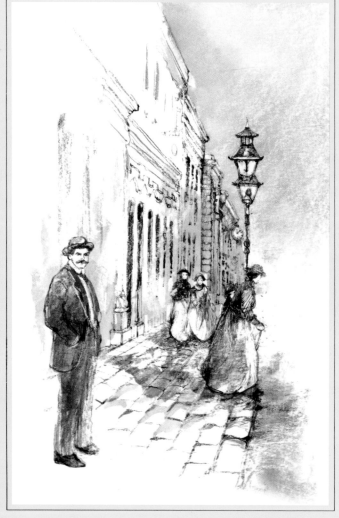

Left *Street lights and cobbled pavements were all too slow in coming to the city.*
Right *Ships riding at anchor on the bright sea at the foot of Adderley Street continually beckoned to the wide world beyond Cape Town's modest limits.*

of the mêlée of cabs, wagons, cycles and carts, and, later, the odd juggernaut of a traction engine. As the condition of the pavements was far from uniform, it was often wiser to make one's way on foot along the street. Accidents occurred all too often, particularly when the Cape Doctor whipped up such a choking and impenetrable cloud of dust that neither pedestrian nor driver could see more than a foot before him.

The tempo of life speeded up and the city's population doubled and redoubled, putting increasing pressure on outmoded facilities and conveniences. An impatient community insisted on a new and efficient urban mechanism … immediately. The water supply could not keep up with demand: most Capetonians had to get their own water from public pumps and summer shortages and rationing were chronic. They even ran out of ice at the City Club during the dog days of February.

In the rainy season an excess of water was the problem. The canalisation of various streams that tumbled off Table Mountain during the wet months had to be upgraded: it was unthinkable that the burgeoning business centre should still be subject to winter flooding. The roads, hopelessly behind the times, were reduced in winter to dangerous quagmires. In 1878 a girl attempting to cross Longmarket Street had bogged down, waist-deep in clinging mud, and had to be rescued by a couple of men. Heavy vehicles exacerbated the situation (often bogging down too) which was one of several good reasons for preventing large wagons from coming through the centre of town. An adequate supply of electricity for rate-paying businesses and for street lighting had to be provided. The days were numbered for the once familiar sight of a man with a ladder solemnly plodding from gaslight to gaslight, lighting each for the night and returning to extinguish them in the morning.

Public transport had improved by leaps and bounds. By the turn of the century the electric tram ran to all parts of the suburbs and the line of railway to Sea Point proved immensely popular. In spite of fears to the contrary, there was still plenty of custom for livery stables (where horses and a variety of wheeled conveyances were to be hired) and the city's huge population of cabbies. Cabs were registered and cab fares had been standardised. In 1897, for example, a cab cost half a crown for the first hour regardless of the number of passengers, and a florin for each additional hour. The charge for two passengers over a distance of half a mile was sixpence. The fare from the cab stand at Cape Town Station to the New Somerset Hospital was 1/6. These fares were not inconsiderable when one considers that a teacher, for example, could expect to earn £50 a year in the late 1890s. There were cab stands at the station, at the corners of Bree and Waterkant streets, on Stal Plein and on the corner of Wale and Long streets.

The most visible of the 'small' business people were the cabbies, pedlars and flower sellers who brightened Adderley Street with their huge bunches of proteas, heaths, arum lilies and the blue disas and painted ladies that grew in profusion in Platteklip Gorge. The bigger fish in the commercial sea made themselves visible by their increasingly grand premises.

Structurally, the city was undergoing a series of rapid transformations – only temporarily slowed down by intermittent periods of economic depression. One by one the old residential houses that had once been a feature of Adderley Street were converted to business premises or demolished to make way for new buildings. One after another city firms displayed their affluence by erecting extensive new buildings of great architectural value and sometimes as many as five or six storeys high – irrefutable evidence of the competition for trade and the increase in the value of land in the city centre.

As architectural commentator A.G. Howard noted at the turn of the century:

> ❝If street architecture progressed slowly during the first two decades [1870-1890], it moved fast enough during this the third one, and especially was this the case during its latter half. The conditions prevailing were most favourable to the evolution of a superior order of building and architects during this decade had chances they never had before. People had been educated to appreciate the beauties of the 'Fine Art' aspect of Architecture. The employment of steel framing also helped, as an architect could obtain greater architectural effects at less cost when he had not to take into consideration the necessity for thick walls to support the upper floors …
>
> 'As, when one looks at a landscape, he sees the distance, middle distance and foreground distinctly separated; so it is with the street architecture of Cape Town today; one can see the distant past, the middle distant past, and the foreground of the present, each quite distinct and recognisable. As we pass through a thoroughfare like Long Street, bristling with architecture of modern times, we can see down the vistas of the side streets, remnants of bygone days, even the time when the Dutch and not the English were masters of the Cape … Some of the old people still remain, but, like the buildings of other days, hiding in back streets, they have retired from public to private life; others still shine in the front ranks, even as some of the old buildings still adorn the front streets.❞

The old Supreme Court building at the top of Adderley Street was one of the most venerable of these enduring old structures. This was originally built as a lodge for the slaves employed in the Company's Garden. In the mid-eighteenth century a second storey was added and, towards the turn of the century, the architect Thibault designed an impressive new frontage with a curved entrance foyer and a grand double staircase sweeping up to the first floor.

After the liberation of slaves, the building was converted, again by Thibault, to serve as government offices. He added a pediment to the Parliament Street end of the building. This was embellished with a parody of the British royal coat of arms: the unicorn is looking perplexedly at the lion who has dozed off. The old slave quarters were converted into judges' chambers and the rear section housed a fine Assembly Room. A courtroom was the last addition. The building was known as the Supreme Court for the remainder of the century.

For a year or two in the early 1870s Cape Town was without a single architect. Then a young man named Charles Freeman who had been working for the Public Works department in Natal, moved to the equivalent office in Cape Town. In his own time, he prepared drawings for the Houses of Parliament which had been in discussion since 1860. Various sites had been suggested including the paddock halfway up the Avenue, Caledon Square, Greenmarket Square and a site facing the Grand Parade on the Adderley Street side of the Drill Hall. By 1874, the existing site had been settled on, plans drawn by the Colonial Engineer had been shelved and a competition was announced. Freeman entered under a pseudonym and his design won.

A spectacular Masonic ceremony for the laying of the foundation stone was held in 1875 but shortly after the construction work began it was discovered that deeper foundation were necessary and that draining the ground was essential. The budget of £50 000 would only cover an estimated half of the real costs. Freeman was accused of miscalculation (although the Public Works Department had ratified his estimates) and of plagiarism. The latter accusation was absurd because he had merely worked from standard late Victorian set books, as all colonial architects were expected to do, combining details and elements into a pleasing whole. By 1876 Freeman was out on the street, as it were, and a young man named Greaves had been imported as clerk of works for the building of a watered-down version of Freeman's rather splendid plan. In 1884, the building was finally ready for use. It cost a total of £220 000.

Freeman had quickly found his feet again and within a few years was one of the Cape's busiest architects. Almost more influential on the city's skyline were his imports of ready-made iron mouldings for the 'enrichment' of existing and new buildings. These were ordered by customers from catalogues and included finials, lace-work for roof ridges and veranda eaves, slim pillars and curly brackets, decorative features like urns and eagles. Pre-fabricated units could be combined to make entire verandas and balconies, bandstands, follies and conservatories.

Riebeeck Square, as the old Hottentotsplein had been renamed, was always a well-patronised outspan place.

Capetonians, like other colonials throughout the Empire, fell completely under the spell of these easy-to-apply features and hardly a building of the name escaped some kind of application. Even the dignified old rectory attached to the Lutheran Church in Strand Street was updated with a decorative wrought-iron veranda and balcony.

Mansion House, the new premises of J.D. Cartwright on the corner of Adderley and Darling streets, was among the most impressive of all the new iron-lace and concrete buildings. The *Cape Argus Weekly Supplement* of 3 February 1897 gave its readers a preview: The company's existing shops and stores on the site were to be demolished in stages as the new building took shape so as to disrupt business as little as possible.

The building was divided into two sections, according to the writer, one with Darling and Adderley Street frontages and occupied by Cartwrights. A two-storeyed veranda balcony 10 feet wide sheltered the two street fronts from rain and sun and the new structure boasted a basement of nearly 8 000 square feet particularly suited to cool storage. The ground floor was given over to handsomely fitted shops; the second floor was also one large showroom and the remaining storeys above this area were used as warehousing.

A grand staircase and an electric passenger lift gave access to the upper showrooms and a separate goods entrance and goods lift serviced every floor. As Cape Town's plumbing had been somewhat archaic up until now, much was made of the sophisticated lavatories included in the plans for this modernistic edifice. There were well-appointed conveniences for lady shoppers on a special mezzanine floor and, as the writer noted with interest, separate lavatories for the workers on the warehouse floors.

The second section of the new building was known as Mansion House Chambers. The upper floors were divided into 60 well-lit offices of various sizes, arranged either in suites or singly according to requirements. The office entrance took the form of an elegant arcade, paved with tiles and mosaic, which led into a large hall with a staircase and another of the new electric passenger lifts. The prime offices faced Adderley Street and had bay windows leading on to balconies or balconettes. More modest premises faced into a central courtyard lined with white glazed bricks. Ladies' and gentlemen's lavatories were provided on the fifth floor; they were tiled and furnished throughout in the best possible manner.

Well-lit shop premises were offered on the ground floor below the chambers, each with a frontage either on Adderley Street or along the central arcade.

'The façades,' wrote the *Cape Argus*, 'are designed in the Free Renaissance style, the three lower storeys forming a base supporting bold Ionic pilasters, crowned with a massive cornice and enriched pediments and

Cecil Rhodes presented a handsome bronze statue of Jan van Riebeeck to the city before the Jameson Raid soured his relationship with the Afrikaner Bond.

gables. An octagonal domed turret, 16 feet in diameter and 144 feet in height from the pavement to the top of the flagstaff, supported on eight Ionic columns and an inner drum of red brickwork pierced with eight windows forms a striking feature in the design and gives an air of importance to the whole structure. Imported red facing bricks will be used above the second floor and the whole of the dressings and the ornaments will be executed in Portland cement. Electric light will be installed throughout.'

More weighty and, appropriately, more serious in mien than the Mansion House was the Standard Bank building on the next corner. Opposite this, opulent premises designed by Freeman to house the department store of Thorne, Stuttaford & Co. issued a compelling invitation to the shopper. From the opposite side of the street, the eye was irresistibly drawn to the massive iron tracery spelling out the name of the company against the sky. From the pavement in front of the shop, 'impressive glass-panelled doors led through to the delights of the shop within. The tea-room on the first floor had french windows of stained glass leading out onto a veranda of elaborate iron-work'.

With ambitious and profitable commercial buildings of this magnitude making an appearance, no old structure, however antique or historically valuable, was entirely safe from the demolisher's hammer if it happened to be situated in the centre of town or to occupy a prime business site. There was even talk of removing the Castle and using its site as an additional parade ground. Serious consideration was given to a suggestion that Government House be knocked down to make way for a new Supreme Court.

In 1892 the Commercial Exchange Building, another prominent landmark between Adderley Street and the Parade, fell before the march of progress. For 71 years the Exchange had contained the city's largest hall which had been the scene of many historic gatherings and functions. Now it was expropriated by the government for the erection of an imposing General Post Office building on the site.

Of the demolition, A.G. Howard wrote, 'As I saw the old place fall piecemeal under the axe of the destroyer, it was like witnessing the death of an old friend.'

The new General Post Office was designed by the Public Works Department. It was the largest building in the colony at the time — a massively grandiose monument of a structure in the Victorian-renaissance style much favoured for public buildings. Four storeys high with an attic above, it was faced with Saldanha Bay limestone. The roofline featured imposing corner towers and clusters of chimneys. An extra square tower above the main Adderley Street entrance bore a flag pole — the flag was used to signal to the populace that the mails had arrived. Inside the building was equally impressive with a good deal of weighty mahogany furniture, brass fittings and much fancy plasterwork on walls and ceilings.

The Public Works Department was extremely active and productive in the last three decades of the nineteenth century. An incubator for young architectural talent, the offices also produced other buildings as impressive as the General Post Office, the contentious Houses of Parliament and the new railway terminus among them. The Adderley Street frontage of the building was square and powerful-looking very much in the idiom of the Florentine renaissance palace. The platforms were spanned by a splendid curved canopy of glass and iron.

By 1897 an enormous new cold storage complex was under construction on Dock Road. It was so large that a train was installed to carry carcasses and fresh produce about inside. Where, only months earlier, the sea had washed against the old dock wall, clever engineers had sunk the huge girder-and-concrete supported basement of the building well below sea level. Using the ammonia circulation system with brine for extra cooling, the complex included cold storage and ice-making facilities as well as a wholesale and retail butchery.

Amidst the headlong rush into modernity, the new bronze statue of Jan van Riebeeck, donated by Cecil Rhodes before the Jameson Raid and while he was still *persona grata* with the Afrikaner Bond, served as a powerful reminder of the past which Cape Town's renovators had all but erased. Rhodes was in England on 18 May 1899 when the statue was unveiled by the mayor but he would have been proud of the stirring effect this striking monument had on the hordes of Capetonians who had gathered for the ceremony. Van Riebeeck stood at the bottom of Adderley Street on a stone base, 'a sturdy, purposeful figure . . . with his head set proudly back and his keen gaze forever directed at the sheer rockwall of Table Mountain'.

The city was justifiably proud of its overwhelmingly ornate commercial palaces, but the dispassionate eye would never forget that the wild sweep of the Bay, the great bulk of the Mountain and the blue infinity of sky quite dwarfed even the bravest of man's works. The soaring man-made dome atop the new Mansion House might seem to cast a lengthy shadow but it was paltry relative to the scale of Nature's architecture.

Steam traction engines, known as 'Cape juggernauts',
helped immensely with heavy transport but churned up havoc
on unsurfaced roads during wet weather.

THE GRAND PARADE AND GARDEN

 mid the exciting innovations of late Victorian Cape Town, the salient features of Van Riebeeck's *Caabse Vlek* were still visible. The first commandant had been instructed not to try to convert the garden refreshment station into a town, but within a decade this had happened willy-nilly. In the mid-seventeenth century, this remote outpost boasted a parade ground and a fort (around which the Fresh River was canalised) and a straight track, later called the Heerengracht, leading towards the Company's Garden and the Mountain. The garden was a long rectangle with a track up the centre and symmetrically laid out vegetable beds interposed with fruit trees and herbs. The Heerengracht formed the main axis of the hamlet and as other streets and roads developed, they did so at right angles or parallel to the Heerengracht.

In spite of radical changes in the life at the Cape, Adderley Street (as the Heerengracht was now known), the Castle and Grand Parade Ground and the Garden continued to dominate the functioning of the town. Adderley Street was the prime trading area. The Castle, the Drill Hall and barracks, the railway station and first the Commercial Exchange until 1892 and then the General Post Office (built on the same site) bounded the four sides of the Parade.

The main thoroughfare was still the chief mercantile artery of the city and the Parade was the centre of its muscle power and, though the Garden was no longer the vital organ it had been in the 1600s, it was surrounded by establishments of the most serious importance. Government House, the new Houses of Parliament and the Supreme Court flanked its eastern limits. At the Mountain end, the South African College produced future leaders for the colony and the new museum with its handsome face of Saldanha granite housed a record of its natural heritage. Opposite, down at the Wale Street end, the South African Library, in splendidly classical style, pronounced the value of scholarship, while St George's Cathedral, a replica of St Pancras church in London, was a firm reminder of the colony's religious affiliation with the Church in England. Queen Victoria Street (as New Street had been re-named) ran up the west side of the Garden and had

Left *Officers, who were hopefully also gentlemen, added considerable sparkle to the Cape social scene.*
Right *When the Grand Parade Ground was not in use for stirring military displays or rallies and festivities, it served as an informal market and auction area.*

Corporal J. H. Straker and his pet,
the regimental mascot: they saw active service
together and shared similar tastes in beer.

‘The gardens cover 14 acres and 8 or 9 000 trees and plants from all over the world grow there. There is a handsome conservatory with fine orchids, palms and ferns. A nursery is attached to the garden and with the proceeds of the sale of seeds and seedlings to the public and a government grant, the gardens are self-sufficient.

'The Avenue, three quarters of a mile long, leads to the fashionable villa quarter of town known as "The Gardens". Halfway up the Avenue are four squares of lawn where the City Council has erected a bandstand. Once a week in summer the military band in garrison plays here and chairs are placed under the trees for the comfort of spectators.'

The Rutherfoord fountain which had once stood in front of the old Commercial Exchange was moved to a safe and permanent home in the Garden but the dominant monument there was a full-length statue of Sir George Grey.

The Grand Parade, like the Garden, had been reduced in size over the years by the encroachment of new buildings, but it was still the city's most important rallying point. Auction sales were held at the Adderley Street end every Saturday. When the circus was in town, its wood, iron and canvas structures were always erected in the middle of the grounds. The fire brigade demonstrated its skills here.

Very special occasions were often celebrated in a way that combined both of these historic open spaces in the proceedings. In 1860, during Prince Alfred's first visit, an evening celebration had been held in the Avenue, romantically illuminated by hundreds upon hundreds of flickering Japanese lanterns hanging in the oaks. When Edward the Prince of Wales married Alexandra of Denmark in 1862, Cape Town went almost hysterical with joy. Days of celebrations included an enormous carnival procession. Whole oxen were roasted on the spit on the Parade, courtesy of the Municipal Board and, while Cape Town's *hoi polloi* feasted there, a splendid breakfast was served to the polite world in the paddock of the Public Gardens. Restraint was not a feature of this otherwise genteel repast – the dessert was a wedding cake so immense that it took a span of oxen to haul it from the confectioners' to the party. That night an Old English Fair was held in the Garden; this time gas lights offered more brilliant illumination. The Avenue was illuminated with 3 000 lamps in all and eight mottoes flashed through the trees by means of gas jets.

The Mercantile Ball held there saw the Parade transformed 'from a dingy workaday market to a fairy palace. The ballroom was very tastefully decorated. The fountain in the centre had prisms placed so that the water fell over them with beautiful effect'.

The Parade was also a great rallying point for public gatherings. As the

been dedicated to learning in honour of Queen Victoria's golden jubilee. The Normal College, where teachers were trained, was situated here and plans had been drawn for a noble structure to house the University of the Cape of Good Hope – the official examining body of the colony.

Both the Garden and the Parade were considerably smaller than they had originally been, but there was never any question that either would cease to exist. By 1892, when the Garden was made over to the municipality by the government, the *Cape Town Guide* described it thus:

political awareness of the city quickened, the Parade was the scene of sizeable get-togethers of like-minded citizens either protesting against this or demonstrating their support for that. Grandstands and decorated platforms were erected and strongly worded slogans strung up from trees and stand-supports. At one pro-Rhodes rally a remarkable stage with complicated architectural features worked in wilting foliage added Gothic splendour to the proceedings.

But before the parties and the markets and the meetings used the space, the Parade was first and foremost a military parade and inspection ground and the scene of stirring massed manoeuvres on high days and holidays. A Trooping of the Colour ceremony was held on the Queen's birthday each year. The community turned out in force to watch.

The Castle, once a fortification against the enemies of the Dutch East India Company, was still the Cape's military headquarters. In 1884 the Voluntary Drill Hall was erected on the north-eastern corner of a piece of ground marked 'Exercitie Plein' on the old maps – it was the old military exercise ground. The first building on this site had been a hospital begun in 1772, chiefly for sick sailors. The area, bounded by Ziekestraat (Corporation Street), Buitenkant and Keizersgracht (Darling Street), was known as Hospitaal Plein until the hospital building was converted for use as military barracks from the late eighteenth century. From then on it was known as Caledon Square and in 1840 was made over to the municipality.

The new Drill Hall was designed to serve the volunteer forces of the Western Division as headquarters, as an indoor venue for instruction and for drilling in bad weather. The municipality granted use of the land on payment of one shilling rental a year and the foundation stone was laid on 2 October. At a parade organised to honour the occasion, medals were presented to members of Prince Alfred's own Volunteer Cavalry, the Duke of Edinburgh's Own Volunteer Rifles and the Cape Volunteer Engineers.

Another special parade in December the following year marked the official opening of the commodious hall and several military bands (including the pipe and drum band of the recently formed Cape Town Highlanders) gave a promenade concert that night to round off the festivities.

'Off-duty', the Parade was little more than an extensive trodden-earth commonage for 'loafers' and *smouse* where the tireless south-easter worried at the lean stone pines on its perimeter and swept up scurries of dust, leaves and scraps of waste paper. And the memories of those frequent military displays surely hovered in the air – the sharp clatter of trotting hoofs, rhythmic tread of marching feet, barked commands, the insistent music of fifes and drums. And perhaps what the south-easter sought as it threw up dust and grime was the swirling flags and pennants of the militia.

ON THE WATERFRONT

'The Cape smells of sheep,' pronounced Baudelaire but the wind must have been blowing off the land when the great Frenchman paid his brief visit earlier in the century. During the first half of the nineteenth century wool was unquestionably the Cape's principal export but certainly late Victorian Cape Town smelt quite unequivocally of the sea and fish. The ocean, with its ever-increasing traffic and its rich harvest, provided more than a poetic flavour to life in the Mother City.

A few hardy sportsmen braved the wind and waves of Table Bay, but their vessels were heavily outnumbered by commercial craft. The yachting fraternity and several of Cape Town's rowing clubs were stationed at Roggebaai (Roggy Bay to the English-speaker), virtually at the foot of Adderley Street. Their slim craft contrasted strongly with the sturdy fishing vessels with which they shared the beaching spot and then the rudimentary moorage once the 'fish jetty' was completed there in 1884.

By the time dawn lit the sky, the fishing fleet was well under way into the Bay. Its return was eagerly awaited on the beach by a buzz of small urchins, brightly garbed fishwives, hawkers with their pagoda-shaped hats and bamboo yokes, perhaps a turbaned imam or two, and dealers with their fishcarts and horns.

Fish were kept alive in tanks near the whitewashed block of a fish market. Others were cleaned and either curried or smoked on the beach under the close and noisy scrutiny of a cloud of squabbling gulls, greedy for offal. Hawkers and dealers roamed the city and the suburbs announcing their wares with the nasal cry of the fishhorn. These unmusical instruments were originally no more than lengths of dry hollow kelp stems, but more affluent hawkers had permanent horns fashioned from tin. The noise they made was the subject of much heated correspondence in the pages of the *Cape Times* during the 1890s. The issue divided the citizenry into different camps: those who damned the infernal racket, those who insisted it was an endearing part of the Cape scene and those for whom the sound kept the wolf from the door for one more day.

During bad weather, the fleet stayed in and many poorer Capetonians

---

Left *The elegant clock tower with its tide-gauge became
functional during the 1880s.*
Right *The new Table Bay docks were overcrowded almost
immediately they opened, so great was the need for shelter and
modern loading and off-loading facilities.*

would go to bed hungry. And bad weather was not infrequent at this tempest-torn latitude.

One of the great sea ports of the world, Table Bay provided distinctly dubious harbourage for Her Majesty's fleets of naval and merchant vessels. During the Australian gold rush it was estimated that up to 5 000 people were sailing from Britain a week, but until the mid-1860s Cape Town could offer only the most primitive of port facilities – three simple wooden jetties and one of stone running out into a bay exposed to the northerly gales of the Atlantic. Simon's Bay offered a safer winter anchorage but was not linked to Cape Town by rail until 1890. Scores of ships had been blown on to the rocks and hundreds of lives lost before the new Alfred Dock was opened in 1870 by His Royal Highness Prince Alfred in person.

The need for some sort of protection for shipping had always been apparent. The problem was meeting it. During his governorship, Sir Harry Smith had tried to tackle the labour problem by importing convict labour. But when a shipload of felons arrived at the Cape, the community rose in a body and objected so strongly, even violently, that, after five months, the convicts were sent on to Australia.

It took the catalytic spirit of Sir George Grey finally to force the wheels into motion and the new mailship service considerably strengthened his argument. Shipping was the chief means of intercontinental communication as well as transport between the far-flung chunks of the Empire, and the development of subsidised mail services administered by the Admiralty were encouraged because they used private enterprise to improve sea links. A contract would be awarded to the lowest bidder who offered the fastest service. The Cape mail service first went out to tender in 1850 and the contract was held somewhat falteringly by several different parties until a future giant of the route came on to the scene: in 1857 it was awarded to the Union Line under the chairmanship of Arthur Anderson. Capetonians were thrilled: 'The arrival of the Royal Mail Steamer *Dane* on Thursday has thrown new life and vigour into the community,' announced the *Cape Town Monitor* of 31 October 1857. The *Dane* returned to England with 10 867 letters from homesick Britons.

This was the time of the Indian Mutiny and the *Dane* had shared Table Bay's anchorage with 68 India-bound troopers and supply-ships. Only five of them were steamships, including the two largest in the world – the *Great Britain* and the *Himalaya*. By 1870, 83 per cent of all construction in British shipyards was iron and three-quarters was steam-powered. Nevertheless, for the remainder of the century, the sailing ship dominated the scene in Table Bay. This was partly because many steamers took the shorter alternative route through Suez – an expensive option for sailing ships which had to be towed the length of the canal.

Those maritime greyhounds, the racing tea clippers, passed the Cape as fast as possible. In the heyday of the China tea run in the 1850s and 1860s, the British travelled both ways via the Cape but the Americans went out via Cape Horn and returned via the Cape of Good Hope. Once Suez opened, tea was transported by steamers taking this man-made short cut. The last genuine tea race took place in 1873.

A year earlier, in 1872, the first serious competitor to the Union Line entered the lists for the mailship business. Numerous companies had challenged the Union Line's supremacy on the route but in vain until the Castle Line presented itself. On 2 May 1872 Donald Currie's chartered steamer, the *Penguin*, came into Cape Town in a new record time of 24 days and 18 hours. The Cape Government was delighted and offered Currie every encouragement to stay on the route – including a bonus of £150 for every day his ships saved. The bearded and dignified Sir Donald was to become a prominent figure on the South African scene and his company was affectionately known as the 'Currie Line' by Empire-trotters who patronised it. In 1876, when the contract came up for renewal, it was split between the Union and Castle Lines with the proviso that they did not join forces and create a monopoly. Benefiting from the competition (sometimes bitter) between the two companies, the Cape was served by weekly sailings from then on with the maximum time allowed per voyage given as 26 days until 1888 when a further six days was lopped off the official allowance.

Other smaller lines edged in on the route and competition grew hotter until a freight price war threatened everyone, big and small. Currie called a meeting and in 1883 the first South African Conference was formed to protect shippers' interests. Large numbers of sailing ships were chartered for war deliveries to South Africa and the Conference acquired £1 750 000-worth of the total charter fees of £12 700 000 paid by Her Majesty's Government. So great was the imbalance of power among Conference members that 90 per cent of the cartel's haul went to the Union and Castle Lines. When the mail contract came up for renewal in 1900, no one tendered so the government was forced to allow the Union and Castle Lines to merge and to grant the contract to the combined company.

The activities of the two companies were observed with keen interest by the English and European citizens of Cape Town. Local newspapers carried detailed information about arrivals and departures, and often included full passenger lists. For many Capetonians the mailships meant contact with home, news, mail and parcels. And as the speed and frequency of the mailships improved, so did the distance from loved ones seem to decrease. The record passage from England to Cape Town was set by R.M.S. *Scot* in 1893 – a time of 14 days and 18 hours.

Most necessities were still imported in spite of increased industrialisa-

A new ship, the Thermopylae, *owned by the Aberdeen*
White Star Line, went ashore off Green Point as it entered Table Bay
in 1899. All passengers and crew and two valuable racehorses
were recovered, but the ship broke up, and the shore was littered with
frozen meat which had been her principal cargo.

tion at the turn of the century. Retailers often used the movement of ships as the focal point of advertising. 'Twenty thousand tea pots have arrived,' advised the Nectar Tea Company, warning those desirous of acquiring one of these indispensable items not to delay; the last lot had been bespoken almost before it was cleared at the customs house. (Clearance there was not always a simple procedure. One family of German immigrants, bound for the Cape Flats, had to live in a shed at the docks for three weeks while their papers were sorted out.)

Long sea voyages were very much a part of life and in spite of mailship companies' efforts to create the most sumptuous public rooms and state-rooms featuring the last word in modern luxury — potted palms, grand pianos, brocade and velvet upholstery — the experience aroused different emotions in different passengers. For the young journalist, Winston Churchill, it was a crashing bore. 'What an odious affair is a modern sea voyage! . . . how slowly we travel! In the sixteenth century nobody minded taking five months to get anywhere. But a fortnight is a large chunk out of the nineteenth century; and the child of civilisation, long petted by Science, impatiently complains . . . of all delay in travel . . .' Chafing at the frustration of being cut off from news, even he had to admit '. . . yet even monotony is not without a secret joy. For a time we drop out of the larger world . . . and become the independent citizens of a tiny state - a Utopian State where few toil and none go hungry . . .'

It is perhaps not by sheer coincidence that that canny Scot, Sir Donald Currie, had only brought his little 'Utopian States' on to the Cape run in 1872 once the long-mooted harbour scheme was up and running.

The project had been initiated at midnight on 10 July 1860 when Sir George Grey, serving his second term as governor, hustled the necessary Act through Parliament in the teeth of fervent opposition — mainly from the Eastern Cape. The colony was divided into an eastern and a western section and there was understandable rivalry about where any available funds would be invested. Barely a week after the Act went through, 230 workmen swarmed on to the harbour site, fencing, preparing roads and erecting accommodation and workshops, as well as launching a platform which reached out 100 feet into the sea and from which Prince Alfred would tip the first truck load of stones into the water, thus officially commencing the construction of the Table Bay harbour. From that day until the end of the century, hardly a year went by when further harbour construction was not either being debated, designed or executed. The bulk of the work was done with pick and shovel, while small carts on metal tracks and a motley assortment of animal-drawn vehicles plodded through one wearying day after another bearing loads of earth and rock. Financial constraints necessitated a continuous supply of free prison labour and the breakwater convict station was never short of inmates – some were wretched souls from Cape Town and others bundled in from the furthest corners of the colony, including men accused of illicit diamond dealing.

Fortuitously, the material from a site adjacent to the breakwater proved ideal for building it, so the Harbour Board was able to kill two birds with one load of stone, as it were: the excavated material providing the needed fill and the excavations forming a dock. Some of the looser material was used for ballast in empty ships and some was used to reclaim land on the sea side of the Castle.

The notorious Cape weather threw many a spanner into the works. The gale of 1862 raged for 17 days, damaging the embryonic works and there was much heated debate in the House of Assembly about the pros and cons of continuing. The sentiment that there was no going back prevailed. After three comparatively peaceful years of toil the Great Storm of 1865 struck, sinking many ships. Some 60 000 tons of stone were shifted, but in spite of this grievous onslaught, the beleaguered breakwater afforded significant protection to the jetties in the Bay.

By the beginning of 1869 the breakwater extended 1 790 feet; by 15 June, finishing touches had been made to the excavations; in October the coffer dam was removed to let the water into the man-made dock and on 20 November members of the Harbour Board had the singular satisfaction of entering and steaming round the dock in the tug, *Gnu*.

Predictably, before the harbour was complete, the facilities had been outgrown by the demand – so much for the gloomy forecasts that Suez (officially opened by Empress Eugènie in December 1869) would steal the Cape trade. Suez cut 4 500 miles off the sea voyage between England and Bombay, but as we have seen, it did not provide a viable alternative route for sailing ships. And by the 1870s there was a busy trade in coasters and steamers headed for the Cape rather than simply past it.

Less than 20 days after the harbour went into service, the Board received the first complaint from a coaster that had been obliged to wait more than a week before a berth became available. By 1876 things had come to such a pretty pass that Sir John Coode, the engineer, was called upon to make recommendations both for the excavation of a floating basin on the inland side of the existing dock and for the formation of an outer harbour under the shelter of the breakwater.

Alas, these projects were too ambitious for the available budget which could only stretch to the construction of a wooden jetty 500 feet long and 70 feet wide. This facility was essential for the coaling of steamers of large tonnage and deep draught.

❛. . . a ship in dock coaling is not the pleasantest place imaginable . . .❜ wrote E.E.K. Lowndes of her experience aboard. ❛The steamers usually take in coal at Southampton to last for the voyage out and home again; but this steamer had been up the coast twice from Cape Town with troops, so had used her supply and was obliged to coal [at Cape Town]. A dirty disagreeable job it is and the ship's appetite seems insatiable. When we remember that she burns between 50 and 60 tons a day we are not at all surprised. From eight in the morning until ten at night, working by the electric light, a procession of wagons loaded with coal went slowly by. As they stopped, strong natives, begrimed with coal-dust, each seized a bag and emptied it into a great cauldron, which was swung up by a derrick and emptied into the ship. Canvas was put up and portholes closed; but the coal-dust penetrated everywhere. Our usually dapper stewards looked as if they had been sweeping chimneys, but when we looked at our own faces in the glass after coming down from the deck, we concluded to make no remarks about their appearance.❜

And while the coaling was in progress, the quayside seethed with the activities of loading cargo. There were wagons piled perilously high with wool bales. Each bale would be roped and the derrick would hoist four at a time on to the deck where an officer booked the markings before the bale was rolled down the hatch into the hold to be packed tightly and quickly so that the steamer could get out to sea and allow the next one in.

But the wooden jetty was no solution to the real problem, as the dreadful 72-hour storm of 1878 proved. The continual increase in maritime traffic and the requirements of the enormous new steamers added a commercial urgency to the matter. Sir John Coode recommended alterations that were estimated to cost £350 000 and were directed towards the eventual creation of an outer harbour deep and extensive enough to provide shelter for even the largest of steamers.

In 1879 the Board bought a patent slipway for the inner basin where it was immediately put to use. In the interim, work was in progress on excavation for a dry dock. Progress was slow – there was a nine-year delay in getting the necessary granite from Paarl to line the dock – but the facility was eventually opened in 1882 and named the Robinson Dock in honour of the governor, Sir Hercules Robinson.

Swimming galas and diving competitions were held at the dry dock. City athletes had quickly recognised the recreational possibilities of this facility and the grand structure was the scene of many a lively social and sporting get-together. All the youth and beauty of town, along with enterprising members of the lower-classes, gathered on the stone steps leading down into the water. Boaters were waved as encouraging cheers filled the air and muslins fluttered as colonial swimmers challenged each other in the brine. The novelty races were some of the most popular: it took considerable strength to compete in the top-hat-and-umbrella race – keeping a black topper and open man's umbrella clear of the water, swimmers had to kick and paddle one-handed the length of the dock.

In spite of lean times during the depression of the 1880s, an octagonal, three-storey dock clock and tide-gauge tower was erected at a cost of £3 700 on the southern side of the cut, or entrance to the Alfred Dock. The tide-gauge was situated on the ground floor over a well connected to the sea by a subterranean channel. The rise and fall of the water level was conveyed by means of a float suspended by a copper wire from an ink-filled stylus which traced the tidal fluctuations on a roll of waxed paper. This meant that a captain waiting to sail could check on the time of the next high tide with the minimum of fuss. The middle floor of the structure was occupied by the port captain's office. Affording a 320 degree angle of vision, 13 sash windows topped with pointed arches and wood filigree work allowed the incumbent an unequalled perspective on the outer anchorage, the cut, the basins and the southern jetties. The floor of this splendid chamber was tiled with Italian terracotta and the ceiling, the window surrounds and the

wall facing the stairwell were decorated with fancy mirrors and small tiles. Two more turns upwards of the narrow wooden stair with its reassuringly solid balustrade led to the highest eyrie which housed the mechanism of the clock that topped the tower.

By 1889, the economic tide appeared to have turned. The Transvaal goldfields were operational, the depression appeared to have run its course, trade was once again on an upward trajectory in Cape Town and congestion at the harbour chronic. The Cape Parliament rose to the occasion with the sensible offer of a £300 000 interest-free loan to the Harbour Board and Sir John Coode's proposals of 1883 (slightly modified) were consequently acted upon.

The new outer harbour added 62 acres of enclosed water and some 5 000 extra feet of quayage to Cape Town – not an inch too much according to the statistics. In 1889 the tonnage of vessels entering the docks exceeded one million.

By the turn of the century, the Table Bay Harbour offered an anchorage sheltered by a 3 640-foot breakwater, a 1 700-foot South Pier offering berthage to the large mail steamers, 64 acres of inner basins, the iron Loch Jetty and a graving dock with sheer legs capable of lifting up to 50 tons. The harbour was illuminated by electric lights at night and was served by its own efficient fire brigade.

The massive industrial complex was an enduring memorial to all the nameless men and animals who had toiled to shift hundreds of tons of earth and rock, spadeful by spadeful, to create a fitting maritime gateway to South Africa.

Swimming galas held in the Robinson dry dock were not always of an entirely serious nature. Novelty events like the top-hat-and-umbrella race drew wild applause from large audiences ranged on the stone steps of the dock.

SUBURBS– A STRING OF COUNTRY VILLAGES

The old tracks that traversed the Peninsula were punctuated by outspans which became the logical place to establish travellers' inns and eventually small settlements. Improved communications transformed these drowsy backwaters into busy hamlets in the mainstream of progress. Cape Town's burgeoning population as well as new road and rail transport meant that more and more people who worked in the metropolis could live at a distance from its hustle and bustle and insanitary dust storms.

A string of pretty country villages clustered along the railway line which extended as far as Wynberg by December 1864 and all the way to Simon's Town by 1890. Once Sea Point, a mere four miles from the centre of the city, was a remote seaside retreat. Wynberg in the early decades of the century was a country hideaway to trek to for the summer holidays. The iron horse changed all that, enabling men to commute to work even from the more southerly settlements on the Peninsula. Cape Town's energetic speculative builders wasted no time in taking advantage of this broadening in their scope of activities. Rural areas adjacent to the city were converted to residential villages with a speed that prompted rhymes like:

God made the country,
Man made the town;
But who made the suburbs
Is not yet set down.

During 1882, in spite of the depression, an estimated 800 new buildings were erected between Sea Point and Wynberg. Mass-produced housing was part of the scene from 1870 on, coincidentally about the time when there was an influx of architects to the Cape. They built business premises for the rich, then mansions, then even grander mansions for themselves. It was left largely to speculative contractors to put up terraces of dwellings and semi-detached houses for the general population.

The desirability of moving away from town was unquestioned. The noise and bustle were trying on the nerves; the insanitary conditions aggra-

Left *A fisherman in pursuit of dinner in the Liesbeek River near Mowbray Bridge.*
Right *Gracious old farmsteads mouldering away in obscurity suddenly became desirable country residences as railways and roads made it possible to work in town and live in a suburban village.*

vated by overpopulation in slum areas and the frequent choking dust storms whipped up by the wind made it an unhealthy habitation for genteel people. Naturally, working-class people tended to congregate in the new residential areas closer to town. The mass-produced dwellings of District Six sheltered a huge population of all sorts and conditions, including many freed slaves, the lowest on the social scale invariably to be found congregating in Seven Steps Lane. Maitland, Salt River and Woodstock boasted a better class of resident: well-to-do working-class people and merchants.

Woodstock was originally known as Papendorp because one Pieter van Papendorp had settled there in the mid-1700s. When, in the early 1800s, the first village management board called a meeting to decide on a new name, the fishermen, who formed the majority of the population at that stage, voted for Woodstock after their favourite hostelry. The other proposed name was New Brighton in honour of another local watering hole.

As early as 1874 the old Woodstock and Altona estates were in the process of subdivision into building plots. Woodstock beach, which stretched virtually from the bottom of Adderley Street to the Salt River mouth, became a major recreation resort, as popular with serious bathers as with local urchins. Helping local fishermen to haul their catch up out of the water added to the fun. Even Governor Sir Harry Smith had been wont to do this, while Lady Juana captured the scene in her sketchbook. Sir Alfred Milner, a strong swimmer even in the most treacherous tides, threw himself more energetically into the pleasures of the surf on the few occasions when his duties allowed him to relax.

Of course there were areas of Woodstock that were not as salubrious as others. In the poorer quarters pigs roamed free, cattle were kept and dealt in, local butchers were numerous. There was a leather factory on the sea side of Woodstock Station. But A. F. Keen, who moved there with his parents in 1896, found it 'just a peaceful country village'. Victoria Road was gravel-surfaced; neighbours all knew each other and small boys could take a big basket up between the sprawling plumbago hedges to Roodebloem (then occupied by the Van der Byls) to fetch hanepoot grapes – pick your own for a shilling a bushel. If they could carry it too, a jug of thick Jersey cream cost a tickey more.

Past the Town Hall, Victoria Walk led off Victoria Road upwards past Mackay's School, the Woodstock Hospital and Leliebloem, the family home of Edward Searle, who, with his brother, once operated the toll to Cape Town. Next door to this grand mansion was the suitably imposing stone House of Mercy, a place of correction. And of course, within easy reach of even a young boy's legs, was the whole unspoilt mountainside with its gay profusion of ericas, proteas, *pypies*, *afrikaners*, *kalkoentjies*, evertrevers, pincushions, buttercups, agapanthus, chincherinchees and watsonias.

Salt River, a residential area mainly for artisans, was less yeasty as far as growth was concerned. Several of the old mills erected by the Dutch for grinding corn still stood. The old inn at Salt River had been an outspan place for wagoners entering and leaving town before or after negotiating the hazardous drift over the Salt River. By the 1870s the Welcome Hotel and other hostelries were outspan places of another kind for seaside holiday makers.

One of the next stations down the line, Observatory Road, was so called because of its proximity to the Royal Observatory and the settlement that sprang up around the station was known by the same name. When an official title for the village was to be settled on, one faction suggested Trilby, in honour of the Trills, a prominent local family. The naming of Trill Road resulted and the suburb was christened Observatory.

The Royal Observatory was established by a Royal Order in Council of 1820 and the first astronomer, the Reverend Fearon Fellowes, arrived in the Cape the same year, unfortunately without funds or credit. The Cape Government gave him temporary shelter in the form of a settler's wooden hut which he erected in St John's Street.

Fellowes chose the site for a permanent observatory (constructed in 1827) on a small hill known as Slangkop between the Black and Liesbeek rivers. There may well have been snakes about and jackals certainly howled there at night, but the important thing was that it was far enough east of the Mountain to be on an unobstructed meridian and it was visible from Table Bay. From the beginning, the primary job was timekeeping for shipping which relied on an accurate chronometer for navigation. (Cape time was one hour behind Natal time.) Originally a brass pistol was fired from the roof of the observatory at a set time. The flash was visible from the signal station in Table Bay where a ball was then dropped from a mast to inform ships in the Bay of the correct time. Eventually a new system was introduced: a time ball at the observatory and a cannon on Signal Hill. Unfortunately charge of the cannon seemed to be thirsty work and drunkenness frequently militated against accurate signalling until 1864. From then on, the noon time blast was fired by electric current from the observatory.

Valkenburg Estate, land acquired by Valk in 1720, lay a short distance from the observatory. Subdivision began mid-century and the remainder of the estate with the manor house was bought by the government in 1881 (with a bequest from the late Honourable William Porter) for the establishment of a reformatory and, later, of a lunatic asylum.

Lying on the mountain side of this development, Mowbray was so-named in 1850. Earlier it had been known as Driekoppen and the local inn sign had three heads on it in memory of the slaying of a European family there in 1724 by three vengeful slaves. The murderers were broken at the wheel and then decapitated, their heads displayed on stakes at the scene of the crime as a warning to other intransigent servants. When Mowbray achieved municipal status its arms showed three cups and three heads, allowing a flexible interpretation of the meaning of the old name. By the late decades of the century it was a modest but genteel suburb. Among the residents of its unimpressive houses was Sir Gordon Sprigg, prime minister for four terms but dependent on his official salary for subsistence.

Rosebank's rural charm was interrupted only by its busy match factory. It lacked the fashionable appeal of Rondebosch, next suburb down the line and among the oldest of all the southerly settlements. Within five years of Van Riebeeck's arrival, cornfields and orchards had been established here. By the end of the nineteenth century the village was justifiably famous for its exquisitely pretty gardens and orchards as well as for the overshadowing presence of Cecil Rhodes and his splendid Groote Schuur estate.

For a time Mowbray, Rosebank, Rondebosch, Newlands, Claremont and Wynberg were combined as the Liesbeek Municipality, but this later broke up into four separate units. Many members of Cape Town's 'aristocracy' and financial élite had their country retreats here; gardens were large and planted with exotic trees and sprawling flowering shrubs. There were lengthy avenues shaded by firs, oaks and bluegum trees.

One ecstatic visitor reckoned, 'I do not believe that prettier retreats are to be found on the face of the earth.'

Bishopscourt was one of the showplaces of Newlands and the bishop frequently granted permission to Capetonians wishing to picnic amid the sylvan beauties of its surroundings. The walk up from Newlands Station (famous for the adjacent Western Province Cricket Club grounds) was a treat in itself, leading along tree-shaded lanes and then up a magnificent

avenue of pines. Thanks to its reliable water supply, Newlands had also become a centre for the brewing of beer and ale. By the end of the century, a company headed by Anders Ohlsson controlled all the local breweries.

By the mid-century Claremont had already boasted a clutch of small shops, the future springing up beside the past which was represented by an old circle of pines and oaks – all that remained of the old outspan. The village attracted some of the Cape's richest families and avenues with verdant borders led off the Main Road to the bigger houses.

Wynberg was so dubbed when Van Riebeeck established a vineyard there. When Major-General Craig marched his troops from Simon's Bay to Cape Town at the beginning of the first British occupation in 1795, there was a small military camp at Wynberg. The British established a permanent garrison here and it was regarded as the healthiest of all foreign military stations. In the 1840s it became *the* place for Anglo-Indians to take a break from the rigours of the Indian civil service and climate. There could

Between Muizenberg and Simon's Town, village life was very much centred on the seashore and fishing.

be as many as a hundred at a time of these 'Hindoos' (as they were known) with their 'expensive ways and exotically robed and turbaned servants'. And from then on the community remained upper-crust if not downright snobbish. It was said that at Wynberg in the 1880s there were no men, only gentlemen; no women, only ladies; no schools, only colleges or seminaries; no inns, only hotels.

The fertile farmlands of Constantia stretched beyond with the sweep of the mountains to the west and the hazy shimmer of False Bay to the south. Groot Constantia, in spite of the scourge of phylloxera – the disease that struck Cape wine farms in 1886 – was the acknowledged landmark of the area. No visitor to the Cape voluntarily omitted this imposing old manor house from his itinerary.

The estate had been granted to Simon van der Stel in 1685. Within ten years he had increased its size by acquiring neighbouring farms and had planted over 8 000 trees, including oaks, olives and bananas. 'The sweet, luscious and excellent' wines of Constantia became known almost immediately. The estate was in its heyday during the occupancy of Hendrik Cloete who bought it in 1778 and it was he who commissioned the architect Thibault and the sculptor Anreith to enlarge and beautify the homestead and construct and decorate a new wine cellar behind the house.

By the time his great-grandson Hendrik ('Henry') acquired the estate, it was a fraction of its original size. When he sold the farm in 1885 there was little public interest in the property but Professor Daniel Hahn, the colony's most eminent scientist, had propagated the idea that a government experimental farm should be established. The government arboretum at Tokai had shown how useful such a project could be. Politician 'Onze Jan' Hofmeyr was among the influential local figures he had recruited to the cause. So when Groot Constantia came under the hammer it was knocked down to the government for a mere £5 275 and embarked on a new chapter of its history. Baron von Babo took charge and the homestead, still furnished with relics from the past, accommodated his staff and the agricultural students they trained.

Convict labour was housed in the old slave 'barracks' under the homestead.

When Charles Cooper visited the farm in 1895, he was most impressed with the abundance of pears, apples, peaches and apricots produced there. He was told that the malaise that had decimated the orange crop was being successfully controlled with ladybirds that were bred in cages and released to 'eat the insect that was eating the orange trees'.

Growing grapes and producing wine were the most important activities at the farm – it had been discovered that by grafting European vines on to American root stock a resistant plant was produced. Cooper observed with

quiet vitriol: 'The phylloxera does not like the American vine. He refuses to touch it. The fact is a tribute to American repulsiveness.'

His opinion of the old Dutch wine-makers was equally poor – 'they maltreated their grapes as in Ireland milk is maltreated'. He pictured 'the time when, thanks to the care of the Cape Government in teaching better methods of growing and making wine, the nectars of South Africa will jostle with the thin beverages of the Fatherland, and even take a place at home along with the ruddy and generous wines of France and Spain and Portugal'.

The architecture escaped his censure. The homestead he found 'a fine old Dutch building, as comfortable as the most comfort-loving could desire'.

The elegant old swimming pool in the trees on a rise behind the house dated back to the earlier part of the century. But no doubt its guardian triton (the old teak figurehead from a ship) witnessed many a jolly bathing party after a hot day's work supervising the estate's labourers. Alas, the beckoning blue of False Bay and the social pleasures of Muizenberg were too far for Von Babo's students to reach for an early evening bathe.

In 1893 Kalk Bay ('Lime Bay' after the kiln once operated there) and Muizenberg (named after Wynand Muys, holder of the Dutch East India Company's post there in the seventeenth century) had a small permanent population (801 Europeans and 655 'coloured') but an enormous shifting population of visitors. In January of that year over 11 500 railway tickets were issued to the False Bay seaside stations.

Fish Hoek had been granted to a farmer by Lord Charles Somerset on condition that he was not to keep a public house there, presumably because it would delay messengers bound to and from Simon's Bay. In mid-century, Fish Hoek was an eccentric-looking settlement with fences made of whale bones, walls made of vertebrae, steps and stairs of shoulder bones and jawbones arched over the entrances to huts – constructional oddities dating back to the whaling industry that had once been a major source of income for locals. The slaughter of these peaceable sea monsters had all but ceased by the later decades of the century because they had become rare and permits was prohibitive.

At the end of the line, Simon's Bay, named in honour of Simon van der Stel – the first to use it as a safe winter anchorage – was the site of one of the earliest Company gardens. It was linked to Cape Town by telegraph in 1860 and by rail in 1890. The colonial seaside variation on most house-building themes of the Victorian period were to be seen along the main road. Wooden and cast-iron balconies offered residents ample opportunity to relax while enjoying the view and the benefits of ozone.

Of course for Capetonians desirous of sea air, travelling from the city in the other direction towards Sea Point had been a favoured option even before there was a reasonable road. Sea Point was already known by that name in 1766 when one of Captain Cook's commanders, Sam Wallis, encamped his men there, a safe distance from the smallpox epidemic raging in Cape Town. By mid-century all the old estates had been sold for division into building plots – Weltevreden at the corner of Regent and Church roads, Goede Verwachting on the Green Point side of the Rump and Zwagers Hoek in 'the most agreeable and wholesome part of Sea Point'. But by 1900 Bellwood, a fine old veranda house, was still the only residence on the actual mountainside.

As was the case with the southerly suburbs, the names of villages here gave clues to their history. Botany Bay, one of the prettiest coves on this marvellous stretch of coastline, was named at the beginning of the century when Dr F.S. Liesching had established a botanical garden above the bay near the Camp's Bay road. Camp's Bay got its name from Ernst Friedrich von Kamptz of Mecklenburg who arrived in 1778. He had worked his passage under the alias 'Otto von Kamptz'. Put ashore sick, he eventually married a widow who brought with her the farm Ravenstijn on the exquisite half-moon bay which became known as 'de Baai van Von Kamptz' and eventually contracted to the easier Camp's Bay. The property was sold to the government in 1782 and the bulk of the farm was let at the beginning of the second British occupation in 1806 and, on the remaining land, an official seaside residence was established. The first governor, the Earl of Caledon, occupied it for a while but, because of the difficulties of communicating with Cape Town, he was limited to using it as a holiday house. When he succeeded Sir John Cradock as proconsul, Lord Charles Somerset used public money to restore the house and repair the road. He also acquired the Round House in Kloof Nek on Roodezand estate which he used as a hunting lodge.

The government had sold Camp's Bay in 1828 and by mid-century building plots were being sold on the New Brighton estate – aptly named for Camp's Bay was regarded as having the potential to become the Brighton of South Africa. But right to the end of the century development was very slow and there were no proper contoured roads laid out. The heathery slopes sweeping down from the Twelve Apostles to the rocky shoreline were scarred only by the road leading down from Kloof Nek.

The late nineteenth-century visitor was advised to hire a conveyance from one of the city's livery stables and sample the delights of the new Victoria Road – rated one of the finest drives in the world by Colonial Secretary, Lord Carnarvon. The road led above Green Point Common, affording a good view of hundreds of handsome villas *en route* to Victoria Road and Sea Point. Botany Bay was followed immediately by a rocky promontory

The Boshoff Gates in Paradise Road, Newlands, announced to the world that the owner of this property had arrived.

called the North Lion's Paw, Klein Kalk Bay and the South Lion's Paw. The *frisson* of risk was now added to the thrill of the landscape for the road was literally carved out of the cliff which plummeted 300 feet to the cruel surf below. Around the 'corner' of Lion's Head, the ground levelled somewhat and the gloriously rugged vista of the Twelve Apostles was revealed to the bemused gaze of the traveller.

The road skirted Camp's Bay, a broad crescent of white sand between points of large recumbent boulders, then continued to Oude Kraal with its old farmhouse and excellent fishing, and then led higher and higher to the 'nek' from where a splendid view of the Hout's Bay valley spread out before the visitor. This little fishing village on a bay teeming with fish, boasted a very good hotel popular with Capetonians in search of an escape from the city. Honeymoon couples might stay here for as long as a month. Inspiring scenery on a grand scale encircled the spot compensating for its isolation and the fact that, in spite of its name, the valley boasted hardly any trees of reasonable size.

To complete a circular trip, one could then drive up out of the valley eastwards to another nek and an impressive view of the Cape Downs. On the downward run, the route wound through many well-known vineyards including Constantia and thence to Wynberg and the main road back to the metropolis.

CAPE TOWN'S PEOPLE

'No one can be at Cape Town for a single day without being struck by the infinite variety of the human race encountered in the streets. Indians, Chinese, Malays, Bechuanas, Hottentots, Creoles, half-castes of many kinds, Negroes of every variety from the East and West coasts of Africa, and Europeans of all countries, form the motley population of the place.'

So wrote the explorer Charles J. Andersson in the mid-nineteenth century, and by the end of it, this southerly 'tavern of the seas' was playing host to a veritable league of nations.

The discovery of diamonds in 1866, and the declaration of the Transvaal goldfields 20 years later, attracted a flood of adventurers from the four corners of the earth. Always an important temporary roost for all the birds of passage who plied the southern oceans, Cape Town now became the point of departure for many venturers into the interior. And all the world and his wife were to be encountered in the vibrant — if also hot, dusty and noisy — streets that led up from the Bay into the metropolis. Each national community contributed its share to the colour and life of the capital.

Founder members of the population were the indigenous people first encountered by European visitors to the Cape — people who called themselves Khoikhoi in the Namaqua dialect and Kwekwena in that of the Cape. Both appellations translate as 'men of men'. The word 'Hottentot' was probably picked up by whites from one of the local dance chants and by the eighteenth century had become a derogatory term. The Khoikhoi pastoralists shared the territory with Sonqua or Uniqua ('strandlopers' or beach rangers) and, inland, with the San (or 'Bushman') hunter-gatherers. These were all regarded by Europeans as sub-species of Hottentot.

Khoi herders were in the habit of camping in Table Valley for a certain period each year. Within days of his arrival, Van Riebeeck found the lower slopes of the mountain covered with browsing sheep and cattle. It was not long before a degree of interdependence grew between nomads and newcomers. The strandlopers were the first to take up employment as fishermen, wood-gatherers, domestics and intermediaries in bartering. Some permanent Khoi camps were established adjacent to the white settlement

Left *Built by Baron Willem van Reede van Oudtshoorn, the old Saasveld House in Kloof Street spoke of long-established Dutch culture.*
Right *The large Malay community brought colour, music and a good deal of talent to the Cape scene.*

Many black Capetonians aspired with all their might and meagre resources to attain gentility, but alas, the heartless social canon pronounced that one could not be black or poor and be a gentleman.

— the most notable being just above the open space called Hottentot Square until it was renamed Riebeeck Square in 1880.

By the second half of the nineteenth century, the Hottentot population had been decimated by successive epidemics of smallpox, typhoid and measles. Most of the few survivors were confined to the lowest of the working class, in a melting pot with the poorer classes of blacks, freed slaves, Asians and half-castes.

The Dutch, who had put down their first tentative roots in 1652, still far outnumbered any of the other European nations represented. Legal and

common-law marriages with slaves had introduced eastern blood into the community. Huguenots, who had found new homes at the Cape during the time of Governor Simon van der Stel, had been virtually assimilated into the community, their French names, family treasures and cultural heritage enriching the more austere Dutch style. Early German and Scandinavian and, in the nineteenth century, some Scottish immigrants had also become, to all intents and purposes, part of the now-heterogeneous Dutch community, speaking the local patois referred to as 'the *taal*'.

English feet had trodden the Peninsula's beaches off and on from 1615 when a small number of condemned criminals had been dropped off at the Cape, the intention being that they should start a colony. They failed in their task and those that survived were eventually removed. An English flag had been hoisted on Signal Hill in 1620. But this isolated gesture was not followed by any substantial claims until 1806, the time of the second British occupation and the subsequent annexation of the colony, after which the English settled at the Cape in increasing numbers. Initially the soldiers far outnumbered the bureaucrats. Then came the shopkeepers and the working-class folk — usually imported *en masse* for special projects like stone masonry. Cockney and Irish cabbies enlivened the clatter and hub-bub of the city's street-life with their wisecracking humour and the flamboyantly sentimental names they gave their conveyances: 'Forget-me-not' and 'Light-'o-my life' were among the most favoured. The opening up of the diamond and goldfields brought an increased through traffic of adventurers and, in their wake, the kind of riff-raff the colony had tried to bar by refusing to accept imported convict labour in 1849.

There was hardly a European country not represented at the Cape. There was an established community of Jews of English and German origin who lived in suburbs like the Gardens, Oranjezicht and Tamboerskloof. They were members of the Gardens Synagogue which was consecrated in 1863 — the first in South Africa. Then, from 1881, the influx of East European (Russian and Polish) Jews began to arrive. They were refugees from pogroms, economic hardships and prolonged military service. Most of them passed through the Poor Jews Temporary Shelter which had been set up in London by the London Jewish Board of Guardians and spoke Yiddish and little, if any, English. As it was relatively inexpensive to live and work in District Six, so many of these so-called 'litvaks' gravitated there that it was sometimes referred to as the Jewish quarter. They built synagogues as soon as they could: the Beth Hamidrash in Constitution Street was consecrated in approximately 1897 but many smaller places of worship were established in houses or rooms. Groups of *Landsleit* — people from the same towns and villages in Eastern Europe — attempted to maintain their identity, forming their own congregations and *Landsleit* societies.

A handful of Greeks had quickly established a reputation as purveyors of household provisions and fresh produce. An Italian contingent – doughty seafarers and fishermen – had set up a home from home in the region of Somerset Road which they shared with the odd Spanish-speaking Filipino who had strayed from the main settlement of his kin at Kalk Bay. Other Italians, like Antonio Chiappini, chairman of the first Chamber of Commerce, distinguished themselves in business.

There were Americans too, working mainly as missionaries. In 1889 the headmistress of the Bloemhof Seminary for young ladies in Stellenbosch was an American as were the two founder-teachers of the Huguenot Seminary in Wellington.

Most prominent representative of the Scandinavian countries was Anders Ohlsson, a Swede born in Norway in 1841. He served as consul-general at the Cape for both those countries. The Irish were to be found at 'Irish Town' in Newlands and also at Woodstock, some working in the railway yards and at the docks in the 1880s, others keeping the productive dairy-cows that the suburb was known for. The Irish and Germans formed expatriate associations which offered group security and identity. If they did not put up their own candidates, bodies like these were assiduously courted for votes at election time.

There were Germans at 'German Town' in the region of Leeuwenhof and near the Bo-Kaap. Among the distinguished earlier representatives of this community was the Bleek family of Mowbray. Dr Wilhelm Bleek, a German philologist, had encountered Bushman convicts who had been sent from the Kenhardt district to work on the Table Bay breakwater. A relationship of mutual respect developed and eventually some of the men fetched their families from the Kalahari and came to live with the Bleeks. Bleek and his sister-in-law, Lucy Lloyd, took down nearly 12 000 pages of verbatim accounts of Bushman life, ritual and myth. Each page had a parallel Bushman and English text which involved developing a suitable phonetic script for recording the actual Bushman words.

Some of Bleek's countrymen found life at the Cape less satisfying. In 1878, a community of Germans had been settled willy-nilly on the Cape Flats by the current Prime Minister, John X. Merriman, and Squire Cloete of Groot Constantia. These two influential citizens had decided that the industrious agriculturists and tradesmen to be found on the Luneberg Moors would solve what was known as the Cape Flats Problem. The natural vegetation of this vast no-man's-land had been thoughtlessly exploited for decades by those seeking fuel for their lime-kilns, so that by the 1870s, when Merriman and Cloete laid their plans, the wilderness between the Hottentots Holland and Table Mountain ranges had been reduced to what seemed an all but unnavigable sea of shifting sands and morasses. The Ger-

mans, it was decided, would transform this desert into a kitchen garden for Cape Town.

Lured by extravagant promises, the first party of hapless immigrants arrived in 1878 to be met by instant disillusionment. Their desperate pleas to be sent home were ignored and they were deposited in the middle of nowhere with only tents for shelter. They had been instructed to bring their own implements because the authorities had burnt their fingers during an earlier attempt to settle a consignment of Irish on the Cape Flats. The canny Celts had quickly summed up the situation and high-tailed it off to the diamond fields, taking with them the picks and shovels provided by the colonial government.

The first Germans, whose numbers were swelled by a second importation in 1883, doggedly set about making the best of a bad job. Most of the young girls went into service immediately and many of the men went out to work too, leaving the older women to start farming operations. Establishing windbreaks was obviously a priority and with the aid of Australian imports – Port Jackson Willow, hakea and so on – the taming of the Flats began. Time also had to be found somewhere to erect wattle and daub shelters with reed roofs before the winter rains engulfed them. Two years after the Luneberg farmers had arrived, a candid official report gave them their due: it had not been work for the majority of Germans on the Flats. It had been slavery, drudgery and slavery, from morning until night, week after week, year after year.

By 1892 they had made such phenomenal progress that they were able to display the fruits of their labours in the first Fair and Show of the Cape Flats' Farmers Association held at the Claremont Town Hall on 7 April. One newspaper reported that not the least interesting exhibit was that which had no place in the catalogue, viz., the quaint personality and dress of the industrious peasants and their families.

Other hard workers – Scottish stonemasons and Cornish miners – were imported to construct the storage reservoirs and water tunnel on top of Table Mountain. They settled in a village of stone cottages erected in the immediate vicinity of their work and, apart from sorties down to civilisation via a perilous cable car plummeting towards Camp's Bay, made themselves very much at home up among the mists and heathers of their windswept eyrie. A football team was established. They had several musical instruments including a piano and some mandolins, and formed a choir for their own entertainment. Fierce rivalry was exhibited during a competition for the best cottage garden at this elevated settlement where regular visitors included ramblers and mountaineers. Once the work of reservoir-building was complete, the masons left, some to settle for married bliss with colonial sweethearts. The village was razed – except for two huts which were retained for the use of the Mountain Club and a house occupied by a waterworks official.

The black population had grown to at least 10 000 by the turn of the century. Labour was constantly being imported and though the official view was that each worker would return to his home after his period of indenture or contract was over, many did not do so and settled permanently in the Cape.

During the border wars with the indigenous peoples, black prisoners had been brought to Cape Town and sometimes men, women and children were transported in reprisal raids. Some black people actually walked overland to the Cape in search of relatives who had been taken there. Between October 1879 and July 1882 14 groups of Berg Damara from central Damaraland, totalling about 300 in all, were contracted. The Damara Commissioner, William Coates Palgrave, insisted that they should come as families and he predicted that 50 per cent would remain in the Cape once their indentures expired. Hildagonda Duckitt refers to buying vegetables in the 1890s from Damara women living at Constantia.

Between November 1879 and May 1882, 2 400 men were imported from Delagoa Bay on three-year contracts. Less than half of them returned home. By the beginning of 1881 some had deserted for the open wage market and were living with blacks from the Eastern Cape in the outbuildings of the old police station at Altona, Papendorp, as well as in a stable in Roodebloem and wherever else they could find a corner to creep into.

Tension between the two African communities led to open conflict in 1881 after a black man from the Eastern frontier had picked up a purse dropped by Jan Jonas, a Mozambican deserter from the docks. In September that year a regular free fight developed when about 200 blacks from 'locations' in the vicinity of Papendorp rose in a body and were attacked by a mob of whites and 'coloureds' who proceeded to destroy African property. This once again roused public debate on the provision of a supervised black location − something which had been discussed since the 1850s. (Separate facilities for worship for whites and people of colour had been adopted by the synod of the Dutch Reformed Church in 1861.)

In the 1890s about 1 400 Mfengu from the Eastern Cape were contracted to work for the Harbour Board. By 1893 a few of these men had brought their wives and families to town and it was hoped they would put down roots and become the foundations of a black working class. Besides the Mfengu and Xhosa, new arrivals in the 1890s included 1 900 Tswana captured during the Langeberg rebellion of 1896-97 and transported to the Cape for indenture.

By the turn of the century the black population of the Cape was too sizeable and too permanent to be simply assimilated. Talk of a separate location became more serious but it was not until the bubonic plague outbreak of 1901 that black people, always a convenient scapegoat when insanitary conditions were discussed, were finally forced to relocate themselves at Uitvlugt (Ndabeni) on the Cape Flats.

Much earlier was the arrival of the first 'Malay' people who had been brought to the Cape by the Dutch from their eastern trading posts. Many in fact were not Malay; the term was used loosely for Muslims. Some came as slaves, some as free servants, also registered as slaves or bondsmen, and others came as soldiers and guards. Among the early arrivals were Malay aristocrats and religious leaders deported to the Cape as political prisoners. They influenced the existing local population greatly to the good, welding the community together and heightening its sense of identity and self-respect. According to a nineteenth-century writer, the Malays soon won the affection of the 'aboriginal Hottentots', and the other 'coloured' people by attention and kindness. 'A natural quickness too, which approved them to their new masters, and the good example they set by abstaining from intoxicating drinks gained for them some privileges in addition to the free exercise of their religion.'

By the mid-nineteenth century, Cape Town's Malay community was well established and prosperous. Its members were to be found in all walks of life, and in general displayed skill in whatever they turned their hands to. The Cape boasted of several Malay property magnates and a number of businessmen amassed considerable fortunes as greengrocers or smallware merchants.

The working-class Malay women earned a living as cooks, washerwomen, nursemaids or housemaids and as milliners and dressmakers. Many of the men were fishermen while others earned their living as shopkeepers, masons, carpenters, wagoners, tailors and cobblers. They were regarded as being excellent coachmen and the best artisans available, 'displaying the great virtues of intelligence, sobriety and industriousness' − truly a valuable section of the population of Cape Town.

Right up until the end of the century, Malay people tended to maintain the traditional forms of dress. Working-class men sported coloured vests, long tunics and wide, shortish trousers. *Kapparings* (wooden sandals with a button between the first and second toe), bright neck-scarves and a small turban under a pagoda-shaped straw hat (*toering*) were common attire for streetwear. Some of the priests and the hadjis (those who had made the pilgrimage to Mecca) wore full turbans, cashmere shawls and long robes.

Malay women had adopted the full-skirted, tight-waisted skirts of their European cousins, but displayed an unrestrained colour sense which considerably brightened Cape Town's workaday street scenes. They kept their hair long, brushed smoothly back at the temples and fastened with decorative clasps and bodkins. They never wore bonnets, preferring colourful oriental scarves gracefully draped over small pillboxes.

Happy, sociable people, members of the Malay community were fond of donning their brightest finery and jaunting out in their gaily painted Cape carts on high days and holidays. A particular grassy knoll right on the Camp's Bay beach was a favourite spot for picnics. No sooner had the company alighted, when the string band would strike up and couples start to waltz energetically in the bright sunshine. Companies of Malay musicians performed at most Cape parties – from Government House balls downwards.

The Malay habit of celebrating New Year with song and dance and street parades of musical troupes is thought to date back to 1834 when slaves were liberated. The style of the celebrations was greatly influenced by the very popular American group, the New Christy Minstrels, who had taken the Cape by storm when they visited it in 1887.

The heartland of the Malay community, known as Bo-Kaap, was on the flank of the Lion's Rump where the first mosques were built and consecrated. Many Christian denominations set themselves the task of converting the Malays, inviting them into church precincts with the temptation of free education, but the gloomy feeling was that as many Christians (mainly women) 'perverted' to Islam as converts were won. Hadji Samoudien, for example, was married to a Miss Williams who had been born on St Helena of Welsh parents.

Not all infidels were susceptible to the call of Islam, though. In 1888, the house at 203 Longmarket Street was occupied by a Christian family who pelted the muezzin with stones when he gave the call to prayer from the wooden minaret on the mosque next door. To put a stop to this, Hadji Abdol Kaliel simply bought the house, issued notice to the Christians and leased the place to his daughter.

But little displays of power like this were the exception not the norm in Cape Town between 1870 and 1900. White English-speakers formed the dominant class both politically and socially. The higher purpose of Empire

was to influence rather than be influenced; to Christianise and Anglicise and, thus, to civilise the rest of the world. So, though the Victorian eye loved few things better than the exotic and the curious, not much of the rich cultural variety which blessed the Cape found expression in prevailing modes. Quite the contrary: African and Eastern people did their level best to ape the dominant English fashions in dress and lifestyle because these clearly indicated success and power.

Non-white people had an irrepressibly bold colour sense which was noted with indulgence by white colonials who would smile sardonically at their efforts to get it right. One popular satiric picture postcard showed a black couple dressed up to the nines in the latest European style. The caption read: 'Cape Lilies.'

The imported 'lilies' did their best to keep their skin white – very difficult in the Cape summer when even the reflection of sunlight on a white wall can add a tinge of colour to the cheek. As the century drew to an end and more and more women sought political, professional and sporting freedom, the fashion for fragile beauty diminished, but milky skin was still a prized asset.

Much of the Peninsula was still under cultivation and, for many, suburban life meant rural subsistence.

THE VERY POOR

*P*overty was not regarded by the ruling class as the central issue in Cape Town's seething, stinking slums. The filth and 'moral decay' and the very real possibility that disease and pestilence would spill over into the respectable parts of town were the concerns of the middle-class Cape Town colonial.

The cost of living in Cape Town was very high and housing was at a premium, but nonetheless the middle-class view was that the city's lower classes crowded into noisome nooks and crannies because they were too lost to any sense of decency to aspire to anything better. In these areas lighting was minimal and the city's notoriously poor drainage was worse than ever. Nightsoil was not removed regularly, water had to be collected from a public pump and the vermin endemic in a harbour town proliferated.

J. Easton, as a self-styled 'concerned citizen' who had researched the situation, told an audience in the Y.M.C.A. hall in 1887:

> Surface drains are the death traps of the slums . . . but I did not expect to find a sluit running through the inside of a house . . . This sluit was cut so as to run alongside the wall of the entrance passage until it terminated at what I may be permitted to call the sanitary arrangement at the other end of the passage. Perhaps the worst state of things I came across was a row of houses with no back yard to any one of them . . . In the court through which we had entered were three or four compartments placed in a row and a dilapidated wall was all that separated these sanitary arrangements from a family bedroom . . . the family admitted that through the wall the stench became unspeakably offensive, and, at times, altogether unbearable.

By 1887, the City Council was responsible for the removal of nightsoil, but houses in the slums received a visitation only once a month, or, if they were lucky, once a fortnight. But this was only one of the problems of the 'fever dens' in overcrowded slum areas in Buitenkant, Harrington, Boom, Canterbury, Constitution, Hanover, Waterkant and other streets too numerous to mention. There were filthy rookeries off Long Street and Keerom Street was

---

Left *For the thousands of poor people who huddled in Cape Town's slums, good fishing weather often made the difference between a morsel to eat and a few pennies for tomorrow, and going to bed hungry.*
Right *Seven Steps Lane in District Six served as thoroughfare and playground for tenement dwellers.*

known as The Valley because of an open ditch in the middle used as a dumping ground for every manner of refuse and filth. The Malay quarters around Rose and Chiappini streets were clean but also horribly overcrowded.

On the opposite side of town, beyond Roeland Street, was another sprawling area where indigent Capetonians and new arrivals alike sought shelter in droves. It had been known as District Six from 1867 when the municipality had divided the city into six electoral wards. Perhaps significantly, it was the only ward to be known by number − all the others had names which were more commonly used.

The buildings of District Six ranged in style from some relics of Cape Dutch farms, like Zonnebloem; a few remaining flat-fronted, high-stoeped town houses; and the shabby remains of a couple of elegant Cape Georgian houses. These were all but drowned in the sea of mass housing that sprang up in the last decades of the nineteenth century, product of the need of the homeless and the greed of building contractors who chose quick profit above ethical craftsmanship.

Unlike other parts of the city, District Six had not been laid out according to an orderly grid pattern, but had grown 'organically', following the contours of the lower mountain slopes, with its streets, lanes and squares running at oblique angles.

The squares and lanes were gathering places for residents of the overcrowded dwellings − Wells Square off Hanover Street, Hanover Square, Butler Square off Harrington Street and a tiny square at the intersection of Aspeling and Pontac streets. Seven Steps Lane between Hanover and Caledon streets was always favoured by layabouts and their associates.

Dozens upon dozens of rows of terraced houses, some single − some double-storeyed − with narrow verandas and balconies, zigzagged up and down the steep streets. Tenement blocks, like the terrace houses, were quickly erected with profit in mind and many were quite unfit for decent habitation even while they were still quite new. The use of half bricks as an economy measure meant that walls were prone to collapse in the rainy season.

There was no proper drainage or water supply and the greater part of the District was squalid in the extreme. But the demand for shelter first from freed slaves, then from migrant labourers, refugees and immigrants from England and Europe kept on flooding in, overcrowding the desperately inadequate facilities.

Black squatters were allowed to construct shelters for themselves on the wasteland between Salt River station and the upper Main Road to Wynberg. Some of their fellows huddled together in the stables at Roodebloem and Altona House. Others had established a warren on the tract of land between

the east end of the city and Zonnebloem College, known as the Orange Free State. These people had previously camped out on Dock Road, 'extemporising shelter' by means of tin cases. They were constantly under the threat of the Vagrancy Act in terms of which the homeless (even if they were employed) and down-and-outs could be found guilty of loafing and sentenced to hard labour.

Easton reported:

❝There is dilapidation everywhere, and the rooms are small, ceilings low, passages narrow and the houses situated in courts and alleys, where daylight and fresh air seemed intended to be blocked out … In the course of my peregrinations, two rooms have been pointed out to me, not 12 feet square, in each of which 15 persons, men and women huddled together, have slept for the night, in addition to which the passages have been lined with human beings right through to the back yard and in the yard itself. From 40 to 50 people of both sexes stowed away in this fashion in one house or hovel … the rooms are filthy … almost every adult occupying these premises is filthy in his own person and in his clothing … [and] this class of people are to be numbered by the thousand … reduced to mere animalism …❞

That certainly seemed to be true of the resourceful folk who had sought to make homes of their own, burrowing out shelters for themselves on the mountain slopes. In one burrow lived 'six coloured gentlemen from the dock'. In another a woman had made a home for herself and her extended family for eight years. One house in St John's Street reportedly sheltered 84 people, of whom a dozen were believed to sleep in the old Dutch oven. According to official census figures, this appears to have been an exaggeration, but the official figures were horrific enough.

In a grim comment on the expectation of life in these circumstances, the researcher noted that

❝… there appeared to be no old people, that is, persons of 60 years of age and upwards … [I was told] "Oh sir, they die off; drink and living in such dens is more than the strongest can stand − their constitutions are undermined by the cheap, strong and nasty liquor, so that when disease gets hold of them the system is too weak to throw it off."❞

In short, the slums were breeding grounds for pestilence and thus a threat to good citizens. The smallpox epidemics of 1840 and 1882 had proved that if the frequent cases of typhoid and phthisis had not already done so.

Vice (also contagious) was immovably identified in the mind of middle-class Cape Town with the lower classes. In 1887 there were more than 170 hotel and canteen licences and some 36 bottle store licences in the town. The bottle stores could be regarded as the more pernicious because drink was cheaper there and, in the canteen, at least a man enjoyed some social intercourse and, one hopes, drank more slowly.

⁶The people are great talkers and fond of a laugh and it is their misfortune that they have no better place of resort than the canteen. With them there is no such thing as home life or the family circle, their recreation rooms and places of amusement are the canteens ... the people drink to render their hard lot in life more tolerable, that is, to drown their miserable condition as much as possible in oblivion ... As to the quality of the drink, you have only to taste a bottle of twopenny wine and you will not be surprised that men and women succumb to its potent influence ... Their present condition has not been arrived at in a day, it is the result of living for years in foul atmospheres which have deteriorated their physical systems, so that the daily lack of oxygen has had to be met by daily stimulants at the canteens. With the lack of physical energy comes the disposition to idleness, ending in debauchery and all forms of vice,⁹

stated our researcher.

Brothels were scattered from Woodstock Toll to Buitengracht Street, from Newmarket Street to Mill Street. When the Morality Bill of 1902 was introduced, the attorney-general quoted from the police report on brothels which estimated that 400 of the town's prostitutes came from Europe, 25 from Britain, 75 were white women born in the colony and 100 were 'coloured' women. There had been an influx of Continentals from Johannes-burg since the outbreak of war, but brothel-keepers also imported girls via agents in Europe. White prostitutes were said to earn £2 a day and 'coloureds' 10 shillings. The bulk of the money went to pimps, brothel-keepers and various shady characters (including corrupt police officers) who demanded protection money. Brothel landlords demanded double rent, but concealed the fact by issuing receipts for normal rentals. They were the most difficult in the network to identify and arrest.

Many citizens and clergymen were outraged at the public advertisement of immorality in the streets of Cape Town. On at least one occasion, an enterprising brothel-keeper, fearing a slacking off of business, had her girls dress up in their most flamboyant finery, bundled them into a large open carriage and they drove slowly around some of the better residential streets of town, advertising their services, noisily greeting any male bold enough to venture past and liberally dispensing their visiting cards. Handing out cards to new arrivals at the docks was standard practice.

A chronic housing shortage aggravated overcrowding: many a Cape housekeeper found herself performing essential chores literally in the street.

51

Cape Town's cyclical depressions had steadily increased the population of indigent whites and matters came to a head during the very bad years of the early 1880s. Now the middle classes decided there was poverty to be sympathised with. There were poor people in dire straits through no fault of their own. In the past laziness, extravagance, waste, dirt and independence had been held to characterise the bulk of the lower orders of the working class. But the need of poor whites was regarded as 'real'. A night refuge committee was set up to help unemployed clerks and bookkeepers, but not their families.

On 19 August 1884, the unemployed organised themselves and 400 came together for a meeting. The *Cape Times* stated that the meeting was not a good advertisement for the cause: the cry had been for European labourers and artisans, yet Malays, 'coloured' people and blacks had attended the meeting too. The organising committee put a notice in the newspaper urging all unemployed men to register their names in the Metropolitan Hall, inadvertently or deliberately excluding those who could not write or did not write in western characters. The government and the city moved on this and some relief was offered.

Another meeting was held on the Grand Parade in 1886 and a labour bureau was established where meals were served. A new book for the names of unemployed people was opened. Within a month 929 names had been entered, three-quarters of them those of 'coloured' people. Cape Town's public-spirited were certainly not short of work to which they could turn their energies. Those who cared to, made life somewhat easier for their hard-pressed fellows.

Saul Solomon, who served for 30 years in the Legislative Assembly, was largely responsible for the repeal of the Contagious Diseases Act and the Masters and Servants Act. The former (repealed in 1872 but reintroduced after Solomon's death), which authorised police-supervised medical checks on prostitutes, was tacitly held to 'legalise' prostitution (a gross indignity to women) and to allow men to sin without fear of reprisal. Solomon's opposition to the Masters and Servants Act was one of the campaigns that had him branded as a negrophile but, thanks to his efforts, the servant was no longer automatically wrong in a dispute with a master but the two could come to court as equals.

Unfortunately the ideal of equality in the eyes of the law did not always work out as well in practice as it sounded in theory.

On one extremely unfortunate occasion the entire hunt came thundering on to the smallholding painstakingly created in the wilderness of the Cape Flats by one of the German agriculturists who had been ordered to settle there. Before his eyes, his precious few hens were torn apart. He caught hold of the bridle of one of the huntsmen, begging him in German

to call off the hounds. Intoxicated with the chase or some other elixir, unable to understand a word the man said, and possibly mistaking his distress for aggression, several of the huntsmen dismounted and thrashed the poor fellow with their crops. The farmer sought justice, but when he faced the magistrate he knew his case was lost. And, alas, he was right. The magistrate was a member of the hunt.

Not all top dogs were as callous. Anders Ohlsson, the millionaire industrialist who headed the largest brewery in South Africa, gave selflessly of his time for various humane projects, including improving the working and living conditions of the 1 200-odd labourers (most of them convicts) employed at the harbour on construction and as porters, coalers and stevedores.

In Kalk Bay wealthy spinster sisters Harriet and Charlotte Humphreys and Alice Pocklington did good works among the community of fisherfolk and whalers. They accompanied Bishop Gray on his return from England in 1865 and, from about 1870, lived together at Kalk Bay. Miss Pocklington ran a school and they nursed the sick, fed them in bad times, looked after orphans. They contributed or collected from their families enough to build Holy Trinity Church. The foundations were laid in 1873 and the building was consecrated the next year.

Other places where the needy or disadvantaged could seek aid included an institute for indigent deaf mutes at St Mary's Roman Catholic Cathedral in Roeland Street. The Salvation Army worked tirelessly for the rescue of bodies and souls most others would regard as already having gone to the devil. In 1895 the Council erected barracks for single labourers at a cost of £8 000. In 1897 these were taken over by the Salvation Army and a charge ranging from fourpence to ninepence a bed was made. The Army also ran a rescue home for fallen women; their officers called at the brothels to try to lead others to the light; they established a social farm and home for discharged prisoners at Rondebosch. Canon Lightfoot was a saintly man who was tireless in his ministrations to the sick and destitute, his sense of Christian duty reinforced by instructions from his superiors to win as many converts as possible. In spite of some personal anxiety he never held back from even the dingiest of hovels or dangerous situations like a smallpox ward where the scurge claimed five or six souls a day. He ran a series of night schools with scant assistance from his colleagues. These were intended to lure Muslim converts to Anglicanism so Lightfoot was only partially gratified by the enormous numbers of adult black men and women who were hungry for education and anxious to improve their station in life. Dr Jane Waterston's Free Dispensary and Clinic for slum mothers and others in Barrack Street was the only free medical service available to the very poor.

Another cause of concern to the public-spirited was baby-farming which was rife in Cape Town. The unwanted product of an illicit liaison would be farmed out to foster parents for a few pounds a month. Good-hearted Malay families were particularly prone to the approach of single women fallen on hard times.

❝I have the knowledge of half a dozen white brats gladly received by the Malay baby-farmers who are only too glad when [board and lodging] payments on account of them lapse and they become their own, body and soul. They are not unkind to them as a rule. Living is so cheap, a bit of snoek doesn't cost much, and a corner in a Barrack Street room is not much crowded by an extra brat. In some cases white foster children are married as subsidiary wives, boys go out as low-caste Malays. In one case I know, a red-haired, Irish-looking fellow in a Malay fez was a few years ago sentenced to a heavy term of penal servitude. He was the leader of the most notorious housebreaking, resetting, shebeening and immoral rookery Cape Town has seen and had been one of our missent children. Was it his fault he was revenging himself on society? Who will start a Dr Barnardo home in Cape Town instead of sending money to London? ... I know of another case where a poor little "avant courrier" of an aristocratic and prosperous marriage is playing cricket at paraffin-tin wickets in a slum street while his parents go to Government House balls.❞

This outburst from the ever outspoken *Lantern* magazine revealed the current notion that colour, poverty and criminal tendencies were linked. It was prompted by a letter from a Natalian who had complained that he had written to Dr Barnardo's in London offering to take

'A Little Mother' read the sentimental postcard caption
under a picture of this pair of wretched children.

two youngsters and 'give them a start' which was more than likely a euphemism for 'put them to work'. The organisation had turned down his offer on the grounds that South Africa's population included elements that would be a poor influence on children from a 'weak moral background'.

Other orphanages, both in England and in Holland, had gladly sent out consignments of children for placement through an agency — almost certainly to a life of drudgery. And Dr Barnardo's had, in fact, been the most recent organisation to explore the possibility of a child emigration scheme to South Africa similar to a very successful and long-standing arrangement with Canada. The organisation sought government aid for the setting up of a training farm to which boys and girls could be sent from Britain. They would be kept there for up to two years under strict moral instruction, learning also the virtues of obedience, punctuality and hard work. Domestic skills would be taught to the girls and labouring and carpentry skills to the boys. They would then be available for employment and benefit the colony which was always crying out for good white servants.

With the greatest diplomacy, the governor had turned down the proposition, indicating discreetly that the bad influences from the Cape's particular type of lower class would present a constant threat to the children. Further, the cost of living in the colony was prohibitively high. If Barnardo's was prepared to send out the finished product, ready for service, it was of course a different matter.

Much of the work among these children and the lower classes in general was justified by a sense of Christian moral duty. It was felt by the upper class that if the execution of that duty produced useful workers and servants for the Empire, so much the better for all parties concerned.

53

THE OLD RICH AND THE NEW

The differences between money and class were still very clear in the late 1800s but in the general atmosphere of social *laissez faire* prevalent in a colonial outpost a blind eye was often turned on the finer distinctions. Society in late Victorian Cape Town was simply too limited to permit of too exclusive an attitude. In reality, anyone who had come up in the world and had the astuteness to acquire polite (that is, English) manners could enjoy the benefits of being a bona fide member of society. This state of affairs was deplored by sticklers for convention who understood that, although being very rich might mean a good deal, it was just not quite enough. It had always been understood that a wealthy merchant family could enter the social lists by marrying a daughter off to a sprig of impoverished aristocracy. But now political power and influence were the new admixture that might open the most sacrosanct of doors to new money.

The Rhodes millions were new and he was a man of exceptional personal power. But he was also the right kind of fellow – an English vicar's son and an Oxford man. Who was to say whether it was not these two facts that gave him the social edge over other rich (but not as rich) men like J. B. Robinson? Shipping magnate Donald Currie would not be pressed, let us say, to stay as a houseguest by the same people who had calling cards waiting the minute someone like Baron de Rothschild stepped ashore. The Baron accepted an invitation to stay at Groote Schuur in preference to one from Government House because he was curious about Rhodes. Unfortunately the colossus was occupied with the affairs of his northerly empire at the time and the house had recently been gutted by fire so the circumstances would have deterred a lesser man than the baron.

The Baron's invitation was typical of Rhodes – the imperial team-man *par excellence*. He had an unerring nose for who was right and collected the best of intellectual, creative, business and aristocratic personalities for his batting side.

When he had discovered that Lady Charles Bentinck and Lady Edward Cecil (the wives of two army officers who were otherwise engaged in the north) had moved from Government House to the Mount Nelson Hotel on 19 September 1899, he insisted that they should make themselves at home in Groote Schuur. Mrs John Hanbury-Williams (wife of the governor's

Left *Highwick, the mansion built for Henry Beard in 1896.*
Right *The entrance hall of Kelvin Grove as it was refurbished by architect Herbert Baker.*

military secretary) had introduced Violet Cecil to Rhodes on 28 July when she took her to lunch with him at Groote Schuur and of course he knew without being briefed that she was the daughter-in-law of Lord Salisbury. She found both the man and his house impressive, understanding immediately why he was known both in the colony and England as the only 'big' man in Africa. Her observations of his lifestyle reveal, however, that he did not give a fig for society manners. She was struck (even a tiny bit appalled) by his 'don't-care' attitude to social conventions. On October 2, Violet wrote a letter to her mother, describing her temporary home:

❛Here I am staying with Rhodes in a most lovely house on the side of what is known here as "The Mountain". It is a most amusing house to stay in, being the only real Liberty Hall I have ever come across. You get up when you like, lunch any time between one and two-thirty, no one cares whether you are there . . . You can ask anyone to any meal that you please . . . you have your own pony to ride and your own Cape cart and pair, which you order when you please.

'There is no show, no servants in livery, no proper butler and no housemaids at all, only black boys upstairs and two nondescript men to wait at table, so of course our maids, who are used to footmen and

The summer house on Groote Schuur Estate where all Cape Town was welcome to relax.

56

housekeepers' rooms, are furious . . . Our host's motto is "Don't Bother" – he doesn't bother and his guests don't bother and no one bothers at all about anything . . . Everything in the house is beautiful, very plain but in perfect taste . . .

'Everyone can come in and out and all afternoon the gardens and the whole place is full of people . . . Mr Rhodes has a great many acres devoted to a zoological collection, [so] you may imagine that the whole of Cape Town lives here . . . Rhodes owns one side of Table Mountain, and the drives and rides all about his place are lovely – I don't think I know of any rich man who spends his money a quarter as well and as lavishly as he does. There is an Imperial Magnificence about his way of doing things, and with it all he spends none on personal or exclusive luxuries.❜

Mr Rhodes was not at all like his portraits, she noted years later –

❛a carelessly put together large man with a top-knot of brown hair, turning grey, and complexion that gave notice of the heart trouble that killed him three years later. He had a face you could not look away from, with the blue eyes of a seer, and the mouth of a Roman Emperor. He had a curious voice that ran up and down the scale and a very individual way of expressing himself. No other man of great intellectual power can ever have had a smaller vocabulary, and he would repeat the same thing again and again – "I give you this thought," he would say, and the thought, badly expressed in words of one syllable, was always worth attending to . . . I was interested in everything he said and admired him immensely.❜

Rhodes' ability to read her thoughts impressed Lady Edward Cecil too, particularly as courtesy restrained him from misusing this advantage.

❛He would let one know in a roundabout way that he had guessed what was in one's mind. He did this (once) to me when I was feeling rather disconsolate over the crowds he daily opened his gardens to. Everyone was at liberty to go everywhere at Groote Schuur and one very fine Sunday afternoon – it was my only free time during the week – I was looking gloomily at the throng in the garden and in the fields and woods and wondering whether it was worth while battling my way through them and whether I should find a corner unoccupied. Mr Rhodes looked at me and through the window at the people who were swarming over the hillside. "Some people," he said, "like to have cows in their park. I like to have people in mine."❜

The Ladies Cecil and Bentinck, both engaged in relief work, remained at Groote Schuur while their husbands and their host were all besieged at

Mafeking and Kimberley. Three weeks after the relief of Kimberley, Rhodes came home and Violet reported to her mother that he was in

> ❝glorious health and spirits, very amusing, full of stories, and very pleased with himself and, fortunately for us, with us too. He insists on our staying on here, won't hear of our going away yet etc., also he accepted Billy Lambton with equanimity . . . found him in his bath (Mr Rhodes' own private bath!) before he even knew he was in the house, shook hands with him over the edge of it and seems to take him and anyone else as a matter of course.❞

A little fun returned to life again. The Rudyard Kiplings were frequent visitors – Rhodes was to have Herbert Baker build them a house called 'The Woolsack' on the estate the following year. There were dinner parties: one evening when Lord Roberts was a guest, Violet noticed him go deathly pale halfway through the meal. His staff officer, Colonel Neville Chamberlain, told her, 'There's a cat in the room.' He caught the cat – the first she had ever seen in the house – and removed it. Later he said to her: 'If the Boers knew their business, they would send battalions of cats against Bobs.'

Roberts was, of course, not only titled, but a hero as well, but other military men of a certain rank (like clerics) were traditionally regarded as gentlemen. Some people in the colony would have liked to change this: 'The days when "officer" and "gentleman" were synonymous, went out when the grocers' sons crowded the cramming shops,' sniped *Lantern* magazine, 'but where the prestige of military cads still lingers, as in Wynberg circles, the "rooi Baadtjies" have still "the way we have in the army" with the fair sex. When hubby is at his office in Cape Town, Captain so-and-so calls on wifey . . .' Dilettante purchase officers and other profligate sprigs of the nobility were regarded with justifiable scepticism where 'mere blood has little to do with any man's position', according to the observations of writer J.S. Little who visited South Africa in 1870. Education and business opportunities were open to all and even tradesmen who could afford to live in the same style and chose to behave in the same way as executive officials or merchants were in no danger of social exclusion.

Wynberg Hill was typical of the exclusive locations favoured by this new aristocracy. Walter Searle, head of a successful merchant shipping firm, had Cecil Rhodes' architect, Herbert Baker, build him a splendid manor on 12 acres there. He called it Highlands and mining magnate J.B. Robinson had to look sharp to outdo it with his Hawthornden, a sumptuous renovation with extensive additions of the old house, Oude Wynberg. Set in romantic grounds, the simple exterior of the French-style house belied the overwhelmingly decorated interior. With a mansard roof and verandas of delicate ironwork, the main frontage of the house was on the roadway and approached through scrolled iron gates and a glassed-in porch. Possibly the most striking feature of the mansion was a conservatory-like ballroom with a glass dome. The interior had been meticulously decorated: all was patterned, from the parquet floors, to the papered walls and the beamed ceilings with multi-coloured stencilled designs overlaying the herringbone stripes of the tongue-and-groove boards. Plasterwork scrolls were picked out in gold and there was more gilding on the woodwork of the window recesses; gilt light fittings and a huge marble mantelpiece inlet with tiles and with a magnificent grate of cast iron formed focal points amid the plethora of detail in the reception rooms. The drawing room was of ample proportions and led through a double doorway to the darkly rich library/billiard room, with William Morris wallpaper, artificially grained woodwork and a frieze of gilded garlands of fruit and flowers.

Salubritas on Alphen Hill was built for Wynberg's first mayor. Trovato, in Herschel Walk, was built in 1895 by Baker for Carl Jeppe. The heavy exterior with its stone facings spoke of the sombre responsibilities of power, but the interior was in complete contrast. Opulent in the extreme, there was a great hallway with a ceiling the full double-storey height of the house, peacocks flaunted their glamour on the wallpaper framed in a good deal too much decorative woodwork. Fine woods with inlaid patterns were used for all the built-in cupboards and the bathrooms were fitted out with marble and brass sanitaryware.

Some parts of Claremont and verdant corners of Newlands were also aspired to by the emergent social elite. The architect C.H. Smith created

Capetonians born with silver spoons in their mouths enjoyed all that money could buy and the freedom of a sunny climate.

Eyton on Paradise Estate for F.E. Cartwright of Mansion House fame. *S.A. Architect & Builder* described it thus: 'This house is beautifully situated on about three and a half acres of ground on the highest part of the picturesque locality of Claremont and commands extensive and magnificent views of the surrounding country. The ground floor walls are of red facing bricks and the upper storey is finished in rough cast plaster, gables and other features being treated with solid half timber framing left with rough adzed face – the whole being roofed with English plain tiles.

'One of the principal features is the combination of a large dining room and parlour which forms one large apartment having a central elliptical arch artistically treated the whole width of the room – together with bays and an inglenook introduced with very pleasing results. The main stairs are placed in a central panelled octagonal hall rising to the full height of the building and lighted from above.'

All this rather sumptuous building activity meant that architects emerged too as a small but not inconsequential segment of the affluent class. Charles Freeman had started with a modest residence on Greenmarket Square before building himself a mansion called Thornhill House in wooded grounds at the top of Portswood Road.

C.H. Smith, the architect responsible for Mansion House, built himself a private palace of a house called The Gables in Camp Ground Road. His garden was a maze of terraces and follies all in rustic stonework into which he'd built fragments of Batavian brickwork and other relics 'salvaged' from Cape Dutch houses.

The prolific Anthony de Witt, the author of the Drill Hall and Lennon's Buildings and numerous other public and private edifices, many of them restrained in style, let his hair down for the design of Montana Vista, the house he built for himself in Aliwal Road, Wynberg. A riotous extravaganza in the Swiss chalet style, it had tier upon tier of balconies, some iron, some wood, no two windows were alike (or so it appeared) and atop all this a steep pitched roof was decorated with every possible device for the diversion of the eye. The garden, too, was in keeping; the entrance was through huge gates on a corner, at an angle to the house with its grandiose front steps; there were palms, Norfolk pines and monkey puzzles; one balcony was romantically hung with wisteria.

Gardening was an obsession with a number of notable Capetonians. The most famous of the older gardens were Hamilton Ross's on the Mount Nelson property and the older Ludwigsberg which Baron von Ludwig had developed on the apparently inhospitable ground not far from Kloof Nek. Many of the botanical treasures assembled from the corners of the earth by the Baron found their way into the Public Gardens, when the old estate was sold.

Among private gardeners, Ralph Henry Arderne and his son Matthew were pre-eminent. By the last three decades of the nineteenth century, the family property, The Hill, in Claremont boasted 50 acres of man-made paradise where trees and flowering shrubs from all over the world were arranged in artistic splendour.

The Ardernes were of solid country stock from Cheshire, genteel but not well-off when they'd arrived at the Cape earlier in the century. The family fortune had been amassed through thrift and hard work and won them unquestioning social acceptance. The governor and all the important names on the social register turned out in morning coats and top hats for the garden parties held at The Hill later in the century.

Anders Ohlsson was another example of the successful self-made man. His purchase of Montebello (a local equivalent of a stately home) announced to the world that he had arrived as a man of substance. Success, a genial manner and genuine sense of social responsibility had earned him his place in society (although not quite at the highest level) in spite of obscure origins in Scandinavia which had left him with a heavy accent. Among the causes Ohlsson championed were the 'colour-blind franchise', the ballot, the use of Dutch in the Civil Service and courts, better treatment of convicts and other labourers and improved conditions for lepers and lunatics. He showed proper concern for the arts, being one of the driving forces behind the success of the Opera House. And his sporting interests – shooting, hunting and fishing – marked him as the right kind of person.

Racing, another traditional rich man's pastime, had fallen somewhat from grace in the Cape, largely because owners had found it financially worthwhile to move their strings up to the richer tracks at Kimberley and on the Reef. Race Week in Cape Town was still a major social event and the new Metropolitan Handicap run at Kenilworth was much talked about. Attendance there was almost a little model of the new social order. At the meetings on the old Green Point track, the difference between the nobs and the navvies had been unmistakable. Now middle-class people with aspirations made up the majority of the gathering.

This may not have been an age when all attained elegance, but it certainly was a time when everyone aspired to it.

And in spite of the emerging middle class in its ready-made 'fashionable' clothing, the heights of fashion were still the prerogative of the very rich. The fashionable woman needed boundless energy to keep up with the day's demands for changes of clothing – even before the correct decisions were to be made for the evening. She would slip from dressing-gown into breakfast gown; then a tea gown if she was 'at home'. Other costumes were decreed for public appearance – different styles for walking, shopping and visiting. Sleeves expanded and contracted (the fashionable sleeves of the

The Grange homestead as it looked before Cecil Rhodes rebuilt it as the magnificent Groote Schuur – the job had to be done twice, because after the initial refurbishment, fire gutted the mansion.

1890s took two-and-a-half yards of fabric each); necklines rose during the day and plunged after dark; bustles rose and fell; skirts spread over crinoline frames or were tied back at knee-length with concealed ribbons to make the front hang straight and slim; hairstyles alternated between bouffant and severe with a rapidity during these decades that echoed the rapid changes in politics and society.

It took wit to keep up. When the Princess of Wales (who created the fashion for the 'cuirass' bodice) wore a short, very curly fringe, the clever woman followed suit with a false fringe curled on to a comb. If one cut one's hair in front there was a very real danger of being caught out when fashion changed again. In the early 1870s there was an enormous demand for false hairpieces to create the tangle of curls and braids then fashionable.

Younger women expressed their increasing need to be taken seriously by the end of the century by wearing squarer shoulders with large sleeve-heads, slightly higher heels, smoother upswept hairstyles and small hats with flowerpot crowns to enhance the impression of increased stature.

But along with all the dressing up and dressing down came a general laxness when it came to observing the conventions of dress that distinguished polite society. Perhaps it was the climate, perhaps the distance from England with its arbiters of taste and manners, but in the colony one somehow let things slip. 'Even the Englishmen who came out gave up their sartorial grandeur very quickly,' noted Lady Edward Cecil, 'and I have a vivid recollection of . . . Lord Stanley riding with strings tied round the bottom of his trousers to keep them down, which they did very imperfectly. I don't say he often dressed like this for riding at the Cape but he yielded to this awful incorrectness as part of the *laissez faire* of the country.'

AT LEISURE

eisure time for Cape Town's population was given an inimitable flavour by the beauty of the environment. Even the poorest of citizens could escape from the bustle of the metropolis and gain the benefits of fresh air, exercise and the contemplation of the work of Nature's Great Architect.

The love affair with locomotives showed no sign of abating and an outing by train meant double pleasure. The Cape Government Railways obliged by laying on all manner of special excursions and picnic trains. Even when stricter Christians predicted doom for those allowing and indulging in the sinfulness of a Sunday train service, they were overridden because stronger public opinion was in favour of anything that would help the working classes get out of the unhealthy air of town and into the country – even if only so that they could work harder and longer in consequence.

Mountaineering tended to attract the more patrician types and the Mountain Club was formally created at a meeting in Kamp's Cafe in September 1891. Founder members (under the presidency of Sir James Sivewright) had been active as a casual association for several years before that but when five climbers had been marooned in the mist on the mountain in 1889, a faction under botanist Dr Rudolf Marloth had agitated for the constitution of a club to co-ordinate safety and rescue procedures. Club membership encouraged many a Capetonian to reach new heights, literally. In 1892 S. B. Morgenrood and H. Bishop pioneered Window Gorge, Silverstream Ravine and Kloof Corner. The first ascents of Saddle Face, Silverstream Buttress and Right Face followed in 1894. By the end of the century over 40 new routes had been charted.

Women were active in the Mountain Club too. Negotiating the chains on the climb up Lion's Head was not impossible in a long skirt and petticoats, but an ascent by, say, Platteklip Gorge was obviously more popular. Many groups climbed up the ravine to pay homage to the wonders of nature. One would wait until full moon and then leave at midnight. Each rest stop up the near-vertical path allowed fresh views of the sleeping city and the silvery bay. From Maclear's Beacon, the fixed star of the Robben Island light and the flashes from the Cape Point and Dassen Island lighthouses were visible. Then, at last, came the moment of moments: sunrise.

Left *Burlesque, music hall, pantomime and all manner of other high jinks helped Capetonians, high and low, to relax.*
Right *Picnics provided not only healthful fresh air and exercise, but also a chance to escape the watchful eye of chaperons.*

Bathing was bliss in the heat of summer. Barbed wire kept prisoners of war confined to one spot at Simonstown. In his story, 'The Captive', Kipling described their 'shrimp-pink bodies' in the green water.

A correspondent of the *South African College Journal* described this soul-stilling experience:

❛In the East ... a belt of low-lying clouds ... gleamed purple and black, heralding the approach of morn ... I took some photographs of our party but we never seemed to grow tired of looking out on to the scene ahead of us: it was glorious, for from the sea of mist, like grim piratical barques, appeared the mountain-tops of the peaks ... Paarl Rock, Simonsberg, Helderberg ... and to the east, directly in the path of Father Sol, lay the range of mountains whose highest point is Du Toit's Peak ... Excitement ran high as to who was to be the first to catch the real rays of that other G.O.M. [Grand Old Man] the Cape possesses ... "Here he comes!" was all the cry and exclamation and amazement break (*sic*) from our lips as we watch the effect of the Old Man's genial countenance ... Hey Presto! and the whole scene ... [changes] with the rising of the King of all the Lights ... Trips and excursions of this character are the sort which teach us individually to realise what it is to commune with Nature and to view her handiwork. Wise men talk of Nature's solitude as existing away from the busy turmoil of life ... [but] she will teach you to find solitude where man works, in the city.❜

Similarly uplifting experiences in smaller doses were to be had walking along the new pipe track above Camp's Bay or along the broad tree-shaded pavements of Victoria Road in Sea Point. Closer to the hub of things were the Municipal Gardens and De Waal Park with the added attraction of a military band playing the kind of stirring music that would rouse the dormant patriot in even the most apathetic of breasts.

Each Sunday more energetic and privileged Capetonians bowled off into the country on their cycles. There were inspiring rides along the Victoria Road with the added attraction of ozone and breathtaking views of the Brighton of South Africa.

Walking parties were almost as popular and also offered a discreet escape from strict chaperonage. It was not impossible for a couple to snatch a few moments in private during an outing with a young group that included tolerant brothers and cousins. The Round House, a catering establishment overlooking Camp's Bay, made no bones about the fact that its popularity as a picnic venue was partly due to romantic trysting places in the surrounding 'bosky woods and umbrageous bowers'.

The colony's less stringent (or downright lax) observance of social convention was deplored by sticklers and revelled in by many a modern miss. The fun for visitors and newcomers inevitably began during the steamer voyage out.

Baron de Rothschild, past the age of making hay himself when he came to South Africa on the *Dunottar Castle*, chronicled some of the high jinks in his diary. As they steamed through the tropics the ship was canvassed all over and people disported themselves in 'the most extraordinary costumes – the men parti-coloured flannels without waistcoats and the ladies in all kinds of loose fluttering garments'. In the evening there was dancing and though the Baron found the heat fatiguing he did his duty and danced the lancers. During the day the young ladies played cricket, the young men quoits and the older members of the party whist, nap, cribbage and bezique.

To enliven the evening hours there were concerts and a Fancy Dress Ball. The Baron appeared as Julius Caesar, clad in a tunic and a toga cut by a stewardess from a sheet and crowned with a wreath of bayleaves, courtesy of the chef. The ladies impersonated Japanese, Italian and Welsh peasants, with a sprinkling of Grace Darlings and whist-cards, while the men were rigged out as cooks, brigands, ranchers and admirals. As reluctant president of the entertainments committee, the Baron supervised a day of deck-sports, during which the passengers ran races of every kind and description.

During his first south-bound voyage, Winston Churchill noted that a fall in temperature caused a rise in spirits. It suddenly seemed important to organise athletic sports. 'A committee is appointed, Sir Redvers Buller becomes president. A two days' meeting is arranged, and on successive afternoons the more energetic passengers race violently to and fro on the deck, belabour each other with bolsters, or tumble into unforeseen troughs of water to their huge contentment and the diversion of the rest.'

Crossing the Equator, Churchill wrote: 'Neptune and his consort boarded us near the forecastle and paraded round the ship in state. Never have I seen such a draggle-tailed divinity. An important feature in the ritual which he prescribes, is the shaving and ducking of all who have not passed the line before. But our attitude was strictly Erastian, and the demigod retired discomforted to the second class, where from the sounds which arose he seemed to find more punctilious votaries.'

The serious-minded young scribe would no doubt have been equally disapproving of the traditional carryings-on at the South African College. The College House residents provided the heartbeat for much of the extra-curricular shenanigans endemic to this seat of learning. Highlights on the year's programme of fun included the annual cadet corps camp-out and

The craze for cycling had reached epidemic proportions and showed absolutely no sign of abating.

the watermelon war. Farmer van der Byl of Welmoed, near Faure, delivered to College House, each year, a wagonload of fine watermelons which were devoured instantly and the dripping rinds used as missiles for a mock battle. Other impromptu pranks included duckings in the college water-cask and spats with Henry Bassett, an irascible old soldier who played the unenviable role of janitor. Obviously no young lady with any self-respect would indulge in such antics, but as a full member of the college she was not exempt from freshman initiation. For this madcap ritual, the entire student body took itself off to the Paddock – the playing-field cum meadow for the governor's cows which lay immediately opposite the South African College across the Avenue. The 'old' students formed a double line between which initiates had to pass while they were pelted with acorns. As a concession to gallantry, the ladies were allowed a knight-at-arms to protect them on the hazardous passage.

All sorts of similar tomfoolery was rife on the Peninsula on high days 63 and holidays. On Easter Monday and for Christmas week, for example, the Crown Hotel in Claremont laid on a variety of holiday sports – tug-of-war, bicycle racing, skittle alleys (Claremont against All-Comers), picnicking, dancing under the Famous Oaks to a full string band, Christy Minstrels and excursions by cart to the seaside.

In addition to the traditional holidays, special national anniversaries and local events were celebrated with boundless energy. History was in the making at this southerly latitude and the Cape, with its unmatched sense of occasion, did not let an opportunity for general jollity slip by.

Simon's Town had been the scene of many festivities over the decades because it was sheltered from the winter winds and had enjoyed popularity as a refuge for shipping since the seventeenth century. But, ironically perhaps, one of the grandest celebrations in the little settlement's history was the extension of the railway line to that point.

The event marked a new era in life at the Cape but the energy and enthusiasm with which the community celebrated the opening of the line had as much to do with an incorrigible fondness for a party. The tradition dated back two centuries. On 2 March 1654, for example, a whale was beached in the mouth of the Salt River. Commander Johan van Riebeeck and his wife went down to pay their respects to the dead grampus escorted by a company that included a trumpeter. Johan Nieuhof, a Dutch merchant, was among them.

'It was indeed large,' Nieuhof commented on the creature later. 'We climbed up on to it and had the trumpeter play the tune "Wilhelmus of Nassau".' The whale's spirit, judging by the stench issuing from its remains, had long since departed so it was not able to appreciate the salute, but nonetheless the expedition had been carried off with appropriate swagger. And swagger was certainly not lacking at Simon's Town's great railway opening on 1 December 1890. The whole community was *en fête*. Every ship, building, wall, fence and pole was smothered in bunting, decorations and flowers. A triumphal arch of 'rustic beauty' was erected over the main street. Flags fluttered against the sky. Shopkeepers had entered into informal competition with one another in the line of imaginative displays. Turner's Drapery sported a pink banner expressing 'Welcome to the Iron Horse' in large blue letters. Just for good measure, a miniature railway set was arranged in front of this. The station was opened by the prime minister, Cecil Rhodes, who was accompanied by the treasurer, John X. Merriman, the attorney-general, James Rose Innes, the general manager of the Cape Government Railways, Charles Elliott, and a host of other important personages.

They had thundered out of Cape Town station at 9.35 a.m. on a special train and at every stop more and more merrymakers crowded aboard. At Wynberg the band of the East Yorkshire Regiment was picked up and pro-

vided accompaniment to the music of wheels on tracks. The train steamed triumphantly into the new station, cutting the 'fragile barrier of tape'. The crowds cheered, the Royal Standard fluttered overhead and the band of H.M.S. *Raleigh* played rousing music.

The prime minister and his party were received by Mayor Hugo and Rhodes then declared the line open for passenger and goods traffic in a speech that stirred the patriotism in every heart present. The assembled school children sang 'God save the Queen' and the illustrious guests were driven down the main street to the British Hotel where a grand luncheon awaited them. All the children, regardless of colour or class, were granted the special treat of a free train ride to Kalk Bay and back. After that they trooped off to the green for sports while the adults strolled about, admiring the decorations or picnicking on the beach.

At the luncheon, Rhodes delivered another speech before handing over the floor to Merriman, Rose Innes and several other speakers. Toasts were proposed to everyone even remotely concerned with the line, including the clergy, the Press, and, of course, the ladies.

That night Chinese lanterns flickered all over town, ships were illuminated with electric lights and salutes were fired. The navy then put on a fine display of fireworks, the revelry continuing until midnight. The last train to leave needed two locomotives to pull 25 coaches full of exhausted Capetonians home again.

Huge floral and foliage arches were very much a feature of the show at Cape events, no matter how great the challenge of wind and sun issued to decorators who scorned the challenge of scale. Way back in 1858, when they had opened Thomas Bain's Grey's Pass over the mountains into the Olifants River Valley, local floral engineers had constructed a number of arches of greenery over the new road, each bearing a suitably serious message: 'Be firm in Difficulties', 'A Good Name Shines for Ever' and 'Labour conquers Everything'.

Before the advent of electricity, most gala affairs were arranged during the day though evening displays of fireworks and clowning with the exciting but dangerous firebarrels and fireballs usually followed. Electricity introduced thrilling new possibilities for after-dark festivities and displays. Complicated illuminations were now possible. Public buildings and the new electric trams could be outlined in lights, much to the delight of the populace. It was a far cry from the ride-past of cycles festooned with Chinese paper lanterns which had had to pass for an illuminated display on pre-electric nights.

By the end of the century leisure-time had extended long after dark. More sophisticated lighting and improved public transport gave the theatre industry a much-needed shot in the arm. There was an increase in activity (if not necessarily in professionalism) as far as high and low drama and all kinds of public musical entertainment.

Staple fare was provided on a regular basis by impresarios like the indefatigable Disney Roebuck and Frank Fillis of circus fame; the spice of surprise supplied by fascinating mavericks like Orpheus McAdoo, born in North Carolina to literate slave parents who were able to educate him. He had started his working life as a teacher with the avowed intent to prove that 'the Negro has a brain, and if only given a chance of cultivation, he will show his hidden qualities'. At 27, he'd decided his true vocation was music and he left teaching to make a full-time career of his hobby: singing. He joined the Fisk Jubilee Singers who almost immediately set out on a seven-year world tour to raise funds with concerts featuring Negro spirituals – the 'sorrow songs'.

By 1890, McAdoo had formed his own troupe and set sail for England where he met his future wife, a 'lady tenor' named Mattie Allan. Failing in England, he shipped the troupe to South Africa where he met with success beyond his 'wildest dreams and anticipations'.

The first minstrel shows had been seen in South Africa in 1850 but it was the New Christy Minstrels' visit in 1862 that really caught the popular imagination. 'In the next three decades, blackface minstrel shows became the dominant form of popular white musical and theatrical entertainment in South Africa, and from at least the 1880s found ready acceptance among the Cape Coloureds.' The crude mockery of 'acting the nigger' was the basis of the entertainment but McAdoo and his singers were not confused with this trend. Cape Town audiences hailed them as one of the finest musical groups ever to visit. 'Singing such as [this] . . .' noted the *Cape Argus* 'has never before been heard in this country. Their selection consists of a peculiar kind of part song, the different voices joining in at most unexpected moments in a wild kind of harmony . . . it is without doubt one of the attributes of the race to which they belong, and in their most sacred songs they seem at times inspired, as if they were lifting up their voices in praise of God with hopes of liberty.'

Writing home, McAdoo said he was appalled at the racism he and the troupe encountered in South Africa; he was too socially adroit to express the same feelings here. As one of his countrymen put it: 'In his accent he is decidedly English. He dresses well in the style of the English upper class . . . He wears a few diamonds within the bounds of propriety . . . From all indications he is a thorough gentleman from tip to tip.' Balancing minstrel songs with slave hymns and (after 1890 when Guiseppe Verdi had toured South Africa with an opera company) a few emotional arias, he kept local audiences eating out of the palm of his hand for five years.

Ladies rowing on Table Bay: boats could be hired
at the old fish jetty at the foot of Adderley Street but it was usually
advisable to take an experienced seaman along
in case of treacherous weather.

Arts and Letters

Architecture has its political uses, as that great English architect Sir Christopher Wren had pointed out in the eighteenth century. Cecil Rhodes was fond of adding, 'Pericles through art did teach lazy Athenians to love Empire'. The art he was referring to was architecture. With these views in currency it was natural that architecture was regarded most highly of all the arts in Cape Town during our years.

All of Cape Town admired the splendid building housing the South African Library between the Gardens and Wale Street, but only a small fraction of the population had been inside to read the fine collection of books which had been founded on a priceless donation by Sir George Grey. And those who did enter often seemed to have done so only to enjoy a snooze in one of the comfortable leather armchairs provided. A delightful incongruity had been added to the stately colonnaded halls flanking the entrance hall when one side was occupied temporarily by the South African Museum. And what a stately procession was to be seen when elephant and antelope, giraffe and zebra were carried, along with hundreds of smaller exhibits, through the Gardens to the new South African Museum which occupied the space that was once a meadow between the South African College and the first beds of garden.

The South African Library, designed by Kohler, was in the Corinthian style and based on the façade of the Fitzwilliam Museum at Cambridge. The new Museum was in the Republican style. An open competition was held for its design and Vixseboxse, a Dutch architect from the Public Works Department of the Transvaal Republic, had won the contract. The building cost sevenpence a square foot to erect and Charles Fairbridge, the lawyer, was largely responsible for motivating and financing its construction. The first curator was his friend, Edgar Layard, brother of the man who discovered the ruins of Nineveh.

It was typical of the tenor of the times that the plastic arts did not have an equally grand headquarters erected in their honour.

Sketching and watercolour painting were regarded as necessary social accomplishments but colonials did not have the cash or inclination to

Left *Keeping an eye on high society from the balcony of the Opera House.*
Right *The South African Library provided house room for all manner of curious specimens until the South African Museum was completed higher up in the Gardens.*

66

invest heavily in pictures. Shops in town, including the larger department stores, offered the kind of framed prints necessary for the decoration of a house. The Fine Arts Association and various art unions enjoyed steady but not spectacular patronage. In 1889, for example, the Fine Arts Association advertised an exhibition in its New Street Gallery; it featured 100 new works for which it had laid out £75. In keeping with the art union principle, if one subscribed 10 shillings one got a ticket for the draw and a chance to acquire one of the paintings at the end of the show.

Of the special-interest societies for disciples of the arts and sciences, the Owl Club enjoyed pre-eminence. It was formed in mid-century for the purposes of serious discussion of matters pertaining to the arts and professions. This exclusive coterie played host to many a celebrated visitor, including the American novelist and humorist known as Mark Twain who visited the Cape in 1896. Had the Owl Club not taken him under its wing, as it were, the besotted Cape populace would almost certainly have killed

him with kindness: he was all but mobbed after each of three public lectures at the Opera House. In his further wanderings through South Africa, Mark Twain was guided by Arthur Elliott who was on the threshold of a career as unofficial photographer laureate of the colony.

Perhaps the foremost of all of late Victorian Cape Town's men of arts and letters was David Gill, Her Majesty's Astronomer at the Cape of Good Hope. Born into a family of well-to-do Aberdonian tradesmen, he had entered the family business, pursuing wide-ranging intellectual interests as a pastime. Astronomy was his passion and his 'vast views, greatness and purity of mind, acuteness in detail, conscientiousness and enormous activity' won him a wide circle of friends of a cultural, philosophical, artistic and literary bent.

Sir George Airy, the astronomer royal, became his patron and Gill soon gave up the financial security of a mercantile career for the profession of astronomer. His first office was at a private observatory and from there he

Once the South African Museum building was ready to house them, preserved animals and other curiosities were carried ceremonially through the gardens from their temporary home in the library.

made two field trips, one to Ascension and the other to Mauritius. He arrived at the Cape in June 1879 and, though the observatory was almost the only place from which the southern skies could be studied, he found it a forlorn and neglected spot, with a rough track connecting it to Observatory Road Station.

He and Mrs Gill set about transforming it into a verdant paradise but, though Gill was a notorious worker, he had time to make some influential and enriching friendships. Among these were General 'Chinese' Gordon and Frederick Richards ('King Dick' to his cronies), Commodore of Simon's Bay and First Sea Lord of the Admiralty between 1893 and 1896. He corresponded with astronomers all over the world and, in 1896, entertained Miss Agnes Clerke at the observatory. She had written the definitive history of nineteenth-century astronomy.

The Gills were frequently invited to Government House and Sir Bartle Frere prevailed on the busy astronomer to assume the chairmanship of the philosophical society when Frere's term of office ended. In spite of the passionate earnestness he devoted to his work, Gill was a tireless dancer and an entertaining *conversazione* and dinner guest with a waggish sense of humour. When asked how he had spent his spare time at the Paris Astrographic Congress of 1896, he'd answered, 'I strolled along the boulevards looking at the beautiful Parisiennes.'

In 1880 he'd become president of the Caledonian Society and was never too high and mighty to join them in a fling. After one St Andrew's Night dinner, he accompanied the Highland Regiment back to the Castle quadrangle where they'd struck up the fifes and drums and danced the wildest of reels in spite of the fact that it was well after bedtime. Music was fun as well as a source of serious pleasure for a man like Gill.

No person who lacked the musical knowledge necessary to appreciate the work of the great masters could claim to be civilised. The ability to acquit oneself reasonably on an instrument and to sing were virtually prerequisites too. 'Music elevated to the dignity of a serious science, would become a real power of good amongst us,' wrote a contributor to the *South African College Journal*. 'Indeed, so powerful are the physical, intellectual, moral and social attributes of music, that it is an open question whether Mr Rhodes would not be benefiting this country more by endowing it with a musical than with a Theological Seminary.' Unfortunately, the South African capacity for art was limited, in his opinion, partly because the nation was young and partly because there was too much racial diversity.

Nevertheless, private orchestral societies were formed in order to try to rectify the situation. The 14-strong South African College ensemble met once a fortnight at Professor Hahn's house with the purpose of cultivating and promoting classical music. Another group met to perform and for

An appreciation of Nature's handiwork was edifying to the soul and Cape Town's eager company of landscape photographers were not slow on the uptake.

'earnest discussion' about starting a city orchestra. 'Surely lovers of the Divine Art, who are anxious to have latent capabilities evoked, could do no better than join a society so instructive, and one productive of so much enjoyment?' asked a recruiting notice.

By the last three decades of the century, visiting musicians completely cast thespians in the shade with their terrific popularity. Opera was all the rage.

Gramophones and cameras were among the most popular of the new gadgets. The Eagle Gramophone Company offered 'the most up-to-date and best talking machine, just the thing' for five guineas.

It was hard to imagine life before the sewing machine and the camera. No anniversary, occasion or outing was complete unless it was recorded on a few snapshots. No home could be considered completely decorated without tasteful photographic portraits. Beginners were offered hand models

69

A handsome marble statue of Sir George Grey
provided a suitable frontispiece to the classical façade of the
South African Library, opened by Prince Alfred in 1860.

like the Stopit. For more advanced work the eight-guinea Instantograph, 'the *sine qua non* of the amateur photographer', was recommended. The set included camera, slide, lens, shutter and a polished mahogany stand with a brass top. The camera boasted leather bellows and sophisticated rack-work to allow for fine adjustment. The lens was of the most rapid type and the patent instantaneous shutter worked with great speed too.

But architecture remained the highest art form of all. For Empire-builders, architecture was the ultimate means of expression for that 'lofty Imperial vision' of dominance, permanence and power. In uncertain times, great buildings, however new, seem to stand like rocks in the surf of time. In fact the newer, the better. Cape Town's Castle was both ancient and solid, but regarded as primitive and quaint because it spoke of life outside the

British Empire. And had it not been for the Dutch faction, mobilised on this issue by Marie Koopmans-De Wet, the Castle would have been razed to the ground or at least mutilated before the end of the century.

The widow's house at 23 Strand Street was the meeting place of intellectuals and aesthetes: no visit to the colony was complete without attendance at one of her famous soirées. Everyone, from Cecil Rhodes downwards, paid attention to Mrs Koopmans' opinion and valued her good favour. She was a remarkably accomplished woman who spoke French, German, Dutch and English quite fluently. She and a spinster sister shared the old family house in Strand Street which was virtually a living museum with its stoep and small-paned windows, stone paved hall and steep stair-case. Inside it was a treasure-trove of antiques – silver, Delft china, Dutch pictures and cabinets. She had maintained her father and grandfather's library with its manuscripts and old atlases.

This colonial equivalent of Madame de Staël went to endless lengths to save the Castle, lobbying the Home Government via influential friends in

England and rallying local support through a tireless Press campaign. The old fort was used as headquarters for the army but she felt it should be given over either to the municipality or to some society for the purpose of preservation and for a museum of historical memorials. The old armoury at the Castle had been transferred to London and she made earnest representations for its return.

When Rhodes suggested that chopping off one of the points of the Castle to make way for a new tramline would not radically alter the old pile, she tartly suggested that in that case chopping off that little point on his face – his nose – would not appreciably alter his face either. The point on the Castle was spared and the widow remained vigilant in her defence of South Africa's cultural heritage. A contemporary newspaper cartoon showed her stout black-clad figure clasping an ancient oak in the Gardens while two axemen looked on.

Although Rhodes' imputed part in the Jameson Raid turned Mrs Koopmans-De Wet against him for ever, they were in fact remarkably similar in certain ways. Both believed passionately in the future of South Africa and both collected about them a coterie of influential artists, writers and thinkers. Rhodes had a house called Woolsack erected on his Groote Schuur estate as a refuge for poets and artists whom he wanted to attract to South Africa. His friend and architect Herbert Baker explained: 'The "incoherent" poetry in Rhodes was evident in his love, amounting to worship, of the mountain ... and in his wish to have the beauty he saw ... [there] expressed in art, poetry, and music. Rhodes carried away on a sudden impulse the organist of St Paul's from his luncheon party at Groote Schuur up the mountain to his favourite view ... and said to him, "Put that in your music; it's so big no artist can paint it." He did so, but it was for Rhodes' memorial service at St Paul's.'

Alas, Rhodes the politician often foiled Rhodes the patron. He went to endless trouble to cultivate Olive Schreiner who had won acclaim for her novel *The Story of an African Farm*. She was intrigued at first and accepted his hospitality at Groote Schuur. But an insight into his political ideals and methods turned her against him finally.

Sir David Gill was naturally also invited to Groote Schuur and several exchanges between the astronomer and the Empire builder were recorded by Gill's biographer. Gill had persuaded Rhodes that, in spite of the expense, he should be assisted in measuring the Arc of the Meridian through Rhodesia. Money, said Rhodes, would make it possible.

'A fine thing, money.'

'A finer thing, astronomy,' countered Gill.

'Too damn expensive,' grunted Rhodes.

Suitably, it was through architecture that Rhodes made his greatest con-

tribution to arts and letters, and his greatest discovery as far as talent was concerned. He first met Herbert Baker at a dinner party, listened to his views, took him under his wing immediately and commissioned him to restore Groote Schuur. Baker explained how he had attracted Rhodes' attention:

> ❟In my visits to the old farms on the Peninsula and in the rich valleys among the neighbouring hills I was thrilled to discover the dignity and beauty of the old homesteads that had been built by Dutch and Huguenot settlers; dignified in the ordered layout of house, outbuildings, avenues, orchards, and vineyards; beautiful in the simplicity of the architecture, white walls, solid teak or green-painted shuttered windows and doors, gracefully curved gables with softly modelled enrichments, and quiet "moleskin" thatch ... On the high tiled stoep with a solid curved-back seat at each end, and in the large entrance-hall or voerkammer (*sic*) with its polished red-tile floor and often good old furniture, one always had a hearty welcome ... I carefully studied and made sketches of [all these things] ... and wondered how little their beauty seemed to be known or appreciated ... Rhodes, too, had seen the old homesteads and he knew by a natural instinct that they were good, and formed a living part in the harmony of the Cape landscape. Their beauty was being rapidly destroyed by the discordant methods of building that were fast spreading over the country.❟

Alas, the Groote Schuur restoration was no sooner complete than fire broke out and the work had to begin all over again. But nothing could destroy the 'Cape Dutch Revival' and the re-establishment of a vernacular style of architecture which the combination of Rhodes' money and predilections and Baker's talent had set in motion.

The never-articulate Rhodes instructed Baker to give him 'the big and simple, barbaric if you like' and told him 'I like teak and whitewash'. Baker added: 'He abhorred the small and mean and anything commercial.' He sent his protégé off to scour far-flung Dutch homesteads for old treasures. Baker had been heavily influenced by the Arts and Crafts movement in England so he shared Rhodes' taste for the honest and the genuine in building materials and furbishments but his English heritage showed through willy-nilly. The interior of Groote Schuur particularly owed a good deal to the Tudor style, but even this was much closer to the South African heritage than those cast-iron flights of fancy propagated by Freeman and other Victorian architects.

Guests at Groote Schuur were left in no doubt that they were not merely visiting a province of the Empire but a place with its own character and idiosyncrasies.

71

THE MOUNT NELSON

For the more discerning members of the upper crust and for businessmen alike, the final sign that Cape Town had indeed come of age was the opening of its first really grand hotel quite up to the most sophisticated of European standards. 'High time, too,' was the general pronouncement when the new Mount Nelson Hotel was opened to the public on 4 March 1899. Situated opposite the top end of Government Avenue, it was an imposing four-storey edifice set in superb old gardens with a private deer park. The entrance to the estate was on Hof Street where a large iron gate displaying the hotel's insignia was flanked by two heavy columns.

The grounds were originally part of a sizeable estate granted to Baron Pieter van Reede van Oudtshoorn in 1743. He joined the Dutch East India Company at 29, immediately taking up the high office for which he was equipped by breeding and education. He called his imposing property 'The garden of Oudtshoorn', buying adjacent plots to extend it and establishing orchards, vineyards and vegetable gardens which were irrigated by water from the Fresh River. The baron sold this paradise in 1766 before returning to the Netherlands and in the next years it changed hands and was sub-divided frequently. In 1806 an auctioneer named William Maude bought a three-acre piece of the original estate directly opposite the top of the Avenue. It was graced with a stately home which Maude had decided would make ideal sale-rooms. A patriotic Englishman, he named his new acquisition Mount Nelson in honour of Lord Nelson who had fallen at the Battle of Trafalgar the year before.

He held successful sales of all manner of merchandise – slaves, thoroughbred horses, hardware and household linens, to name a few – before selling the property in 1816. There followed another period during which the place changed hands frequently and eventually the old house was demolished and a new one erected higher up the slopes. In 1843 Mount Nelson was bought by a prosperous and influential citizen, Hamilton Ross, for his daughter and son-in-law, Maria and John Ross. A keen landscape gardener, Ross converted the grounds into a showplace boasting deerpark, a private swimming pool, an aviary and 26 fountains.

In a shake-up connected with the failure of the Union Bank (of which

*Left Almost as soon as the hotel was opened it served as an officers' club, temporary residence for all the idle rich who'd come to watch the war and (**right**) a haven for the wealthy 'uitlander' refugees from the Rand.*

John Ross was chairman) in 1890, Mount Nelson went on to the market again and, together with a couple of adjacent plots, came into the hands of African Lands and Hotels Limited, a company founded by Sir Donald Currie of Castle shipping line fame.

It took nine years for the plan to build a nonpareil of a hotel to come to fruition in the inspired hands of London architects Messrs Dunn & Watson with Herbert Baker as local consulting architect. It was a major investment for the Castle company which denied fervently that its erection had been prompted by the least twinge of rivalry with the Union Line's sumptuous Grand Hotel (opposite Cape Town station) which had opened in 1894. The Mount Nelson was unique, claimed the brochure. It was not in competition with any other establishment but filled a gap that no other colonial establishment had even aspired to.

Almost immediately it was regarded as the only place to stay. There was hardly a luminary who came to town who did not hang up his hat against the richly flocked wallpaper of this smart establishment. Sir Redvers Buller, who was initially in command of the British forces in South Africa, made the hotel his home from home. When Field Marshal Lord Frederick Sleigh Roberts arrived with Lord Kitchener on 17 January 1900 to take over as Commander-in-Chief from Buller after the Colenso disaster, they made the Mount Nelson their headquarters. Cecil Rhodes entertained at the hotel. Lord Randolph Churchill and his son Winston stayed there (though not at the same time) as did Rudyard Kipling and his family. Lady Sarah Wilson (Winston's aunt) enjoyed a room with a view of the Bay for 15 shillings a day with all meals included. H. G. Wells arrived from England to stay at the hotel and Lady Jennie Churchill, Winston's mother, was, upon her arrival in the hospital ship *Maine*, invited to a reception given at the Mount Nelson by a team of American ladies. Arthur Conan Doyle of Sherlock Holmes fame, came out as senior physician with the Langman medical unit and travelling hospital which arrived on 21 March 1900 and was quartered at the Mount Nelson Hotel while awaiting orders.

The likes of maverick war correspondent F. W. Unger could not quite afford it, but he observed:

❦Up at the foot of Table Mountain, at the end of the Gardens Avenue, is the palatial Mount Nelson Hotel, built to cater for the diamond and gold millionaires from the North, the accommodations of which were at that time taxed to their utmost by the throngs of aristocratic officers, with their wives, sisters and sweethearts who had followed the army thus far.

'The persistent absence from the front of many of these officers "on leave" became quite a scandal until the arrival of Lord Kitchener, who stalked through the corridors one day asking all the idlers in uniform why they had nothing to do and suggesting that at his next meeting he would "find them some occupation"; whereupon the red-collared khakis vanished, the scandals ceased, and the ladies languished.❦

A baggage train was laid on to remove the officers and their effects to the lesser delights of Stellenbosch. And to be 'Stellenbosched' became part of the language of town.

Nevertheless, the Mount Nelson continued to serve as an officers' club, with an 'officers only' rule in the bar. Riled by his exclusion, a Canadian serviceman is said to have shot his way in. On another occasion a British journalist, Harwicke Stanford (popularly known as 'Mathilda Chiffon'), was tarred and feathered when he gate-crashed a private officers' party.

The hotel was also a base for those who wished to be on the spot when history was made and a haven for the wealthy Uitlander refugees from the Rand. This last group dubbed it 'The Helot's Rest' after Lord Milner sent an impassioned dispatch to the Home Government claiming that British subjects in the Transvaal were being treated as helots.

'Such a triumph of construction,' the *Cape Times* wrote only a week before the opening of the hotel, 'of decoration, so perfect a blending of a first-class modern hotel, South Africa would try vainly even to imitate, and there is no exaggeration in the statement that London, the capital of the world, would not be able to produce anything superior.'

The cream-coloured façade of the hotel featured long ranges of green-jalousied windows and balconies. Inside, a spacious entrance hall led to the grand salon – 'a gem of the furnisher's art' hung with old engravings of naval heroes and other distinguished men. 'The Chippendale tables and chairs and an inlaid grand piano were, like the furniture throughout the hotel, supplied by Warings, a name which was sufficient to guarantee quality and taste. The salon's main attraction was a bust of Lord Nelson carved out of a solid piece of oak from H.M.S. *Victory*.'

Opposite the grand salon there was a bar and beyond the bar an arched entrance to the dining-saloon with its gracefully domed ceiling, heavy oak wainscoting and gleaming oak floor. The ceiling was decorated with plaster reliefs depicting the national emblems and shield of the United Kingdom, British South Africa, Natal, the Cape Colony, the Orange Free State, the Transvaal Republic and the City of Cape Town. A relief depicting the arrival of a fleet of ships in Table Bay was the main feature over the arch leading to the conservatory.

Accomplished musicians in a musicians' gallery at the inner end of the dining-saloon entertained the diners. At the inaugural luncheon, they played the 'Ungarische' overture; a cello solo fantasia from *Faust*; 'Home Sweet Home' on the piano; violin solo 'Scotch Airs', and Weber's 'Jubel' overture.

The dining-saloon with its gracefully domed ceiling, massive oak wainscoting and polished oak floor was a fitting temple for the masterpieces of international cuisine offered to diners by the Mount Nelson chef.

Adjacent to the dining-saloon was a billiard-room containing two tables by Thurston and Co., a smoking-room and a writing-room. Neville Chamberlain, who was said to have invented snooker, challenged Colonel G. F. R. Henderson, Lord Roberts' intelligence officer, biographer of Stonewall Jackson and author of *The Science of War*, at the hotel's billiard tables.

Off the main corridor near the entrance hall was a private dining-room. Panelled in oak and seating parties of up to 30, it was said to be 'the ideal spot for the wealthy Capetonian who wished to entertain his friends to the best that Europe's markets could offer and the skill of the Mount Nelson chef'. The kitchen was underground. 'Long ranges of wine cellars stocked with over 20 000 bottles of the finest vintages to be found anywhere, were situated next to the "cool chambers" (for the storage of perishable foods) and a bottling-room containing an apparatus for filtering table water according to the famous Pasteur system.'

The laundry in the grounds behind the hotel was fitted with 'Bradford's best in the way of machinery for washing, ironing, drying and folding house-linen and wearing apparel'. Legend has it that the laundry was erected over the site of Mount Nelson's buried treasure. In the 1870s three young Ross swains embarked on a moonlight quest for this treasure. They are said to have dug up a heavy metal trunk before frightening themselves off with the belief that it contained not booty but a corpse.

In a stable next to the laundry horses were kept to transport guests in an omnibus to and from the docks and station. Electricity for lighting and heating was supplied by the hotel's own dynamo house.

75

'Every single bedroom and drawing-room offered a clear view of either mountain or sea and the visitor could take his choice of "sunlight or shades as his fancy dictates".' The more gregarious gathered on a veranda that ran along the entire frontage. Easy chairs and the pleasing propinquity of the garden and vineries, made this the ideal venue for a leisurely after-dinner cigar and gentlemanly conversation.

'The *Carisbrook Castle*, arriving on Tuesday, 28 February 1899, brought the first guests to the Mount Nelson Hotel. Madame Albani and her concert party had the distinction, along with fellow passengers from Europe, of being the pioneer guests at the hotel. From the following day onwards it was open to the public although the inauguration ceremony was only held three days later.

'On this Saturday, 4 March, representatives of the Castle Mail Packets Company, the builders of the hotel, the architects and the Press met at the Mount Nelson and, under the guidance of M. Emil Cathrein and members of the staff, made a thorough inspection of the building and duly admired its sumptuous arrangements.'

A luncheon was then served in the grand salon. The table d'hôte menu included hors d'oeuvres, *Buisson à la Reine*, *Cassolettes à la Metternich*, *Potage à la Reine Victoria*, *Consommé Fleury*, turbot, *sauce riche*, *pommes nature*, *Suprême de Volailles à la Regence*, *Chaudfroid à la Lucullus*, *Faisans truffes en volière*, Pudding *à la* Castle Line and *Mousse à la crème vanille*.

'Mr E. Powell, one of the representatives of Messrs William Cubitt & Co., the hotel's builders, in proposing "success to the Mount Nelson Hotel", said it was not merely an advance upon the hotels in Cape Town, it was an entirely new departure. He did not say a word in disparagement of the other hotels as they had shown considerable enterprise, but those who had seen the new Mount Nelson for the first time, as he had done, must have fancied that they were taking the Continental holiday for which all good colonists longed. The hotel would attract an entirely new class of custom and he did not think it would injure the old hotels very much as [it] was laying itself out for something that had not yet been brought to South Africa and that was the higher class of traveller, people who had money and leisure and would have the best of everything and would go where they could get it.

'Mr Powell concluded that at the Cape there were the attractions of a garrison, a naval station, a magnificent climate and certain British institutions and these would, he believed, bring out the precise class of people for whom this hotel had been laid out.'

M. Cathrein was a Swiss who, according to the *Cape Times*, 'has the advantage of a long experience in his native Switzerland, where he is the owner of several of the largest hotels where the British tourist foregathers in the season. He has all the tact and *savoir-faire*, not to mention the keen practical knowledge, that go to make the perfect manager of a cosmopolitan hotel and under his care, and with the staff of something near 90 well-trained white servants, Mount Nelson will not fail to fulfil its promise'.

'The idea of creating in Cape Town a hotel offering every comfort of a first-class establishment, Mr Cathrein pointed out in his inauguration speech, had not in any sense been connected with an intention to set up a commercial rivalry. It was rather to fill a want long and loudly expressed by the travelling public and by those who sought an easy and comfortable existence. With the evolution of a hotel responding in every way to modern requirements, it was hoped to build up a new clientele and to do something towards making Cape Town a still greater attraction to visitors from all parts of the world.'

Cathrein then described the technical innovations installed in the Mount Nelson Hotel. These included hot and cold running water, electric lighting throughout, ventilation and impressive precautions against the risk of fire. 'Each corridor and staircase was of solid stone, but he should mention that all the ceilings between each floor and every wall which divided the rooms were constructed of asbestine fire-proof cement or solid masonry. An elaborate system of hydrants and waterpipes, fitted to the Cape Town gauge, was to be found on all the floors, and in the event of fire among so much inflammable material, half a dozen jets could be played on the flames within minutes.' The cellars were constructed entirely of Gault bricks which were hard as iron and gave a foundation as solid as rock.

Mr L. MacLean, the chairman, reiterated these views adding that though passengers rarely expressed anything but praise for the quality of the accommodation on board ship, many first-time visitors said 'they would not return to the Cape unless their comfort on shore as well as at sea was provided for. Pressure had also been brought to bear by Government House where the accommodation for distinguished visitors was limited. The idea was that the Company should do what the great railway companies were doing in Europe: provide a first-class terminal hotel at Cape Town. An opportunity had occurred in 1890 to buy the beautiful Mount Nelson estate which was considered an ideal site for a first-class hotel, and it was purchased in case of need; but so anxious was Sir Donald Currie that there should be no interference with local enterprise, that he waited nine years to see whether someone else would not build a hotel similar to the Mount Nelson'. However, although two or three hotels were built or added to, none of them came up to the required standard.

In replying to the toast to the architects, Herbert Baker said that they had, to an exceptional degree, combined the practical and the artistic in their work, and 'to render the effect still more complete, they had designed all the furniture in the building. The directors in London, and specially Sir

Donald Currie's son-in-law, who were famous for the refinement and beauty of their own house appointments, had taken immense personal trouble with this side of the matter'.

'The chairman concluded his speech by pointing out that the Company had been wise, he thought, to seek their manager and servants in the nation of hotelkeepers, a name of which the Swiss might be as proud as the English were of Napoleon's nickname of the nation of shopkeepers, for it implied a genius for thoughtfulness and consideration to strangers. He expected the happiest results from this alliance between two lands of the mountain and the flood – Scotland and Switzerland – in bringing Europe to realise the beauties of a third mountainous country, that of the Cape Peninsula which, to his mind, was in its own way unrivalled.'

Of course many visitors to South Africa at this time came to seek their fortunes, not natural beauty. Because of its reputation, the Mount Nelson was chosen as an ideal base by Princess Catherine Radziwill, the 41-year-old European adventuress who arrived on the *Scot* in 1899 with the very apparent plan to become 'Queen of Rhodesia'. By repeatedly changing her bookings she had made sure she was on the same vessel as Rhodes (her 'poor Colossus') with whom she had already made contact on some slim political pretext. During the voyage, she had pursued him relentlessly.

In Cape Town she was a frequent visitor at Groote Schuur – invited and uninvited. She entertained her fellow guests at the hotel with accounts of Rhodes' friendship, reading out snippets from letters to reinforce the impression that they were to be married. Finally, irritated beyond the point of good manners by her prying into the business that had led up to the Jameson Raid, Rhodes asked her not to talk to him if that was all she could talk of. While he was immobilised in Kimberley during the siege she set about establishing a new 'Anglo-African Party' on his behalf, claiming that he regretted falling out with 'the Dutch side' and approaching his best-known opponents including Sauer, Merriman and Hofmeyr. She sent long reports to newspapers in Europe and was branded by all as a Boer agent.

Rhodes was furious with her when he returned from Kimberley and refused to have anything to do with her party. By this time her bill at the Mount Nelson was said to be £1 000 of which she still owed £160. She sent a woman friend to Rhodes to ask for help and he agreed to instruct his attorney to pay her bills if she would leave the country. She had no choice but to accept and sailed for Europe at the end of April 1900.

Soon she was back in Cape Town, this time staying with friends and making use of Rhodes' absence in Rhodesia to revive the impression of their intimacy. Rumours circulated that he had been a frequent visitor to her rooms in the Mount Nelson. Rhodes returned in October 1900 and the Princess invited herself to visit Groote Schuur with ever-increasing fre-quency. Ill for a month, he was unable to escape her. This no doubt precipitated a climactic confrontation in which the Princess first tried to extract money from Rhodes to start a newspaper and then appears to have threatened him with some compromising documents she had managed to get her hands on. That was the final break in their uneasy acquaintance, but she hired a house and proceeded with her intention to start a newspaper, faking his signature on promissory notes to pay her way.

Several court cases later, the Princess was found guilty of forgery and sentenced to two years' imprisonment in a 'house of correction'. Rhodes died a month before the case came to trial. She served 16 months of her sentence and was released. After a half-hearted attempt to sue the Rhodes estate for £1 400 000 for maintenance for a daughter she claimed had been born in 1897 and for fees for her political agency on his behalf, she retired to live in America.

No expense had been spared in the furnishings and no detail or refinement neglected in the desire to attract people who had money and leisure and would have the best of everything.

Commerce and Trade

Prospectors made a couple of abortive attempts to transform the economy of Cape Town with mineral 'finds' on the mountain slopes surrounding the city, but these were quickly exposed as either scams or hopelessly optimistic – or both. Prosperity on the Cape Peninsula continued to depend on commerce and trade and, to a lesser extent, on agriculture. However, the mining of copper, diamonds, gold and coal elsewhere obviously had a most beneficial effect on the Cape fiscus.

Business enterprise had been given a powerful stimulus in 1861 by a new Act limiting the liability of members of certain joint-stock companies. Obtaining a certificate of registration with limited liability was now a simple matter compared to the expensive and cumbersome procedures which had been required previously. The disasters that had resulted from investing with unlimited liability in risky businesses had made for a cautious market. The new Act had allayed this caution just as the community was beginning to forget the bitter lesson it had learnt from the copper share-mania that had broken many men during the 1850s and just before the glittering prospect of diamonds offered a short cut to wealth.

The city's merchants and businessmen had organised themselves into a Commercial Exchange in 1817 but by 1860 rapid development had changed so much in the economic life of the Cape Colony that it had become necessary to re-define the shape and function of the institution. Thus, in January 1861 (a few months before the 'limited liability' Act), the Cape Town Chamber of Commerce came into existence and John Bardwell Ebden was elected first president, a position he held until his death in 1873.

The old Commercial Exchange now functioned purely as the Commercial Reading Room (a specialised library holding books and periodicals) but still leased the splendid Palladian building on Adderley Street from its owners. Members of the Chamber of Commerce subscribed to the Reading Room, half of the Chamber's annual surplus was voted to the library and, in addition, the Chamber made a £25 contribution towards the annual rent for the room it occupied in the Commercial Exchange building. The Reading Room committee further increased its income by letting out other rooms in the building for lectures, theatrical productions, concerts, balls and bazaars. When a corn exchange was initiated by the Chamber, it too held sales (by sample only) in a side room of the building for a nominal rental of £1 a month. Sales of other categories, including works of art, jewellery and produce (also by sample only), were permitted but at £1 a day. The ostrich-feather boom lasted from roughly 1872 to 1882, and from 1877 to 1885 sales were allowed in an Exchange side room every Friday.

By 1877 it had made sense for the Chamber and the Reading Room to join forces and the combined body proved itself resolute in the face of depressions, droughts and regional wars.

Commercial vicissitudes could also be caused by natural disasters and by economic changes many thousands of miles away. The untimely demise of Hout's Bay's commercial fishing industry was an example. A boom at the small fishing harbour had been set in motion in 1834 when slavery was

Above   *Scales for weighing coinage and minerals symbolised Cape banking.*
Right   *Imposing new Adderley Street headquarters for the Standard Bank.*

abolished and Mauritius began to import indentured labour from India to man her sugar industry. By 1858 there were 120 000 Indians in Mauritius and their numbers increased rapidly until the turn of the century.

A great deal of cheap food was needed for this labour force and dried and salted snoek from the Cape colony fitted the bill admirably.

For three years in succession – between 1884 and 1886 – Hout's Bay exported 2 500 lbs of fish worth £15 000. By 1890 this had dropped to £4 500 and then the boom was over. The cause was twofold: the fish population along the west coast had plummeted and the Mauritian sugar industry had been severely hit by competition from the European sugar beet.

The streamlining of the Chamber did not include accommodation: a building committee still functioned – leasing space to the Chamber until 1892 when the building, expropriated by the government, was demolished to make way for a new post office.

Amalgamation meant that the crucial, but tricky business of co-ordinating accurate hourly shipping information by telegraph to both Chamber and Reading Room members, could now be rationalised and become more effective. The first telephone exchange in South Africa was opened in the Commercial Exchange Building in 1884 and the Chamber lost no time in securing the use of a telephone in lieu of rent, affording its members even better access to vital trade information. Thanks to increased funds, the Reading Room could now afford more reference books and a greater number of journals and periodicals and it became the hub of the city's commercial life. The advertisements of businesses were posted (for a few shillings per annum) on the stoep and in side rooms and members could make arrangements to display samples of seeds, vegetable and mineral products and other organic specimens. Subscribers included most of the influential names of the Cape: Cecil Rhodes, J. H. ('Onze Jan') Hofmeyr, John X. Merriman, David Graaff, John Garlick, Harry Bolus, Walter Searle, William Stuttaford, William Spilhaus, Ludwig Wiener and J. W. Jagger, to name a few.

From its inception, the Chamber had assisted and encouraged the formation of similar bodies in the rest of South Africa. Contact with London was strong and Cape delegates attended periodic congresses of the Chambers of Commerce of the British Empire there. (South Africa's own Association of Chambers of Commerce was constituted in 1894.) Links were maintained with Mauritius and India (both very important to trade); there was some communication with Bengal and Madagascar was courted in the interests of establishing trade. Through the kind offices of a visitor from the Melbourne Chamber, arrangements were made to exchange Cape newspapers for Australian papers. Prices and market reports were exchanged with Yokohama and Rangoon.

The Chamber also worked diligently to expedite any developments that might enhance trading opportunities – the creation and ongoing improvement of the harbour, provision of refrigeration on mailships enabling fruit to be exported, the spread of an efficient railway network and the establishment of a telegraphic link with the main business centres of South Africa and England. A vigilant eye was kept on any 'progress' that might cut Cape Town out. If, for example, too efficient a rail-link were established between the goldfields and Delagoa Bay much traffic would be diverted from Table Bay. Similarly, it was imperative that direct telegraphic contact should be established between the Cape and Britain before, say, Natal was granted a link with the undersea telegraphic cable from London to India via Aden. (The Cape was linked to the undersea cable at Aden by 1879 and the shore end of a second, west-coast cable was laid at Cape Town on 4 April 1889.)

Tariffs were another ongoing concern for the Chamber – there was tireless lobbying for reduction of customs, wharfage, railage, telegraphic, telephone and postal charges and licence fees. It became possible for Chamber members to become active players in the Harbour Board in 1881 when a constituency of people who paid dock dues was permitted to vote for three commissioners to join the four government nominees who made up the board of seven.

The heavy duty Britain levied on Cape wines was the subject of protracted action by the Chamber. The arrival of Baron von Babo, a viticulture expert who was invited by the government to upgrade local standards, was lauded and an excise on spirits was encouraged in order to foster local wine consumption. But the wine industry was one of the Chamber's less successful campaigns: between 1860 and 1883 wine exports had dropped by over 400 000 gallons. On behalf of other members of the agricultural community, the Chamber promoted prizes and shows which in their turn encouraged improved quality and production techniques. Marketing facilities were assessed and upgraded and much attention was devoted to such physical problems as the need for irrigation.

But beyond the deceptively calm and stable proceedings at the Commercial Exchange building, wildly colourful financial dramas were played out, often by the very personalities who held the Chamber of Commerce on a steady course. Mining and its effect on banking and the trade in stocks and shares was the root cause of many of these episodes. During the copper scrip boom of the 1850s, auctioneer L. P. Cauvin had stopped dealing in furniture and land and devoted his daily Grand Parade sales to scrip – Saturday's were extra lively because members of both Houses of Parliament and luminaries like Attorney-General William Porter were free to fill the front row for the auction. By 1882, Cape Town had 26 firms dealing in shares which they advertised in the Press. There were some 111 companies registered in South Africa at the time, 47 of which were involved in diamond-mining. In addition, investors could buy shares in several overseas-based companies including the Castle and Union shipping companies, the Orient Steam Navigation Company, the Eastern and Reuter's telegraph companies and the South African Brush Electric Light Company. In the next few years a rash of new companies was registered – even before the declaration of the Witwatersrand goldfields in 1886 gave fresh impetus to the fever of speculation that gripped the community.

In August 1887, a group met in the Mutual Hall to discuss setting up a share and stock exchange. Among those present were John Ross (dealer and head of the Union Bank), J. W. Sauer and David Graaff. Agreement was reached and a committee formed but the matter was then apparently laid to rest until January 1889 when a similar meeting was convened by a new cast of personalities. Ludwig Wiener, M.L.A. and president of the Chamber of Commerce, was in the chair and the gathering included Charles Lewis of the South African College, William Thorne and Thomas Fuller. A notice advising prospective members to apply appeared in the Press shortly afterwards. But barely three weeks later another newspaper notice announced that a rival stock exchange was to be opened for business at 12.15 p.m. sharp on 15 February with High Change set for 3 p.m. The venture was headed by Mayor John Woodhead and the ranks included Adrian van der Byl, Wiener's partner. John Ross and C. C. Silberbauer were among the directors and members included R. Melck, the horse-breeder, and William Rawbone, the gunsmith. The 'Woodhead Exchange' had premises on St George's Street. The opposition 'Wiener Exchange' went into operation a few days later in a side-room of the Commercial Exchange.

By 1889 the goldfields were in recession and the amusement of watching two stock exchanges compete with each other was one which the market could no longer afford. In July that year both Woodhead and Wiener withdrew and the two bodies became one. The market collapsed, but somehow trading limped forward in the uncomfortable environment of a converted warehouse. Within a year, gross irregularities in the secretary's office had been revealed and membership had dropped by half. In spite of thrift measures (including abandoning a cable service and negotiating a reduction in rent) the stock exchange was insolvent. Fresh finances were cobbled together and the exchange continued to function until the outbreak of the Anglo-Boer War. Many members of the Johannesburg Stock Exchange joined the flood of refugees from the Rand and trading in Cape Town boomed for a couple of heady years.

The highs and lows of stock trading were echoed more drastically on Cape Town's banking scene. From 1836 locally managed and funded district and private banks proliferated in the Cape. By the time diamonds were discovered, there were no fewer than 29 banks in the colony, mostly well managed and reasonably prosperous. But few were strong enough to weather the coming financial revolution or the competition offered by the great Imperial banks which had started to establish themselves at the Cape from 1861. The first, the London and South African Bank, was followed in 1862 by the Standard Bank of British South Africa. One by one the local

The Commercial Exchange, for decades the heart of
Cape Town's commercial and social life, fell to ruthless progress
and a grand new General Post Office building rose in its place
between Adderley Street and the Grand Parade.

Commodities like tusks, ostrich feathers and hides were traded up and down the coast and fetched handsome prices on the London market.

banks were liquidated or taken over as injudicious loans and investments and shaky record-keeping weakened their already limited assets. By 1893, the Stellenbosch District Bank was the only local bank still in existence.

The small man, woman or child placed his or her savings for safe-keeping with the Cape of Good Hope Savings Bank Society (opened in 1834, the year of the emancipation of slaves). The minimum deposit was sixpence and four per cent interest was paid annually on units of 12/6 as long as the total investment did not exceed £100 in the first year and £50 in succeeding years. Only charities and benevolent societies were exempt from this last rule. The Society used its funds for mortgage bonds at a rate of six per cent and no loans were made without the security of immovable property. The government offered a similar service through the Post Office Savings Bank, but when the Society decided to bow out in the 1890s, there was such a public outcry that business resumed in spite of managerial scepticism about the viability of operating in the face of a stiffly competitive market.

There was an outcry of a very different kind to two other bank closures which went ahead at the same time.

The Union Bank, like many similar institutions, had been conducting business comfortably since its foundation in 1847 and was always run by like-minded people with similar interests. Administrative staff were young and inexperienced and the 'big' men who took advantage of the conveniences of the service did not encourage over-zealous bookkeeping.

John Ross, then resident in the old Mount Nelson mansion at the top of the Gardens, was chairman of the bank when it crashed in mid-1890. The disaster was precipitated by a forged signature on a bill of exchange for £151 000 purportedly due on the account of Alfred Beit. The mining magnate was a life governor of De Beers and a founder of Rhodes' Chartered Company so his credit was assumed to be impeccable. Further, he had allowed two earlier bills signed in the same way. It transpired that the forger was a cousin and Beit had allowed the earlier bills to avoid family embarrassment. Amid frantic telegrams to Beit in London and his office in Kimberley and consultations with Sir Henry Juta, the attorney-general, the bank was forced to close its doors on 29 July 1890. But the full seriousness of the situation for shareholders only emerged subsequently.

The bank had been registered as an unlimited liability company. One third of the original capital had never been paid up and large sums of money had disappeared from the books the year before. Losses sustained in 1886 had been glossed over while directors, including Ross, discreetly reduced their shareholdings. The manager confessed to the directors that he had advanced £160 000 to other parties in Kimberley without security and a committee of investigation discovered that the bank had operated without auditors or a system of inspection. An interdict was hastily placed on one of the directors for trying to protect his assets by selling a house to his daughter for a nominal sum. And while successive details of the scandal rocked South Africa the liquidators calculated the liability of each shareholder, taking individual wealth into account. Twenty-eight of the 135 were ladies 'understood to have few reserves' and only a dozen or so of the shareholders were rich and would thus have to carry the brunt. William Marsh had only 15 shares, but he had to pay £80 000.

This disaster naturally caused nervous ripples to run through the financial community and even long-established quasi-government establishments like the Cape of Good Hope Bank (as distinct from the Cape of Good Hope Savings Bank Society) saw fit to reassure its customers that the stability that had been maintained since the bank opened in 1836 remained unimpaired. Yet on 19 December 1890 the chairman, Charles Eaton, was to be seen at the cashier's desk, publicly withdrawing £20 000 in gold from his personal account. The news spread like wildfire and depositors large and small tried to rescue their funds. Cape Town's Anglican clergy lost their entire funds of £20 000 − on the day of the closure, the dean had withdrawn the total, but had not insisted on cash, accepting instead the bank's own notes which were no longer legal tender.

Hardly a single prominent family or business was not affected by these crises, inspiring a local satirist to rhyme:

When Auntie's bank just folded up
She did not suffer all alone;
the Social Circle drained the cup
And gave the whole affair a tone.

From ducal fief and vast estate,
And ancient lines without a stain,
The money of the good and great
And noble − all went down the drain.

And as for the Directors bold,
They too were men of highest rank;
Their crests and families were old
As their ideas − which smashed the bank.

The Cape Banking Act of 1891 was an attempt to prevent their repetition. From then on, every bank was to publish a quarterly report in the *Cape Government Gazette*; 'surprise statements' were to be demanded by the treasury without warning; instead of allowing a bank to produce its own notes, the treasury would henceforth supply notes once the bank had deposited securities in the form of paid-up capital and reserves.

The legislation served only to reinforce the process that had started mid-century: the weak growing weaker and the strong growing stronger. The Standard Bank had been one of the stronger since its foundation in Port Elizabeth in 1862. Within a year a branch was opened in Adderley Street in the premises of a pastrycook called Cairncross. By 1877 the Standard had taken over the London and South African Bank and was doing the honours for the governments of both the Cape Colony and the South African Republic. In 1882 it won the City of Cape Town account as well. In 1883, when the mayor opened the Standard's new home − a neo-classic palace designed by Charles Freeman − he observed that the bank was '... indeed the national bank of South Africa ...'

New businesses meant more prosperity for the emerging middle classes. An architect as busy as Charles Freeman employed a number of clerks, draughtsmen and junior architects.

83

THE POLITICAL SCENE

An independent political spirit had started to stir in the Cape Colony with the successful anti-convict campaign of 1849, a crisis unwittingly precipitated by the governor, Sir Harry Smith. Mindful of the urgent need for harbour works and the shortage of labour, he had asked the colonial secretary to declare the colony a place to which convict labour could be sent. The heavily laden convict ship, *Neptune*, was under way before the community was even informed of the decision. But Smith had underestimated the power and solidarity of local sentiment. While the *Neptune* stood at anchor in Simon's Bay, an unprecedented campaign of resistance was waged in the Peninsula, fired by propaganda – the new weapon – and armed by a free Press. Using tactics that some observers felt were 'disgraceful and un-English', the Anti-Convict Association won the day and the *Neptune* sailed for Hobart after five months in Simon's Bay.

The colony may not have been ready yet to set up a representative government that could reach consensus, but it was clearly high time that a movement in that direction be made. As a concession to local initiative, municipalities and district road boards were invited in 1849 to suggest members for government nomination to the legislative council. It took a further three years of lobbying, debate and agitation before, in March 1853, a colonial ordinance gave the colony a representative system with two elective houses.

These two bodies could criticise and check the legislative action that was still the prerogative of the Crown in Parliament in London. The Assembly sat in the banqueting hall of the Goede Hoop Lodge at the top of Grave Street while the Council sat in an upstairs room in the Supreme Court at the top of Adderley Street. Early debates were characterised by confusion and lack of information. As part of the legacy of Somerset's Anglicising campaign, proceedings were in English until 1882 when the use of Dutch was also permitted; whereupon, as Mark Twain put it, they could argue in both languages and agree in neither.

Attendance by out-of-town members was bad and resignations frequent. The colony was poor and very far-flung. It cost a good deal more than the one shilling a mile travel allowance and £1 a day subsistence

Left *John Xavier Merriman, locally bred colonial statesman.*
Right *The new Parliament buildings symbolised the weighty import of responsible government, the statue of the Queen affirmed the Cape's ultimate allegiance.*

allowance to come to Cape Town and simply sit for four months during the lambing or planting seasons. There were dire security problems on the eastern frontier and a degree of ignorance about conditions in various constituencies prevailed. Consensus and strong leadership were complicated by the laudable emphasis by members on independence and freedom from party ties. Honourable members were expected to vote on issues according to the dictates of conscience. Andries Stockenström, the member for Graaff-Reinet, was the quintessential private member: he belonged to neither the Anglican nor the Dutch Reformed churches, and was disaffected from the commercial interests of Cape Town and Port Elizabeth. As late as 1894 members like Anders Ohlsson were still winning votes through claims of complete independence of a party line.

In spite of all these difficulties, a constitution involving the greater autonomy of responsible government was granted in 1872. Enthusiasm for this development was not unanimous in British circles. The historian, J.A. Froude, noted bitterly in 1875 that 'Cape politicians strut about with their constitution as a schoolboy newly promoted to a tail-coat while we are to defend their coasts and keep troops in order to defend them in case of a Kafir (sic) insurrection'.

The first prime minister of the Cape Colony was Sir John Charles Molteno whose dourly powerful personality had earned him the sobriquet 'the lion of Beaufort'. He was installed during the governorship of Sir Henry Barkly and he and his ministry were dismissed in 1878 by the new governor, Sir Bartle Frere, because he disagreed with Whitehall on the subject of 'native affairs'. Molteno felt these domestic matters should be left to the colonial government; the imperial authorities felt otherwise. Sir Gordon Sprigg became premier in his place and was to occupy the 'hot seat' four times, including a term of office during the Anglo-Boer War when the constitution had been suspended and so he governed without a parliament.

Up until 1872, the office of the colonial secretary had been the medium of communication between the governed, the government and the governor. The function was largely taken over by a so-called 'prime minister's department' established with responsible government. In 1886, for example, the Colonial Office still controlled the Deeds Registry, divisional courts, education, hospitals, asylums, postal services, the police and the departments concerned with defence. The office of Secretary of Native Affairs, also established in 1872 to control all matters relating to the 'aborigines' of the colony, was abolished in 1893 and the work transferred to the prime minister's department.

All male British subjects who met the franchise qualifications were eligible to stand and to vote, regardless of race, colour or religion. The 'coloured' population of the Peninsula and the Fingoes, who were under Brit-

ish protection, were among the people who might technically qualify: by the end of the century some 20 000 out of a total roll of 182 000 voters were not white. Voters were apathetic, some believing that if one did not vote one would be exempt from taxes.

To qualify for registration as a voter and hence for election to the lower house, the Legislative Assembly, a man had to earn £50 a year or own property with a minimum rentable value of £25. Fifteen members were voted to the upper house or Legislative Council.

Until 1892, the cumulative vote was in force — each voter in the colony was allowed the same number of votes as there were members of the Legislative Assembly for his district. The Capetonian, for example, had four votes, all of which he could 'plump' on one candidate if he wished — and a show of hands decided the issue. Voting by ballot came into force in 1892 by which time the whole system had become more sophisticated with party political allegiances and greater financial considerations bringing urgency and acrimony to the proceedings.

Up until 1892, a candidate would be approached by a number of voters who 'requisitioned' him to stand, pledging their support. For the 1884 elections, Anders Ohlsson's requisition was signed by 1 500 voters, including a number of Malays and at least one black man. The requisition and the candidate's reply as well as the names of all involved were often published in the Press. If the candidate accepted, an election committee of his supporters would then form. On the official nomination day candidates would be proposed and seconded by the audience of voters present to a returning officer. A show of hands decided the result which was then declared. If there was an objection, all the candidates for that district had to agree to cover the cost of holding a poll, those who refused being automatically excluded.

The state of polling was announced at regular intervals through the day. Some voters deliberately refrained from voting until the last minute and, to tap this 'reserve', candidates produced a succession of new pamphlets as new results were released. Candidates like Ohlsson released pamphlets in Arabic with the assistance of the Malays on his election committee — Achmat Effendi, Jaliep Mohmoed and Gatiep Taliep.

The method of open voting was an invitation to intimidation and bribery. Treating — the free supply of food and drink to voters on election day — was regarded as justifiable. When the Irish League's candidate, T.J. O'Reilly, accused Ohlsson of treating at the 1884 polls, the *Cape Argus* suggested that 'although the consumption of Ohlsson's beer on an unusually thirsty day was copious . . . we do not believe the law was broken'.

The revision of the voting system before the 1894 elections coincided with the announcement that Achmat Effendi, Cape-born scion of a distin-

Even as a young woman, Marie Koopmans-De Wet had been a staunch supporter of local cultural tradition. At her hearthside many a pro-South African sympathy was expressed.

guished Muslim family, intended to stand for election. Effendi referred to himself as a European (he had Turkish roots) and a British subject. In the two previous elections, Achmat Effendi had worked on Anders Ohlsson's committee. Now Ohlsson backed Effendi's stand and initially declined to stand in opposition.

But in other quarters his announcement caused an unpleasant flutter. Rhodes and 'Onze Jan' Hofmeyr were too canny to openly take a stand on behalf of the government that could be interpreted as racial. Only a fool would antagonise a vote as sizeable as that of the Cape Muslims. So the Constitution Ordinance Amendment Bill was left to J.M. Orpen to introduce as a private member's motion. In essence, the Bill was designed to restrict 'plumping', or cumulative voting, in Cape Town. There was no need to point out that this was the constituency in which Effendi was most likely to stand or that, given his shortage of campaign funds and geographical location of his prospective voters, the restriction on plumping would impact negatively on his chances of success. Ohlsson stated roundly that as far as he could see the only possible reason for introducing the Bill was to keep Effendi out, simply because he was a 'Malay'. Orpen, he reckoned,

was guilty of introducing what he termed 'class legislation'. Another M.L.A., H.T. Tamplin, also voiced opposition. The House, he said, must not be persuaded to take a retrogressive step through fear of the Muslim population. The ever-direct Saul Solomon said the preamble to the Bill should have read: 'whereas it is expedient to keep Mr Effendi out of the House of Assembly, be it therefore enacted . . .'

J.W. Sauer, perhaps voicing the inner opinions of many of his colleagues, was unequivocal that Effendi would not and should not get in. This was probably a good thing because there was no reason why the Malay community should receive special treatment; indeed, they were probably better off as they were, he said.

Feelings ran high in the Bo-Kaap and a petition registering protest was drafted and submitted to Parliament via Barney Barnato, the member for Kimberley (where Effendi was resident at the time). Nevertheless the Bill went through; Achmat Effendi failed to win a seat in Parliament and left the country shortly afterwards. He was the first and last person of colour to stand for the Cape Parliament.

The House of Assembly had picked up its mace (a replica of that used in the House of Commons but kept in a box made of Van Riebeeck thorn, said to predate the first çommander's arrival by 80 years) and moved to the new Parliament buildings in 1885. The facilities there, including dining-rooms, reading rooms and billiard rooms, were enthusiastically patronised and did a good deal to keep members in good humour – by 1889 there were 76 members of the Legislative Assembly, 21 of the Legislative Council.

Outside these venerable halls of debate, day-to-day conversations among the politically minded of Cape Town concerned events on a stage that ranged from Downing Street to Delagoa Bay, from Damaraland to Mashonaland. Many believed that English influence ought to prevail up to the Zambezi, if not all the way to Cairo. Was it not desirable to get control of Delagoa Bay so that the Dutch republics did not have an alternative route of import? Securing both the port at Delagoa Bay and Damaraland would ensure that no foreign power got a toehold on the subcontinent. Many felt, like a later governor, Sir Hercules Robinson, that the Natal and Cape colonies should unite and that Bechuanaland should be annexed. The pros and cons, hows and wherefores of a customs union for South Africa were pitched about endlessly. In the interests of a unified policy too, it was strongly felt that the job of high commissioner for South Africa and governor of the Cape Colony should not be separated.

The office of high commissioner for South Africa was introduced in 1877 when Sir Bartle Frere became governor of the Cape. It was obviously a preamble to the creation of an amalgamated South Africa.

And below the surface currents of politics was an uneasy division between Capetonians of Dutch origin and those of British descent. In 1889, Sir Henry de Villiers, Chief Justice and president of the Legislative Council who had declined to be nominated president of the Orange Free State on the death of President Brand, told visiting British M.P. Stanley Leighton that there were three factions in South Africa: first, an English party that would quarrel with the Dutch; secondly, the Afrikander (sic) party which would support separation; and, finally, the loyal party which would unite both the others, retain the flag, modify the connection with Downing Street. Manifestations of all three found expression in everyday life. In the interests of conciliation between white people, Professor William Ritchie had even added an optimistic stanza to the South African College anthem:

Our blood varies much,
We are English, French, Dutch,
And German in pedigree,
But whatever our race,
Racial feuds we efface
In love of the old S.A.C.

Dutch-based culture had some ardent and influential supporters, the doyenne of whom was Mrs Marie Koopmans-De Wet who knew everything that was going on politically and was quite 'behind the scenes'. Before the Jameson Raid she was enthusiastically patriotic and very loyal to the English connection ('professing the strongest possible attachment and devotion to the flag'), but 'very resentful of any slight put upon the Afrikaner'.

Everyone, including Cecil Rhodes, found it expedient and worthwhile to attend Mrs Koopmans-De Wet's salons. He once said he feared her more than the whole of the Afrikaner Bond, with whom he had worked closely during the early stages of his political career. After the Jameson Raid he asked her if he might present himself and explain events to her. She refused to see him, saying that the explaining should be done to the whole country.

The Dutch 'element' found a rallying post in 1879 with the formation of the Afrikaner Bond. The victory of Transvaal forces over the British at the Battle of Majuba in 1881 had restored the northerly republic to independence and stoked the fires of nationalist fervour among Dutch-speaking South Africans. The first inter-state congress of the Bond was held in Graaff-Reinet in 1882. Extremists in early Bond factions in the two republics and the colony advocated a radical course of action that would recover them their rights and 'chastise proud perfidious Albion', ridding the subcontinent of British sovereignty and the English language for the good of all. Their rallying call was translated into English as 'Africa for the Afrikanders' and their banner included the flags of the republics and the slogan 'Unity is strength'.

J.H. ('Onze Jan') Hofmeyr, soon undisputed leader of the Bond in the Cape, was a pragmatist and an economist as well as a nationalist, and hence more effective than his hot-headed compatriots. Like other influential political figures of the century (John Fairbairn, Saul Solomon, and Rhodes), Hofmeyr controlled a newspaper, *De Zuid-Afrikaan*. He carefully avoided drawing the political battle-lines along conventional English/Dutch divisions and Bond members were exhorted neither to do nor say anything that might discourage English speakers from joining.

A financially independent but not rich widower with no children, he lived quietly with his mother in the Gardens. He ran the Bond 'show' from behind the scenes, never putting up a Bond ministry though in the 1880s, for example, his men held some 29 seats out of a house of 72. It quickly became impossible for any ministry to dispense with the support of Bond members. Avoiding any overt show of power which might unite the British into a phalanx, he endeavoured to widen the divide between the long-established British settlers and the newcomers and fortune-seekers, recruiting the former to the cause of a united South Africa where old differences and disagreements would be merged in a new consciousness.

This gave him common ground with men like Cecil Rhodes who also had a Machiavellian eye for the main chance and for whom a love for all things South African (with the possible exception of the black population) was an informing principle. Their alliance was mutually fruitful and lasted from the beginning of Rhodes' parliamentary career until the Jameson Raid when it was no longer possible to gloss over the fact that Hofmeyr wanted a united South Africa under its own flag and Rhodes wanted the same thing but under the British flag.

The Jameson Raid, as it came to be known, was purportedly an action supportive of oppressed British subjects on the Reef. Uitlanders ('foreigners') who had flooded to the Transvaal goldfields outnumbered the Boer *volk* and President Kruger was understandably chary of giving them the franchise even though their activities had brought terrific prosperity to his territory. The subject had been a point of disagreement between the Z.A.R. and the Crown for some time as many of the Uitlanders were British subjects. Things were said to have come to a head by late 1895. The Uitlanders, it was rumoured, were planning a rebellion.

In support of his 'beleaguered' countrymen, Dr Leander Starr Jameson, who was chief executive of Rhodes' Chartered Company which governed Matabeleland, gathered a force of 500 men ready to spring from a vantage point in Bechuanaland. But the Uitlander rising was bungled. Jameson, marching on Johannesburg, walked straight into a Boer ambush.

In one move, Boer and British interests in South Africa were polarised. The Raid was interpreted as an act of aggression; Rhodes was implicated, as was the governor, Sir Hercules Robinson, and even colonial secretary Joseph Chamberlain. But Rhodes' admirers felt the Raid was a mere bagatelle in the light of his splendid ambition to annex Africa from Cape to Cairo for the Empire.

When he passed through Cape Town in 1896, *en route* from Rhodesia to London and a tricky enquiry involving the Raid, supporters threw a banquet of Roman proportions in the Drill Hall in his honour. It was attended by 400 ladies and 600 gentlemen. A good deal of whisky was consumed at the main table and a great many grandiloquent speeches were made.

Rhodes and Jameson returned from the hearings in London unabsolved. Many people felt, like Lady Edward Cecil, that 'they had both held their tongues when they could have saved their reputations because, as Mr Rhodes said at the time "we don't matter, it is the British Empire that matters"'.

Not all Capetonians of the day felt quite the same. The reactions of Miemie Rothmann, one of the young women studying at the South African College in the 1890s, are a poignant reminder of the fact. Although Miemie came from a Dutch family in Swellendam, she had at first failed to understand Professor Logeman's eccentric interest in 'the *taal*' (a Dutch-based patois) spoken by members of Dutch families like hers. In a memoir, she noted the fact that he never wearied of the subject which he regarded as a growing phenomenon, a new language even. With Bessie Shaw, whose father was headmaster of the South African College School, Miemie would often slip off down the Avenue for a stolen hour in the House of Assembly watching and listening to Cecil Rhodes. On several occasions she observed another of his admirers, Dr Jane Waterston, sitting in the Distinguished Visitors' Gallery, chin on hand, eyes fixed on the prime minister's face. The white-haired missionary-physician was a fiery imperialist whose admiration for Rhodes was far from unquestioning. Miemie was outraged by the report that Dr Jane had pronounced, 'He ought to be spanked,' when she disagreed with one of Rhodes' decisions. She and Bessie were entranced by the power of his personality and they persuaded themselves that he sometimes looked up at them in the gallery. One of Miemie's more foolish dreams was to serve one day as his private secretary.

Then the Jameson Raid brought the curtain down on this harmless interlude in Miemie's life. She experienced a sense of desolation equal to loss of innocence. She and Dutch classmates like Charles de Villiers and Flippie van der Merwe never discussed the news but they exchanged long bleak glances. A new awareness of her identity and new allegiances stirred in Miemie's heart. She stopped writing to her mother in English. And when she established a career as a journalist, calling herself M.E.R., she wrote only in 'the *taal*', Afrikaans.

Even once the House of Assembly was established in a grand new permanent home, the Parliament buildings at the lower end of the Gardens, members continued to argue in two languages and agree in neither, as writer Mark Twain noted.

THE GOVERNMENT HOUSE SET

overnment House, the official residence of the governor of the Cape Colony and high commissioner for South Africa, was the focus of attention for anyone with social ambitions. But in spite of the preordinations of protocol and an official social diary, inevitably the life in this sprawling and unpretentious manor took on something of the character of the current incumbents. Several of them went further, making radical structural alterations.

As early as 1674 the site was occupied by a modest garden house for the storage of tools and equipment. In 1697, Van der Stel decided to erect a guest house there. This was after he had learnt a salutary lesson in security from a group of passing Jesuits he had entertained at the Castle. They had returned the courtesy by treacherously relaying information about the fortifications to France. The Garden guest house was duly built and from 1682 all official guests were housed and entertained there.

The house was constructed around a central hall with openings on to Stal Plein and the Garden. There was one small salon on each side of the hall. The flat roof was surrounded by a balustrade and a central pavilion provided shade for those who wished to admire the view. By 1710 materials from the original fort had been used to add an extra storey to the house, following the same configuration as that of the ground floor. From then on, the house was continually being repaired, altered and added to. It was known as Government House from 1797 and when Lord Macartney moved in two years after the first British occupation in 1795, he found it large and attractive with many rooms including servants' quarters, and accommodation for guards and slaves. The front façade, facing the Garden, was an extravagant combination of decorative elements. Four elegant pillars supported the long balcony and flanked broad entrance steps. On the first floor, a pierced balustrade with decorative urns broke the upward journey of the eye to the figures of Poseidon and Mercury who supported a banner bearing the V.O.C. monogram of the Dutch East India Company. On either side of this splendid central feature, classical urns graced the roof-line.

The patrician Lord Charles Somerset took one look at this façade and the somewhat neglected house that it fronted and pronounced it unfit for his

Left *Competitive dressing for the Cape season stimulated trade for local importers.*
Right *Anyone with any kind of social ambition aspired to join the select inner circle entertained in the rarefied precincts of Government House.*

habitation. He duly settled into the new summer residence, Newlands House, while the official residence was refurbished to his specifications. By 1826 the architect on the job suggested that it would be cheaper and more practical to raze the old house to the ground and start afresh. But under the indomitable Lord Charles he soldiered on. The north wing was demolished and a much-needed ballroom constructed in its place. Decorations that harked back to the Cape Dutch style were plastered over or built in, lying hidden and waiting for rediscovery one day. Long Georgian windows were added as well as a low-pitched slate roof. What, to English eyes, had once been a foreign-looking residence, had been converted into a tasteful Georgian country house appropriate to the status of King George IV's proconsul.

Outwardly, the house remained unchanged for the rest of the century. The ballroom had to be virtually rebuilt in 1874 and extra office space was added in 1887. In 1890 a proper banquet hall replaced the wood-and-canvas Exhibition Hall previously used for the purpose. Electric lights were installed in 1899 just in time to aid that notorious burner of the midnight oil, Sir Alfred Milner.

The results of these efforts were not universally regarded as successful: the author of 1897's *Cape Town Guide* described it as 'an ugly block of irregular proportions and wholly unfit for the purposes to which it is devoted'.

The reception for Sir Henry Bartle Frere in June 1879 was a good indication of the social importance of the proconsul and his household. A 55-strong committee, including several leading politicians, worked for weeks to organise the event. The railway station was specially decorated for His Excellency's arrival at noon on 6 June. Admission to the precinct was by ticket only. Ladies' seats were arranged on the arrival platform and gentlemen's on the departure platform. A Royal Artillery salute was fired as the train approached the Castle and another salute was timed for its approach to the station.

Members of the reception committee and delegates from various towns received His Excellency on arrival and a guard of honour stood by. Once the governor had stepped on to the platform, various deputations were introduced and addresses read and presented. An escort of the Duke of Edinburgh's Own Volunteer Cavalry accompanied the governor's carriage and Cape Town's volunteer regiments mounted a guard of honour along Adderley Street.

At the town arch leading to Government Avenue, the mayor and city council received the governor and presented an address. As the official carriage stopped at the arch, massed schoolchildren on either side started to sing the national anthem. The Good Templars, Odd Fellows, Foresters, Ancient Druids, Free Wrights, Gardeners, Mechanics and various other Friendly Societies lined the avenue up to Government House as a guard of honour. The hadjis, imams, belals, and other representatives of the Muslim community were grouped at the entrance to the residence. A further guard of honour composed of Royal Engineers saw His Excellency to the door of his new home. A banquet in Sir Bartle's honour was held at noon the following day in the Exhibition Building in the grounds of the nearby Good Hope Lodge.

During the Frere tenure, the governor's wife and daughters created a family atmosphere in the residence. The young women were great sketchers and decorated the doors of Government House with their wild flower studies. They made lifelong friends including Hildagonda Duckitt whom they had encouraged to publish the first book on Cape housekeeping. Mary Frere did a drawing for the book and the sisters helped Miss Duckitt to get it published. She spent many happy hours helping with the garden at the official residence. Once they returned to London, the Misses Frere helped Miss Duckitt to establish a brisk business exporting the white chincherinchees that grew wild round the Duckitt family farm near Darling.

Mrs Marie Koopmans-De Wet, Cape Town's other first lady, was a frequent visitor during this time too, though later, when Anglo-Boer relations grew increasingly strained, she declared Government House to be the grave of her friends. Whoever visited there was no longer welcome at her house at 23 Strand Street, famous as a meeting place for influential intellectuals and politicians.

Charles Cooper, editor of the *Scotsman*, attended a Government House ball on 28 December 1894 of which he had 'nothing but delightful recollections'. Sir Henry and Lady Loch were resident at the time and the ball was a little out of season for they had been in England during the southern winter, which was the correct season at the Cape.

The Government House ballroom was too small for the number of guests invited so the function was held in the nearby Good Hope Hall, 'a spacious and handsome room . . . with a capital floor and well ventilated'. Music was provided by a military band and a 'coloured' string band. Cooper found the young ladies present 'so sweet, so frank, so fair, so joyous, that it would have been a sin not to admire them'.

Naval and military uniforms brightened the room, the blue-coats entering with more vigour into the dancing than the red-coats, in Cooper's opinion. 'It would surprise me very much to learn that no masculine naval heart was broken at the ball. Said heart did not "sit out" much; but it was eloquent in its frequent dancing, and in the eagerness with which, with certain partners, it pressed for "another of the same". I believe that sea has a healing effect in such cases. Under its benign influence, the broken pieces of the heart may be brought together again, only, alas, to be again shattered at the next ball.'

There were grave men present . . . who also danced. The Speaker of the Legislative Assembly footed it featly on the floor. A chief justice of one of the South African states was in great request. A puisne judge of the Supreme Court at Cape Town, stately in court dress, danced with grace and manifest pleasure.

The governor and his lady dispensed gracious hospitality and when the programme of dances was exhausted 'extras' were called for and readily granted. The manager of the government railways had thoughtfully arranged for special trains to run to the suburbs in the small hours of the morning because even the most indefatigable of revellers had to go home eventually.

Alas, setting the social tone was only a minor function of the governorship. Once good public relations had been established an onerous burden of responsibility remained. By the 1890s the job had become a hot potato.

When Sir Hercules Robinson (then in his second term) heard in 1889 that eight men had turned the job down, he is said to have snorted, 'I really did not know there were so many men in England who knew enough of South Africa to refuse.' Mark Twain reckoned that 'The South African question was a very good subject for a fool to let alone'. The newly knighted Alfred Milner, before he arrived in the Cape as governor, wrote to a friend: 'It is an awful job, tho' I never hesitated when asked to undertake it, and without the favour of the High Gods, it cannot successfully be dealt with.' Milner succeeded Sir Hercules Robinson who was made Lord Rosmead during his last term in office.

Before his departure from London, Milner had to appoint staff, choose horses, buy a carriage, plate and furniture and visit the College of Heralds

A degree of pomp and ceremony were appropriate to the governor's movements, though Milner preferred to ride to his office from his summer residence at Newlands.

for a grant of arms. Major John Hanbury-Williams was to be his military secretary and Mrs Hanbury-Williams played hostess very graciously for the bachelor Milner. Ozzy Walrond, young son of a friend, was his private secretary and in due course Lord Belgrave ('Bendor') came out as A.D.C., a post he continued to hold after he succeeded his grandfather as Duke of Westminster. (Lionel Curtis, who met him in 1900, described him rather disparagingly as a 'gilded youth'.) The important post of colonial secretary was only filled several months after Milner's arrival in the Cape.

The new plate and carriage and the new team were only some of the changed aspects of life at Government House under the new regime. Both the Robinsons had been known for the bluff humour that often set people's backs up. Stanley Leighton, a British M.P. who visited the colony, recorded some of the local stories about the vice-regal pair.

For example, when they were ushered into Government House on their arrival, Lady Robinson said, 'I suppose this is the back door?' Shortly afterwards, she showed some lack of attention to some important people; on being told of the omission she excused herself: 'Why, I thought they were Dutch.'

At a Government House reception she said to Lady Sprigg, wife of the prime minister: 'I have not time to shake hands, but my good woman, there are some refreshments in the next room.' When her daughter made herself agreeable at a Government House ball, Lady Robinson reminded her, 'Didn't I tell you, you were not to be intimate with the people?'

Milner had an overtly different approach to the job. As a keen Empire man, he had watched events in South Africa for a number of years both from London and from his desk in the foreign service in Cairo. He had met Rhodes and Jameson in London and was very friendly with W. T. Stead, who was well informed, if somewhat partisan, about events in this southerly colony. Milner started learning Dutch on the voyage out and in Cape Town (he arrived on 5 May 1897) took further lessons from Adrian Hofmeyr, the dominee at Wynberg who happened to be a cousin of 'Onze Jan' Hofmeyr.

During Milner's term, the threshold of Government House was crossed more frequently by political, administrative and military personalities than ever before. But both because of the age and personality of the governor and because of the political situation, the atmosphere was more masculine. Milner was a keen swimmer and rower and believed daily exercise was essential to total wellbeing. In the company of members of his 'family' – Ozzy Walrond and later Lionel Curtis – he walked (climbing on Boxing Day 1897 to the top of Table Mountain), cycled in the Gardens and made a point of riding as often as he could for relaxation. In summer he moved to the governor's summer residence, Newlands House, which he described in a letter as 'our little country house, inconvenient to get at and a mere box, tho' awfully pretty'. When he was in residence there he travelled into town by train in poor weather but preferred to ride the six miles or so coming via Rhodes Estate. The horses at Government House during his time were the best in the colony.

Inevitably, the Government House set was a kingpin of the Cape hunt. 'I am bound to say we all rode . . . [his] horses,' Lady Edward Cecil wrote in her memoirs. She specially favoured Milkman – 'a splendid steady grey who never put a foot wrong and who could jump a house . . . He and a small flea-bitten grey of Mr Rhodes's has Basuto blood and these Basuto ponies were descended from the China ponies brought into the Cape in the early polo playing days. They could go all day and keep themselves on a mouthful of sand, and they were far better for riding [in the Cape Colony] . . . than the Argentines and Walers that the British Government used for re-mounts . . .'

Pursuing jackal on the Cape Flats might have seemed to Britons at home to be a poor substitute for the real thing, but nonetheless it offered a splendid day's sport.

Milner himself was too busy to hunt regularly. Although in the early months of his tenure there were the occasional quiet evenings when members of the household and perhaps a couple of intimates might play whist or billiards, there were also numerous official dinners, a levee and ceremonies for the Queen's birthday and at least one ball ('the cotillion, rather experimental, was not a success, but otherwise people seemed to enjoy themselves').

Although he came from fairly obscure beginnings and did not regard himself as rooted in England, the tall lean Milner with his serious expression exuded a dauntingly patrician air. He did not conceal a clear moral distaste for the lifestyles adopted by some colonials and, in spite of his genuine interest in people, he always remained in essence an Anglophile.

He said that one of the job's disadvantages was living among uncongenial people and after three months in the Cape wrote to a friend: 'Apart from the work the life here bores me to death. It is a hundred thousand times less amusing than Egypt . . . my only personal interest is in my English friends and my only amusement hearing from them.'

Nevertheless there was a constant stream of visitors to Government House and the Milner set were devoted to His Excellency. There were several women among them. Mrs Chapin, an American whose husband had mining interests in South Africa, made friends with Milner during the outward voyage after his spell of home leave and they remained friends. Violet, Lady Edward Cecil, who had met Milner in England through her father-in-law Lord Salisbury (the British prime minister), was a staunch ally. While their husbands were besieged in Mafeking she and a friend, Lady Charles Bentinck, stayed as Rhodes' guests at Groote Schuur but were very much part of the Government House set.

In Lady Edward's view, 'the community in the Cape … was sharply divided into three parts – those who were loyal to Britain and to the Crown, those who hoped for Boer supremacy in South Africa, and a number who meant to be on the winning side wherever this was. At the moment this last group was clinging round the knees of the governor and swearing fealty'.

Among Milner's official colleagues he numbered many genuine friends. Colonel Robert Baden-Powell was one example. His book *Aids to Scouting*, published in 1899, was extremely popular with the public although it had been written to assist in the training of soldiers. The subjects covered included Tracking, Reporting, Spying, Reading the Spoor, Keeping Yourself Hidden. Hundreds of copies were issued to British troops embarking for South Africa and the work was later serialised for the first boys of the Scout movement. Baden-Powell stayed at Groote Schuur (an overflow station for Government House guests) after the relief of Mafeking and gave rise to more 'mafficking' (a new word coined by the riotous celebrations that followed news of the relief on 19 May 1901). Crowds had gathered outside Government House cheering Milner. Baden-Powell received a standing ovation when he attended a performance in the Opera House. A crowd tried to mob him when he was recognised in Adderley Street and he had to seek refuge in Thorne, Stuttaford & Co.'s department store.

The architect, Herbert Baker, was another member of the inner circle. Baker had fallen under the blustery spell of False Bay and built himself a beach house called Sandhills which became a favoured retreat for many of his eminent cronies. During the height of the War, after the Battle of Spioenkop, the exhausted Milner escaped from his horrific responsibilities for a weekend at Sandhills.

On the Saturday evening, as the two friends walked along the beach, 'we saw what looked like a large man-of-war off Simon's Bay; when it suddenly vanished we realised that it was but the little flat penguin-haunted rock there raised up, a mirage in the breathless air. We thought of Marryat's story of The Phantom Ship, which appeared to mariners off the Cape in calms before storms, foretelling their doom'.

Other contacts, like chief justice Sir Henry de Villiers, Milner admired, but did not quite trust. The chief justice had often expressed a belief in the possibility of uniting Boer and Briton but at Government House he was known as Black Henry.

General Sir William Butler, commander-in-chief of the British forces at the Cape, was an Englishman with whom Milner most definitely had nothing in common. The two men held diametrically opposed views of the situation – Butler believed the Boers were being shabbily treated and was determined to avoid any action that might provoke them. Milner wrote to Joseph Chamberlain that the General was 'out of sympathy with my policy … cordial co-operation between us is impossible'. Butler was finally recalled at the end of August and General Sir Frederick Forestier-Walker who took his place fitted in with the official viewpoint more amenably. Violet Cecil described him as 'a charming man, desiring above all things a quiet life, and quiet lives were not to be had in the Cape Colony in 1899'.

On 10 January 1900, when the Lords Roberts and Kitchener came out to assume command of the fighting forces, they too stayed at Government House and, at a dinner held to welcome them, Milner said, 'At least now I feel we shall not be shot sitting.' The days when the Government House set was a leisured social cabal were gone for good.

Some of the finest horses in the colony were to be found in the Government House stables and well-connected equestriennes like the Duchess of Teck lost no time in acquiring a mount there.

In Council

apid increases in population and in strategic resources strained Cape Town's limited and rustic resources to bursting point as the nineteenth century drew on. (Some facilities, most notably the antiquated sewers, did in fact break down.) The city doubled and redoubled in size. The total population of Cape Town and nearby suburbs in the mid-1890s was set at about 90 000; its revenues increased from about £37 000 in 1880 to £184 662 in 1898.

Maintaining some semblance of order and hygiene now was a far cry from the relaxed tasks of the old Municipal Board, established in 1840 to look after the rudiments of small-town management. It had been responsible for ensuring that the streets were clean and for lighting them. In addition, an Act passed in 1861 specified that 50 gallons of water should be supplied to each household each day 'as soon and as far as may be practicable'.

All had jogged along happily, enjoying interminable contests of mild bickering until the discovery of diamonds in 1866 changed the tenor of life. The finds were many dusty miles away in Griqualand West, but ripples of prosperity went out from there to the whole country. The Mother City certainly enjoyed a generous share of the spoils.

As the capital of a colony whose government was growing in power and activity; as a port whose harbour was being improved by increased government expenditure; and as the railway terminus for the Cape Western system, and the main southerly starting point for Rhodesia and all points north, Cape Town became an extremely busy commercial centre. It attracted the headquarters of banks and land and insurance companies and enjoyed a rich injection of capital.

So what had been little more than a village management board was thrust into the status of a full-scale municipal authority with an elected City Council running the show.

The city was divided into six districts for voting purposes, voters in each electing three representatives. Up until 1882 there was only one ballot box – at the Town House in Greenmarket Square. Aspirant city fathers who relied on the support of middle-class citizens believed that this 'better'

class of voter did not enjoy coming to the old Burger Watch House where he would have to mix with franchised members of the *hoi polloi*. Polling booths, they recommended, should be positioned in each of the six districts.

Females did not vote, and although a colour-blind franchise brought a reasonable cross-section of male citizens to the polls, it did not guarantee councillors with no social, personal or commercial axes to grind. Public spiritedness was diluted with ambition and self-interest in varying degrees amongst those who held office and it was perhaps not surprising that money was the root cause of a major division in the ranks which characterised Council proceedings up until the turn of the century.

In earlier times when money was scarcer, the problems were correspondingly less significant. But in less than 20 years the Council had been transformed from a financially insignificant body into a conspicuously wealthy and powerful one. The bitter lessons of periodic recessions had left untarnished the general assurance of a golden future, and the unassailable creditworthiness of the municipality. New possibilities for raising loans in the colony and overseas were taken as encouraging signs of progress, at least by the more progressive-minded who wished to increase the borrowing powers of the Council from £20 000 to £150 000. And they

---

Above *The Prince Street pump: supplying water was*
one of the most important and challenging municipal obligations.
Right *The old Burgher Watch House in*
Greenmarket Square where the City Council met.

wanted to increase the funds they could levy in rates from tuppence in the pound to thruppence. The conservative faction led by 'Onze Jan' Hofmeyr grudgingly accepted the increase in the rating power of the Council but adamantly opposed the increase in borrowing powers because they feared it would lead to extravagance which would in its turn necessitate yet another increase in rates.

It had been generally acknowledged for years that all the facilities for which the Council was responsible needed radical improvement if not complete reconstruction. But any matter which threatened to cause an increase in rates polarised opinions among property-owning councillors. The vital issues of water supply and drainage and cleansing were at the centre of the dispute.

The conservatives, dubbed the 'Dirty Party' by their opponents, were mainly landlords with extensive properties which lay within the city limits and were thus subject to municipal rates. A typical 'Dirty' councillor would derive the bulk of his income from rents. In 1881 M.J. Louw, who was described as a 'large' landed proprietor, owned 11 houses and a tannery with a municipal valuation of £8 545. C.A. Ashley also owned 11 houses of a modest sort in District Six – they were valued at £860 in 1880. This group was supported by Kinsley's householders and ratepayers who included L.P. Cauvin, an auctioneer with property worth £10 694, Grocer Prince who was worth £3 760, R.H. Arderne worth £7 490, and J.C. Wicht who was worth £15 630 in 1881.

The reformers, or 'Clean Party', on the other hand, were merchants or successful businessmen, possessing fluid capital, often living outside the municipal boundaries and with their stores and places of business in the centre of Cape Town. Councillor Farmer told the Standard Bank that he was worth £170 000 in 1881 – he was a partner in the mercantile firm of W. Anderson & Company, and boasted extensive shareholdings, including shares in at least one insurance company, banks, diamond scrip and the City Tramways Company. Councillor Bolus was a partner, with his brother William, in Cape Town's chief stockbroking firm. By 1890, Councillor MacKenzie, already a vast property owner, also had sizeable holdings in diamond scrip and other shares and a lucrative business as a landing agent at the docks.

Later councillors, John Garlick, John Woodhead, William Thorne and Thomas Fuller, were all connected with mercantile activity. Fuller had originally been invited to come to South Africa as editor of the *Cape Argus*, Garlick was a member of the department store family and Thorne was managing director of Thorne, Stuttaford & Co. D.P. Graaff, an attorney with Combrinck and Company, although initially mistakenly grouped with the 'Dirties' by the *Cape Times*, could soon be seen to be on the other side. This

was hardly surprising for a man, described by Merriman as one of the new breed of pushy urban Afrikaners, who was rapidly becoming one of the Cape's most successful businessmen.

Reform suited these men who stood to gain more than what a small increase in rates would cost them. Their businesses would benefit from all the development and improvement the Council could afford. Better communications and service would bring an increase in trade, and as most of the proposed reforms would enhance the centre of the city, the value of their business premises would be enhanced. The resentment of the 'Dirties' towards the use of public money for these developments was understandable, but as the local English Press depended on the 'Clean' business community for their advertising revenue, it suited them to have a field day with the 'Dirties'.

During the smallpox epidemic of 1882, the *Lantern* launched a vitriolic campaign against the 'Dirties', publishing cartoons and scornful ditties such as:

> Sing a song of smallpox
> Hofmeyr gone askew;
> Ashley, Louw and Zoutendyk
> In a pretty stew!
> When the scare is over,
> These rascals will begin
> Their dirty tricks, to stop the bricks
> Who would clean a town win.

It also suggested that the opposition depended on the lower class voter: 'The flying brigade of the Dirty lot are all abroad . . . enrolling Japies, Salies and whipping up the whole crew of their dependants for the fray.' With this kind of propaganda and the real horror of smallpox stalking the streets, it is small wonder that the 'Clean Party' won the day and secured dominance of the Council for the next couple of decades.

The 'Cleans' proposed abandoning the free supply of 50 gallons of water to each household which dated back to the days of the Board. Instead proprietors would be obliged, when called upon by the municipality, to supply every house with a hundred gallons a day and to pay for this.

The proposal met with howls of outrage from the conservatives. Landlord Councillor Arderne said, 'I believe that dry dirt is comparatively innocuous, and I believe it is the waste of water in all the little lanes and alleys that has been the source of more annoyance than anything else can possibly be. When these people (i.e. the tenants) had to go to the public pumps they did not waste the water.'

But progress, though slow, was not to be halted. Cape Town had relied on water stored in two small reservoirs in Orange Street and the Hof Street Water House. As the town grew outwards and upwards, these three storage units proved too small and too low down to cope with the demand. Consequently, once Parliament had passed the appropriate Bills, the springs on Van Breda's farm were sequestered, the farm Oranjezicht was purchased and the construction of one or more reservoirs contracted out.

One reservoir named after Sir John Molteno, first prime minister of the Cape Colony, was completed by March 1881. Construction had commenced four years earlier and necessitated excavation and the raising of embankments. The work created an ugly scar on the mountainside that drew unfavourable comment from all who sailed into Table Bay.

The first problem cropped up when there was barely two feet of water in the dam. It had to be drained and the fault repaired. In the next months three further faults were discovered, and each time the reservoir was drained again and repaired. On Sunday morning 27 August a serious leak occurred. Water rushed down into the city, flooding several streets. In 1884 engineer Charles John Wood was appointed to report on the reservoir problem. At his recommendation it was drained and lined with concrete at a cost of £37 346/7/2. So the reservoir was finally safe and usable in 1886. It had cost a total of £98 000.

The jinx upon the ill-fated pond had been laid to rest. Or so it seemed until 1900 when it claimed a human victim. One Isadore Michaels made a much-publicised hot-air-balloon ascent from the Goodhope Gardens. A high wind swept the balloon towards the mountain and Michaels prudently abandoned ship with the aid of a parachute. Alas, the wind carried him too far away from the park where he intended to land and dumped him in the reservoir. He had become entangled in the ropes of his parachute and drowned before he could be rescued. Once more, the reservoir was drained.

As early as 1858 a faction of far-sighted citizens had called for the construction of storage dams on top of Table Mountain, but it wasn't until 1890

The fire department was also a Council responsibility.
This spanking new fire engine went on display
at the Woodstock Show.

99

that it was officially decided to construct two reservoirs that would take advantage of the high rainfall on the 'back table'. A tunnel, 700 yards long, was driven through the Twelve Apostles range of mountains above Camp's Bay, at Slangolie Gorge, and a pipeline was laid from Kloof Nek down to the Molteno Reservoir. By 1900 two service reservoirs had been constructed – one at Kloof Nek and the other at Sea Point. At last Cape Town could rely on a reasonable supply of water.

In the shadow of the Mountain, heed was paid to the general ambience by the city fathers. Trees were continually being planted and a park was laid out beneath the Molteno Reservoir. A French forester, Count de Vaselot de Regne, was appointed Superintendent of Woods and Forests in 1889 and he was responsible for many reforms including the ban on the lighting of picnic fires on Table Mountain.

Along with these more pleasant tasks, some effort was made to rectify the problems that had earned Cape Town its title 'the city of stinks'. These included inadequate street cleaning by private contractors; open drains and raw sewage discharged into the sea.

Citizens of all classes were affected and at a meeting in the Commercial Exchange in 1887, voting was so strongly in favour of modernising the city's drainage system that it was even decided to delay the construction of a new City Hall if there were not funds for both. New drainage would put an end to the offensive smells and also reduce the risk of epidemic.

But while excavations for the modern new drains were very much in evidence in the smarter parts of town, the situation grew steadily worse in the backstreets. Some 5 000 householders paid private contractors two shillings a tub for nightsoil removal; in the poorer districts people cleared their own buckets. By 1887, the City Council was responsible for the removal of nightsoil but houses in the slums received a visitation only once a month, or, if they were lucky, once a fortnight. The health department had a hopelessly inadequate staff of two who checked that the contractor met his obligations in this respect. The cost of nightsoil removal at the time was estimated at £6 720 per annum as against £4 000 budgeted for the running of the police force.

The maintenance of roads in the city was a constant source of contention. Dust storms in summer and flooding in winter exacerbated other problems of doing business in the city centre. Responsibility was laid squarely at the door of the Council. Messrs Thorne and Stuttaford wrote to the *Cape Times* on 10 May 1890:

Dear Sir
Seeing no mention in the Town Council's report of the disgraceful state of our Cape Town streets, which, for this last week, have been a sea of mud & dirt, we think it is time that the rate-payers, or else the government, should bring pressure to bear on this serious state of Municipal negligence. Ladies complain of the impassable state of our leading thoroughfare, Adderley Street: they have to walk through mud ankle-deep to join cab, carriage or bus. Even the crossings are neglected and dirty . . . Adderley Street should be paved with wood similar to Darling Street.

The fire brigade was also a Council responsibility. In 1891 this organisation moved into new premises on the site of the old theatre in Burg Street. It had five horses – two so intelligent and well trained that when the alarm sounded, they trotted up to the engine on which was fixed a patent automatic harness.

Cape Town first saw electric lights in September 1870 when a showman named Henry Edwards demonstrated arc lighting, and despite the cost and fire hazard of these bright lights, the railways became the first bulk consumer in 1883 when the Anglo-African Electric Light Company was formed. It supplied the docks with 22 lights and the railway station with six. Only three years behind the British Houses of Parliament, the Cape House of Assembly was illuminated with arc lights on the outside and on the inside with the newer and safer incandescent lamps.

For these and the few other consumers in the Cape there was no centralised supply – each had its own separate plant which produced the electricity required. The Cape Town Corporation and its neighbouring town councils had monopolies of water supply and other services and electricity increasingly came to be regarded as a comparable municipal public utility.

Until 1895 Cape Town bought its supply from the Cape Peninsula Lighting Company, but in that year it established the first municipal electric undertaking in South Africa – the Graaff Electric Light Station. The station was sited near the Molteno Reservoir and opened by Mayor Smart on 13 April 1895. It was designed to supply electricity for lighting purposes, making the town safer because it was better illuminated, but it also provided the municipality with a source of revenue and a means of ensuring that the cost of electricity could be controlled. Generation was by water or steam and overhead and underground wires were laid to a distribution point in Dorp Street.

The very first official occasion on which the Corporation supplied electric light was a banquet in honour of Sir Hercules Robinson on 4 June 1895 at the Good Hope Hall. The Corporation had not monopolised the supply of gas and no powerful vested interests were involved in the gas industry, so demand for electricity was unhindered and grew swiftly. In the first year there were 20 consumers but by 1904 the number had increased to 1 300.

The public reception of the new electric communication systems was less enthusiastic. In 1873 the Cape government had acquired the telegraph lines which had been constructed – the first in 1860 to link Cape Town and Simon's Town – by private companies.

But the telegraph was not generally recognised as an amenity for the ordinary citizen. A private individual could send a telegram from Cape Town to Grahamstown as early as 1863 but few took advantage of the convenience. The telegraph was at first classed with 'electro-biology' and 'animal magnetism' and other crazes of the early Victorian period, a subject that might serve as entertainment for the curious. Telegraphic communications with Natal came in 1878 just in time to alert the respective colonial governments on the menace of the Zulu war.

Nor were telephones perceived as much more than a novelty and a luxury. In 1880, even in Cape Town, there were only 11 privately owned instruments so a telephone exchange was not regarded as a necessity until 1884. It was some years before even police headquarters in Burg Street boasted a set.

For Cape Town's sizeable population of newspapermen, the telegraph and telephone were to prove invaluable, particularly during the Anglo-Boer War. Instead of remaining purveyors of editorial comment, advertisements, domestic intelligence, Council and shipping news, the city's periodicals could now evolve into newspapers proper.

To alleviate Cape Town's chronic water shortages, water was redirected from Disa Gorge via the Woodhead Tunnel into a pipeline that fed the Molteno Reservoir. This was no mean engineering feat, involving the construction of several tall aqueducts.

PRESS AND PERIODICAL

'The local newspapers were not lacking in enterprise,' wrote Frederic William Unger, American war correspondent extraordinary in 1900. 'Naturally, in a city half full of Boer sympathisers, surrounded and occupied by Imperial troops, every bit of news from the front was eagerly looked for. As each new telegram from the front arrived an "extra" of "dodger" size, eight by ten inches, was issued from the newspaper offices. While the presses were still running, the engineer would open the whistle-valve and an agonising scream would pierce every ear for miles around. Then windows and doors opened and heads protruded, followed by half the body. Men and boys, hatless and coatless, tumbled out, rushing like mad down town, every alley and street vomiting its contribution to the dense mob which assailed the newspaper offices in a mad fight for the penny extras: — a splendid speculation for the proprietors. Then the crowd would break up and disperse, streaked with swift-running newsboys selling copies to the laggards, all reading, as they slowly returned to work or went to meals...'

Local newspapers were certainly not lacking in enterprise even before the Anglo-Boer War placed the country in the forefront of world news. Neither did local newspapers lack readers, for that matter.

In 1858, Cape Town boasted eight newspapers issuing something like 21 000 copies over a week. (Grahamstown maintained no fewer than five papers.) The ladies' special interests were catered for in the *South African Ladies' Companion*.

The circulation of newspapers only hinted at readership because in the early days many papers were read in clubs and refreshment rooms and each copy might pass through perhaps a score of hands. Among the successful Press campaigns which illustrated the power of the printed word was the anti-convict protest waged by John Fairbairn in 1849. With the governor, Sir Harry Smith's, blessing a consignment of convicts was to be off-loaded from the ship *Neptune* at Simon's Town for labour. But in a highly organised and completely unprecedented campaign, kept at fever pitch by Fairbairn's fiery editorials, the populace blocked the move. They would not budge from fiercely maintained boycotts, until at last, after five months, the ruling had to be reversed and the wretched felons were sent on

Left *The typewriter helped to streamline communications and create clerical jobs for young men and women.*
Right *Newspaper vendors at the Salt River branch of the Central News Agency.*

to Australia. It was the first time the colonials had united in action and the first indication of the viability of local government, not to mention the power of the Press.

It was hardly surprising that vociferous and politically ept newspapermen, with their detailed knowledge of parliamentary procedure, would take an active part in local legislature, as indeed they did. Fairbairn, F.S. Watermeyer, Saul Solomon, and Thomas Fuller were just a few of the newspapermen who served as members of the Legislative Assembly and helped to raise Parliament above the level of the debating club it was always in danger of becoming. The years 1857 to 1861 saw an influx of professionals into the local newspaper scene and South Africa's first daily, the *Cape Town Daily News*, made an appearance.

The youthful *Cape Argus* quickly earned the nickname 'The Cape Thunderer'. It first issued from the steam-presses of Saul Solomon on 3 January 1857. Saul Solomon's other publications were the *Cape of Good Hope Gazette*, the *Cape Mercantile Advertiser* and the *Shipping and Mercantile Gazette*. His firm undertook all the government printing and at its peak employed a staff of 300 employees including 'a large number of girls who specialised in folding, stitching, and correcting the printed sheets. The wages bill rose as high as £14 000 a year and the annual turnover ranged between £50 000 and £60 000'.

With R.W. Murray in the chair, the *Cape Argus* soon acquired a distinct style. His parliamentary reports under the nom-de-plume 'Limner' gave vivid and unforgettable portraits of Cape administrators. He was followed by the great Thomas Fuller whom Solomon had personally recruited as a relatively unknown journalist in Britain.

The mutual friend who introduced the two men had warned Fuller that Solomon was 'somewhat smaller in body than other men, but not in other respects'. Fuller recalled that he was not 'in the least prepared for the diminutive figure which entered the room, and for a time the feeling of wonder almost paralysed every other'. Thus began a fruitful working association which was to last nine years unmarred by anything but gentlemanly and sincerely friendly interchanges.

Mrs Marie Koopmans-De Wet, a tireless campaigner for the preservation of the Cape's indigenous cultural heritage, waged her most successful campaigns through the Press, among other things, saving the ancient Castle from a fate worse than total destruction.

Some years before he became prime minister, Cecil Rhodes had bought controlling interests in the *Cape Argus*, an investment which was to play dividends on several occasions. The Logan Scandal of 1892 was a case in point. James Logan had given up his life at sea for a job as a porter at Cape Town station. In the twinkling of an eye he had risen in the world, making

a name for himself as a hotelier and owner of refreshment rooms including one at Matjiesfontein in the Karoo. He also ran a wholesale malt and spirits business and traded in hides, feathers and other negotiable commodities. He was eminently qualified for the 15-year railway catering contract awarded him by one of Rhodes' most intimate cronies, Cabinet member James Sivewright. But the process whereby he obtained this profitable monopoly was suspect. Sivewright had not observed the proper procedure and ignored other tenders. Under pressure from the attorney-general, Rhodes allowed that the agreement should be cancelled, whereupon Logan announced his intentions to sue for breach of contract. Rhodes was travelling at the time and realised the seriousness of the situation only when Sauer, Merriman and Rose Innes all threatened to resign from the Cabinet if the premier did not force a satisfactory explanation from Sivewright. By May 1893 things had come to such a pass that Rhodes resigned as a matter of principal. The *Cape Argus* blamed the hostility between Merriman and Sivewright for the break-up and Rhodes was returned with a resounding majority during the 1894 General Election.

The 1890s were the great days of the comparatively youthful *Cape Times*. In 1890, the first editor, Frederick Yorke St Leger, still had five years to run. He was succeeded by Fydell Edmund Garrett, master of the lively, humorous news report.

All papers put more emphasis on sport than on cultural matters. They were slow to see the wisdom of journalist, Sam Sly (William Layton Sammons), who insisted that subjects of popular interest, for example music, should be covered in the pages of a newspaper.

Advertisements, lifeblood of the industry, allowed creative expression to both display artists and writers. Some advertisers preferred to rely on the visual impact of decorative type and some lithographic illustration. Others liked to disguise their advertisements as news stories.

A particularly engaging beer advertisement, written by 'H. Rider Haggard Junior', appeared in *Lantern* in February 1889 under the headline: 'Saved from a Horrible Death Through a Bottle of Ohlsson's Stout.' It took the form of a first-person account by a Woodstockian who was wont to return to that 'salubrious suburb' for his dinner at midday. On the day of his close shave, he arrived to discover that his wife had procured a quantity of mussels, knowing how much he liked the 'luscious bivalve'. There were probably sufficient to feast the entire standing Free State army and he felt quite up to the task of despatching them. But mussels without stout were an absurdity. 'Yes, I would get a bottle of Ohlsson's stout and with this relish the dinner would be complete. I had just time to go to the nearest hostelry and procure the needful.' With the bottle anchored securely under his arm, he was about to make for home when a fellow Woodstockian rushed in, exclaiming, 'Mr Brittain has just died. That makes three.' One half of Woodstock was poisoned through eating mussels.

'Great Jehosaphat!' cried 'Mr Haggard', rushing home as fast as he could travel. Fortunately his wife had eaten only a few and escaped with 'a severe shaking-up'. The deadly molluscs were thrown in the refuse bucket.

But alas, 'a retriever dog belonging to mine host of the New Brighton, while engaged on a foraging expedition, came across the mussels and disposed of the lot. Returning to his master's yard, he was seized with vomiting and the pigs and ducks gathered to the feast. The result: one dead retriever dog, one ditto pig, one ditto cat, 14 ditto ducks.

'Had I not been so fond of Ohlsson's I would have shared their fate. I could easily point to a moral, but it will be obvious to an intelligent reader.'

Neither the decorative typographical advertisement nor that of a more literary or humorous turn were unduly affected by the advent of photographic reproduction and weekly illustrated supplements in the 1890s. Advertisements maintained a style all their own and advertisers simply benefited from the increased readership of periodicals offering this novelty.

During the second half of the century a number of eminent journalists and writers had visited the colony drawn by the frenzy generated by the gold and diamond mines. But it was the Anglo-Boer War that really brought the writers to town. From the established big names like Rudyard Kipling to the maverick adventurer like Unger, they all wanted front-row seats as history was made. Some of the visiting scribes had already established international reputations, others were chancers. Journalism was not an easy field to break into as newspapers and magazines had their own hand-picked men and additional competition was provided by the established South African news media.

The young Edgar Wallace had volunteered to do his bit for the Empire and found himself posted as medical Staff Corps orderly at the Simon's Town Hospital. During his stint there he met his future wife: Ivy, the daughter of Rev. and Mrs William Caldecott of Simon's Town. He was starting to establish himself as a writer and fortuitously one William Andrew Timbrell decided to found, publish and edit a Saturday paper called *The Simon's Town and District Chronicle* in the interests of the community at *Old Snoekie*, as the settlement on Simon's Bay was known. The first issue appeared on 11 August 1899 and the last on 15 September 1900. The maiden issue carried a poem by Wallace entitled *Evening at Simonstown* and several more of his poems were later reproduced from other papers. Two months

Woolvin's Pagoda – the telegraph office on the corner of Darling and Adderley streets.

Photography presented exciting possibilities for journalists and publishers but equipment was cumbersome and exposure times too slow for capturing news events.

after its inauguration, the *Chronicle* acknowledged 'we feel that no small amount of the success of this paper is due to the fact that we were fortunate enough to secure the services of Mr Edgar Wallace as assistant editor'. Wallace helped at the paper until he was transferred to the front.

Throughout the war, competition was extremely fierce between reporters, photographers and news artists. In the last-named field, W.H. Schroeder who worked for *Lantern* was South Africa's most successful cartoonist.

Unger was one of the unknowns and had a hard time of it at first, which explains his reactions when he first saw the great Kipling: 'Late in the afternoon ... I saw an open carriage pass my boarding-place drawn by two beautiful, swift-trotting horses. The livery of the footmen and the crest on the carriage-door I recognised as being those of Sir Alfred Milner, Governor of the Cape Colony. Seated in the carriage were a gentleman and a lady: on the opposite seat a little child. The man wore heavy spectacles and had very dark eyebrows. He seemed to see everything on both sides of the street at a glance. Though I had never seen him before, I recognised him from his pictures as Rudyard Kipling, whose arrival the papers of the day before had announced. I frankly confess that as the carriage turned the corner I envied Mr Kipling all he had acquired ...'

Eventually the American more or less thrust himself upon Kipling. He was rewarded for his temerity with a most cordial reception.

Frustrated by the red tape involved in trying to get official accreditation via the complicated censorship system that was in operation, Unger cut some corners which inevitably landed him in some tight spots. On one occasion, expulsion from the lines seemed inevitable when someone suddenly remembered Kipling's mentioning him – a kind act which saved his professional bacon.

Sir Arthur Conan Doyle, known to millions through his immensely popular Sherlock Holmes series, had been watching events in South Africa closely. It was natural for a man of his temperament to be part of the great drama, noted his biographer. As it was for so many Britons, Black Week in December 1899 was a turning point for him. He decided he would take up the challenge to play some part in the War. He could go as war correspondent for the *Westminster Gazette* or he could volunteer. On Christmas Eve he decided to volunteer. His mother was appalled, reminding him that the pen was mightier than the sword, but he was impelled by his sense of duty. He felt he was honour-bound because of the tremendous influence he wielded over younger men like Rudyard Kipling to whom he could give a lead. And apart from the unique opportunity to take part in a major historical upheaval, it was an adventure too good to miss.

He failed to enlist because he was 'not suitably qualified' (possibly by his lack of youth) but when he offered his services as a medical doctor, he was accepted immediately. At Cape Town, Conan Doyle, like so many officers, stayed at the Mount Nelson Hotel before taking the train to Bloemfontein where he was placed in charge of the hospital services.

He established a hospital on the local cricket pitch and daily contact with war-wounded gave him access to unique material which he collected assiduously. By September he had completed a book called *The Great Boer War*. Within two months of publication 30 000 copies had been sold, indicating the British reading public's hunger for words from South Africa. In October 1901 a new edition of the book was published bringing the action up to date.

The censorship system tightened up and, once Roberts and Kitchener had arrived in Cape Town on 10 January 1900, it became almost impossible for a newsman to acquire the necessary permit from the militia. Kitchener loathed the Press in general.

One notable exception was G.W. Steevens who died of enteric fever during the siege of Ladysmith. A professional war journalist, he published five highly acclaimed books in his short 30 years. They were *With Kitchener in Khartoum, In India, The Land of the Dollar, With the Conquering Turk* and *Egypt in 1898*. His record of the Anglo-Boer War was unfinished but was published nonetheless. Perhaps it was prophetic that when he had first arrived in Cape Town, he remarked that the Mountain looked to him more like a coffin than a table.

When the news of his death became known, Lord Roberts cabled Steevens' London paper: 'Deeply regret death of your talented correspondent.' Kitchener's reaction was more surprising. He is reported to have said to one of Steevens' colleagues: 'I am anxious to tell you how very sorry I was to hear of the death of Mr Steevens. He was with me in the Sudan, and, of course, I saw a great deal of him and knew him well. He was such a clever and able man. He did his work as correspondent so brilliantly, and he never gave the slightest trouble — I wish all correspondents were like him. I suppose they will try to follow in his footsteps. I am sure I hope they will. He was a model correspondent, the best I have ever known, and I should like to say how greatly grieved I am at his death.'

In fact the journalists 'Bobs' and Kitchener were so averse to were the intransigents who did not understand or did not care to understand the functioning of the Empire and its higher purposes. (Edgar Wallace, for example, broke the embargo on the Vereeniging Peace news and was barred for his troubles. Nevertheless he returned to South Africa within months to edit the new *Rand Daily Mail* newspaper.)

The compatibility and combined usefulness of loyal men of the sword and of the pen was neatly expressed in this verse from *The Struwwelpeter Alphabet* published in 1908:

> *Men of different trades and sizes*
> *Here you see before your eyeses:*
> *Lanky sword and stumpy pen,*
> *Doing useful things for men;*
> *When the Empire wants a stitch in her*
> *Send for Kipling and for Kitchener.*

While it was left to public figures to wield sword and pen for the Empire, closer to home, at least one journalistic maverick criticised society in the microcosm. Outspoken, argumentative, often libellous and reactionary, usually racist, Thomas McCombie of the controversial weekly *Lantern* worried terrier-like at what he perceived as social ills.

One of his more flamboyant exercises in character assassination had earned him a conviction for defamation and three months behind bars as a guest of the colonial government. He put the time to good use, researching the stories of his fellow inmates who included paupers, felons, lepers and the mentally disturbed.

From then on he never let up on the subject of prison reform. Publishing genuine or specially composed letters to the publication was one of his methods of drawing attention to the conditions behind bars. This is a particularly distressing example: 'Knowing you have taken an ardent part in the cause of prison reform in the Cape Colony, I desire to draw your attention to the case of a friend of mine now and for the last month confined, being upset in his mind, in the common gaol of Cape Town. He is a most respectable tradesman who has had the misfortune to have become upset in his mind and has been placed in the common prison. When his wife last saw him … the poor fellow was roaming about in the exercise yard, uncared for, with his hands and feet literally swollen to double their natural size, and his face blistered almost beyond recognition. The poor fellow cried to her, and pointing to his horrible hands, said: "I have got the leprosy."'

Rudyard Kipling perches on a table to proofread a wartime news report: he believed that journalism, like poetry and fiction, should further the aims of Empire.

CLUBS AND PUBS

ince the earlier days of the second British occupation, gentlemen's clubs (attached to other establishments) had been formed and these of course served as arbiters of social acceptability.

Men who did not have an office to go to and men who did needed a place where they could enjoy the company and conversation of like-minded people. Young men who were still climbing the ladder of success were unlikely to entertain colleagues at their places of residence and a club solved the problem.

They brought disadvantages with them as well, according to social reformers who railed: 'Fashionable clubs are springing up like toadstools from the rank soil of luxury, idleness and sensuality.' Blame was laid at the door of the club for much alienation and unhappiness in aspirational middle-class couples: 'Husband; the club, a taste for French cooks, expensive courses, fastidious epicureanism, late hours, estrangement, profligacy, misery.'

South Africa's first gentlemen's club of the London type dated from the foundation in 1859 of Maritzburg's Victoria Club. It was followed by the Durban Club in 1861 and Cape Town's Civil Service Club and Grahamstown's Albany Club, both in 1862. These were never the stronghold of political parties, but they were places where colonial opinion could be measured on any subject of general interest. The avid reading of local and overseas newspapers featured largely in the daily routine of members.

Many aspects of the 'proper' life were similar to those of the earlier versions – like the African Club based in what was known as Subscription or Society House on the old Heerengracht (later Adderley Street). A writer of 1822 said, 'The charm of the Society House lies in its situation, so prime for gossip, being in the centre of the Heerengracht, traversed by everyone going to the Parade, to the Government offices, to the Custom house, or to the wharf, so that, between the hours of eleven and five almost everyone may be seen from the door of this house. Physicians, lawyers, civil servants,

military officers, merchants and gentlemen from India congregate during the whole morning. Early in the day some one or two regular posers occupy the green seats in front... The talk commences, and that which is, or is not, being reported, gains currency for the day.'

Talk of opening the Civil Service Club was rife by the late 1850s. One of the founder members, Mr John Blades Currey, wrote in his memoirs later in the century that the idea of forming the club was that it should be 'a means of raising the tone of the Government Service and creating a stronger *esprit de corps* among the younger members by giving them opportunities of mixing freely with their elders and, if possible, keeping them out of public bars. In this I was warmly supported by the Heads of Departments...'

In August 1861, one newspaper referred to 'a club, not a billiard and beer room: a club with a coffee room, reading room, library and all other conveniences and luxuries which make up the arrangements of those admirable institutions at home. Verily, a club of this kind is most desirable to an English gentleman, and in no place can I imagine it more acceptable to him than in Cape Town. And a club is to be attempted forthwith. It is to be confined to the Civil Service, Consular, Diplomatic Services, Army and Navy and the three learned professions'. The exclusiveness of this pseudo club brought down the ire of eligibles and non-eligibles who derided it alike. As a palliative, it was suggested that merchants be allowed to join as

---

Above *The City Club provided everything a gentleman could desire of such an establishment, including a comfortable smoking room* (**right**).

honorary members. But the high entrance fee and subscription would keep out a lot of civil servants. A circular was sent out by the promoters which said 'the best elements of Colonial Society are now to be so combined as to create a standard of public opinion and conduct ... After much deliberation the promoters decided to vest the government of the club exclusively in the Civil Service, not from any desire to suggest invidious distinctions, but solely because civil servants, as a body, are the only class of the community for whose permanent position there is any official guarantee'.

This stimulated further criticism and one Augustus Fitzgerald Snobkins Esq. was moved to submit some highly satirical pieces to the local Press on several occasions making much of the implication that government was permanent where the church, commerce and the legal profession were not.

Eventually a compromise was reached and the Civil Service Club opened on New Year's Day 1863 at 7 Roeland Street but at the end of 1865 moved to 'very roomy and comfortable premises' in Church Square. The starting rent of £210 per annum was reduced to £160 after two years, no mean incentive to continued tenancy.

The pub at the Altona Hotel in Victoria Road, Woodstock,
served as a club for Cape Flats farmers wending their weary way
home from the early morning market.

In January 1877 another group of city gentlemen met in the Commercial Exchange and agreed on the formation of their own City Club. The newspaper report on the meeting said the rationale for this move included the fact that 'the tramway to Sea Point and the railway to Wynberg have so scattered the population of Cape Town that there is less unity of movement in the city than in any other colonial town that we know of. The new club will do something, we hope, to counteract the disintegrating process which has been going on for so many years'.

The two clubs co-existed side-by-side with the City Club slowly but surely overtaking the Civil Service Club in status and in the importance of its visitors.

The Civil Service Club embraced all gentlemen (either actively engaged or on the retired list) on the fixed establishment of the Imperial, colonial, and foreign civil services as well as justices of the peace. In the 1880s gentlemen holding appointments on the staff of the governor joined the list of eligibles. Other gentlemen resident in the colony were eligible for all purposes excepting membership of the committee and proposing the admission of new members, but these exceptions were removed in the 1880s. Officers of the Army and Navy, and gentlemen not resident in the country, were admitted as honorary members. The admission and use of the club by honorary members evidently caused some dissatisfaction in the 1880s when the comfort of members was threatened by an influx of strangers.

At first five guineas was payable by each member for admission and five for subscription. In the 1880s the subscription was raised to 10 guineas. Members (and they were many) who were tardy or failed to pay their subscriptions when due had their names posted and failure to pay within three months meant erasure from the list of members. In 1890 reciprocity was declared with the Victoria Club and the Royal Naval Club. As early as 1868 the suggestions of members were noted in a book kept for that purpose and in 1873 the arrangement became formal in a volume called 'The Complaint and Suggestion Book'.

In the early days, one member suggested that 'a bill of fare be put on the dining table every evening to enable the members to "pick and choose"'. The secretary wrote beneath it 'Under Consideration' but a wag of the club could not resist adding 'Now they chews first and picks afterwards'. In the minute book it was recorded that one member suggested that 'a damper be provided, in order that members writing letters and closing envelopes in which they put them, may not be obliged to injure their constitution by licking the gum on the envelopes'. The record proceeds that 'it was decided that a damper be procured, a hope being expressed at the same time, that the complainant's health was not seriously impaired by anything he had licked up at the club'.

In 1880 a member wrote: 'The small boy "Henry" is useless, unornamental, unkempt and altogether anything but a credit to this club. Most of his time is occupied in playing "peg top" in front of the club with street arabs.' The secretary wrote against this entry: 'Discharged.'

In the 1880s a member 'submitted that five pence for half a glass of brandy with a modicum of ice in it is too heavy a charge', and the next day pointed out that 'ice is purchased at 3d per lb and it is seldom, if ever that a ⅓ lb is placed in a glass of anything ordered'. A couple of years later there was a complaint that there was no ice in the club, to which the reply was that there was no ice to be had from the factory due to the scarcity of water, a perennial summer problem in Cape Town. In 1882 a suggestion was made that 'a filter be purchased, the water from the water bottles being at times undrinkable'. This member was fobbed off with the comment that 'water as a beverage never having been popular with the members of the C.S. Club, it would be as well to get the names of the water drinkers before incurring the expense of an elaborate filter'.

The only games allowed were chess, whist and billiards, the last named with limited stakes. In the very popular billiards, a pyramid pool was sixpence during the day and ninepence at night, while black pool was reduced to thruppence a ball. The card room was limited to members only and outside it cards were forbidden. Only cards supplied by the club were to be used; no game of hazard could be played nor dice used.

From the beginning the fine for bringing a dog into the club was five shillings. At first smoking was permitted only in the smoking room and a fine of five shillings was imposed on any man who smoked on the steps of the club house, in the entrance hall or any other part of the building. In the 1880s the steps were removed from the regulations and smoking was also allowed in the billiard room. By the 1890s the tables had so turned that rooms had to be set aside for non-smokers.

A few blocks away, in the City Club, business proceeded in very much the same way with an important difference: its members had been looking for a site upon which to build special premises. In 1892, the year the Civil Service Club first suggested amalgamation with the City Club, several sites were offered, including St George's Home near the corner of New and Wale streets. The idea of amalgamation was agreed to in principle but the two clubs could not reach consensus on common rules. The New Street site was turned down because it was not central enough. Ironically, after four more years of debate on the pros and cons of various properties, the City Club bought Miss Tennent's property next to Poole's Hotel in New Street. Herbert Baker won the competition held to decide upon a design for the new clubhouse and by the end of 1898 the splendid new building was ready to open its doors.

Members responded generously to a request to help with the decoration of the building. Presentations included a pair of koodoo (sic) horns, a chess set, a picture of London's House of Commons, an aneroid barometer and two clocks. All that remained to be purchased were a bust of Queen Victoria and oil portraits of Sir Alfred Milner and Cecil Rhodes.

By the turn of the century the City Club was probably the prime forum for the exchange of commercial and political news and the servicing of useful personal and professional connections. But the Masonic Order remained stronger than the club network and was never seduced into frivolity. From its inception in South Africa in 1803, it had provided a structure within which many men were able to consolidate their business and professional establishment. Sir George Grey was among the many influential Masons to spend time at the Cape. When he was invited to lay foundation stones both for the New Somerset Hospital and the slipway at Simon's Bay, the ceremonies were performed with full Masonic honours. The foundation of the new Houses of Parliament received the same treatment. Cecil Rhodes was inducted as a Freemason on 2 June 1877 during one of his periodic sojourns at Oxford.

It was essential to spend several hours a day at the club if one needed to keep up with what was going on both in commerce and in the Empire.

THE WORKING WORLD

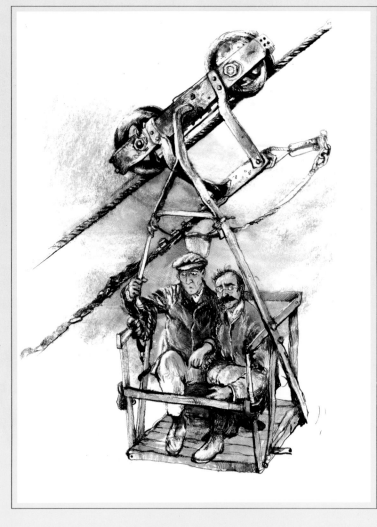

As the Cape came of age the opportunity to get on in the world became a glorious prospect within the reach of more people: more citizens needed to earn money and more and more employers needed skilled workers and labourers. Conditions of service were gradually reformed and the 10-hour working day reduced to eight in winter – even for convicts.

The opportunities for young white working-class people with ambition were greatly enhanced by the many office jobs created as new banks opened, assurance societies were formed and set up their headquarters in Cape Town and the Civil Service grew. The completion of the grand new General Post Office building on the site of the old Commercial Exchange created welcome new clerical positions both for males and females.

Stenography lessons had been offered in Cape Town as early as 1833 and Pitmans shorthand was first introduced to Capetonians in 1844, but by 1887 shorthand still suffered from the absence of a suitably qualified teacher. Typewriters were said to be common in America by 1890, but in the Cape they only crept into government departments, the office of the colonial secretary and the Supreme Court in 1892 and reached the Department of Agriculture in 1896. A papyrograph or copying machine was on sale in 1877 and during 1883 the very latest models in speaking tubes and pneumatic bells came on to the market.

The necessity for training people in the skills demanded by a new mercantile world was not overlooked. Zonnebloem College, which had originally been established by Bishop Robert Gray in 1858 for the education of chiefs' sons, was run by the Anglican Church as a place where males and females, European and 'native', could prepare for university examinations but also learn marketable skills – the boys bookkeeping, woodwork and practical agriculture; the girls typing, dressmaking and cooking.

Nursing was the newest of jobs now suitable for young ladies. When formal training was instituted at the New Somerset in 1885 probationers were not paid but by 1898 they were earning £20 a year. In the early 1890s a trained nurse could earn between £40 and £50 a year (the same as the

*Large consignments of British tradesmen were
'imported' for special projects:*

Left *Welsh and Cornish miners and stonemasons were
transported by cableway from Camp's Bay up to the reservoir works
on the mountain; Irish labourers (**right**) found employment
at the railway workshops at Salt River.*

Young women at work in the Cape Town central telephone exchange.

hospital laundress) and Matron's salary was on a par with Cook's at between £100 and £130 (virtually half the annual stipend for a hospital clerk-cum-storekeeper).

The day staff at the New Somerset commenced their duties at 6.30 a.m. and, with a break of three hours which they took in shifts, remained on duty until nine at night, seven days a week. Trained nurses could apply for permission to leave the hospital for three hours once a week. Standard uniforms had been introduced and the following daily allowance per head was made: a pound each of bread and meat, 12 ounces of potatoes, half an ounce of salt, three drachms of tea, one-and-a-half ounces of sugar, half an ounce of coffee, a gill of milk, an ounce of rice or barley, four ounces of oil, and 20 pounds of coal. Each member of the nursing staff was allowed four pounds of soap a month.

The medical superintendent, Dr Parson, received an annual salary of £300 with accommodation, generous rations for three people and stabling for his horse provided gratis. He supplemented his income by serving as medical officer for the harbour and for the breakwater convict station.

In short, working for a salary was not the way to establish a personal fortune. Many wage-earners tried to alter their fortunes by flirting with Lady Luck on the share market, and in spite of her capricious ways, kept telling themselves that today's bankrupt could be tomorrow's millionaire.

As a columnist in *Lantern* magazine wryly commented in January 1889: 'The very babes at Cape Town breasts are forming lacteal syndicates and booming them; the boys in the street talk scrip in the intervals of paraffin-tin cricket, and the Cape Edwine, having pegged off prospector's rights in Angelina's heart, would hardly refrain from syndicating them on the spot were it not that the owner's claim was under dispute.'

Luck played a certain part in business too, of course, but many a newly prosperous Capetonian had proved that business for a hard worker with the courage to make the most of an opportunity, was the best way to make one's way on in the world. The story of Anders Ohlsson was a case in point.

Ohlsson was 23 when he arrived in the Cape Colony in 1864. He set up as a merchant specialising in the importation of Swedish manufactured goods and timber. By 1869 he was recognised as a man of substance in Cape Town, largely through trade in Damaraland via Walfish Bay. In partnership with a fellow Scandinavian – A.W. Eriksson – he established regional headquarters in Omaruru and stores at strategic points throughout the area, including at Walfish Bay and Rehoboth.

Eriksson had been sent into Damaraland in 1866 as an apprentice to the famous explorer and hunter, C.J. Andersson, and knew the territory very well. He managed the affairs of the partnership in Damaraland while Ohlsson took charge of the business from the Cape Town end. During the 1870s the company flourished, being capitalised at about £200 000. In 1876 20 whites were employed and this number increased to 40 by 1878.

Earlier in the decade, Ohlsson had purchased his own schooner, the *Louis Alfred*, with which he traded goods and transported passengers directly to and from Walfish Bay and Europe. At that time there was no control, tax or excise tax on goods traded between Cape Town and Walfish Bay – except for that payable on guns and ammunition. This trade was highly lucrative. Items sent to Damaraland in 1877 included 600 gallons of brandy, 1 000 rifle barrels, 20 000 pounds of gunpowder, 39 000 pounds of coffee and 51 000 pounds of sugar. These were traded for ivory, animal skins, curios and ostrich feathers. A typical example of the type of cargo exported from Damaraland in the *Louis Alfred* and unloaded in Cape Town included four cases of ostrich feathers, 31 ivory tusks, a bundle of skins, six ox-hides, a box of horns and seven live sheep.

By the end of the 1870s the pickings were not so easy. Commissioner Palgrave had been appointed in 1874 and once the local Damaras and Namas heard that the colonial government was levying tax on wagons and warehouses through him, they started demanding tax too. They also charged higher prices for water and for permission to pass through their territories. And then they fell to fighting among themselves. Trade was seriously disrupted by this war and Ohlsson and his partner could have lost anything between £20 000 and £40 000. But in spite of this setback, the partners wound up their business arrangements and started afresh, each with an enormous capital.

Ohlsson interested himself briefly in the Woodstock glass factory but by 1881 he had decided to buy into the beer-brewing industry although there were already seven other brewers in the vicinity of Cape Town. He bought Annenberg in Newlands and built a modern brewery there which he fitted with all the latest equipment. By the end of the century he had virtually the entire Cape Town brewing industry under his personal control. He had weathered the doldrums of depression so well that he was able to buy out competitors when they faltered. The beer business was vulnerable to economic depression because its market was working class and low wage-earners were always the hardest hit when money was scarce and retrenchment rife.

In fact, all classes of workers were affected by Cape Town's regular depressions. But relief tended to be directed towards whites with some skills. During the worst days of the depression in the early 1880s working-class whites were employed as farm labourers at the standard rate of six-pence a day with rations and some sort of shelter. Twenty-five men were employed in the Roeland Street quarry breaking stones for one-and-thruppence a day.

In good times there was simply not enough labour to go round and convicts (much sought-after because they were not paid and hence meant a considerable reduction in the cost of a project) were at an absolute premium. The Native Depot in Strand Street under the direction of George Stevens, who was re-titled Contracting Officer in the 1890s, attempted to meet the Peninsula's needs for labour by importing people from as far afield as Damaraland and Delagoa Bay. Between November 1879 and May 1882 2 400 men from Mozambique arrived in the Cape and, after they had spent a time in quarantine in a maize store on Newmarket Street, most of them were employed in Cape Town and its close environs. In April 1881 100 were signed on for a three-year contract with the Table Bay Harbour Board. They were paid as little as 15 shillings a month and provided with rations and quarters. They were expected to contribute £4 towards their passages and clothing and on completion of their contracts were allowed £1/11/6 towards their return fare. By the early 1890s the Harbour Board employed mainly Mfengu from the Eastern Cape. They were now each paid 60 shillings a month on one-year contracts.

For most women, whatever the colour of their skin, even these meagre sums were out of reach. In terms of middle-class mores, a woman who aspired to gentility did not accept payment for services rendered — the implication being that genteel people did not need money because they had more than enough already. Payment for any work other than nursing or teaching was simply not proper.

Skilled members of the lower classes could get employment as housemaids, nursemaids, cooks, laundresses. Others worked as fishwives, flower-sellers and vegetable hawkers. But the working world for women was not a place that presented much opportunity for self-improvement.

The Hope Windmill near the Salt River railway junction. The haulier who carried supplies of fresh produce and fodder from farmer to market, the butcher, the miller, the baker and the dairyman plodded steadfastly on through his time-honoured daily chores. For the staples of life were unchanged in spite of progress.

HEALTH, HYGIENE AND HOSPITALS

*T*he poorhouse, the leprosarium, the prison, the lunatic asylum and the hospital, all of which, until relatively recently, had often been accommodated within the same walls, were still frequently confused with one another by citizens who had not kept up with the tremendous advances in the care of the physically sick. Admittedly, the care of the morally and mentally ill lagged woefully behind.

Colonial hospitals were originally intended as refuges for passing mariners, paupers, the chronically sick and the mentally deranged. Citizens of substance took bed-rest at home or hotel where they were visited by medical practitioners. But with the influx of travellers and adventurers from the 1870s on, the need to cater for a better class of patient had grown. The Civil Service List of 1887 states: 'Patients are eligible for admission who are unable to pay for medical or surgical aid at their own homes; who are officers of ships or sailors; who are strangers in the town or colony, having no fixed abode therein; and those who are the subject of a serious injury or accident.' When, for example, Cecil Rhodes' architect, Herbert Baker, contracted typhoid in 1896 he was hospitalised: as a young bachelor he had no one to care for him.

The improvement in hospital services was evolutionary, not instantaneous, so, by the 1870s, the old and new existed side by side in the Cape. There were several hospitals in the Peninsula even before war casualties at the end of the century demanded a drastic increase in facilities.

The Old Somerset Hospital continued to provide a place of safety for the incapacitated, the chronically sick and the aged, as well as a few lepers and 'lunatics'. There was a military hospital near the beach on the Salt River side of the Castle. The Woodstock Cottage Hospital on the lower slopes of Devil's Peak had been built by public subscription, as had Wynberg's Victoria Cottage Hospital. The Lock Hospital for the isolation of patients with venereal and contagious diseases was attached to the town prison in Roeland Street. Most lunatics and lepers were sent to Robben Island where there was also a dog quarantine station and accommodation for convicts. Between Claremont and Newlands, the Seventh Day Adventist Church had acquired a 123-acre property where a medical and surgical sanatorium was

Left *The doctor's box with its patent potions and tinctures.*
Right *A nurse of the Florence Nightingale school attending to a wounded soldier, as photographed in a studio against a painted backdrop.*

116

established, offering all the latest electric and hydropathic treatments under medical supervision.

But of the existing hospitals, the New Somerset at Green Point was by far the best equipped and most sophisticated. It stood virtually on the beach between the Chavonnes Battery and the town and, on completion in 1862, it was the largest building in the area. The imposing battlemented fortress was the first structure visible to mailship passengers as they approached Cape Town. The great façade seemed to rear up into the wind-whipped clouds with reassuring stability. Gulls wheeled in the turbulent air that guaranteed a constant supply of clean ozone to the convalescent.

Unfortunately the roof of the 'haunted castle' (as it was known to irreverent interns) had leaked from the day the first patient was admitted in August 1862. One would have expected better from an edifice that cost £25 000 to erect upon a foundation stone laid with full Masonic honours by none other than Governor Sir George Grey himself.

But in spite of such faults, the average Capetonian was more than grateful for the facility. A letter in *Lantern*, purportedly from an ex-patient, described a happy sojourn there:

> ❝To some people the mere mention of the word "hospital" is like waving a red flag to a bull: it nearly drives them frantic − not with rage, but with fright. Others have a loathing for a hospital but from false pride − caddishness − the fear of the supposed odium that would cling to them as the man, who was "in the hospital, you know"... Dr Parson was my surgeon. Talk about killing a man with kindness! And the nurses too, God bless their hearts! Theirs were like angels' visits. I've read about hospital nurses who could be named Sairy Gamp, who smelled of gin and would swear most horribly at patients and make them "sit up" and give them "what for" while they were in their tantrums. But believe me, there's nothing of that sort going on in the New Somerset. All the nurses are perfect ladies − angels in petticoats I call them.❞

Francis John Parson, resident surgeon at the New Somerset, had been admitted to the Royal College of Surgeons in England in 1860 and in 1870 he had been granted the licentiate of the Royal College of Physicians in Edinburgh. The next year he left England to take up the position of medical officer at the Cape Copper Company's O'okiep mine, a post he combined with that of district surgeon of Namaqualand. His experiences in the northwest had left him permanently disillusioned with the glamour of pioneer life. He advised newly immigrant colleagues to avoid upcountry practice, 'for they all take to drink or morphia unless they become the local preachers'.

When a resident doctor was needed on Robben Island, he volunteered and remained on the island until Dr Wood's death created a vacancy at the New Somerset. Parson, who had acted *in locum tenens* for Wood during his illness, was appointed. He, in his turn, later twice called on the aid of his island successor − first when he was laid up for several months with typhoid fever and then again when he went home to England on long leave.

Dr Parson did a round of the hospital's 13 wards every morning, sometimes accompanied by students gaining early experience before they went over to Edinburgh, London or Leyden to qualify as doctors. The assistant surgeon and visiting surgeons called several times a week. Matron did a morning and an afternoon round.

Although the New Somerset's hundred beds were heavily subscribed, the resident surgeon was blessed with a sprightly sense of humour, not always evident to the office of the colonial secretary, the recipient of his sharp memoranda on hospital priorities. After one official hospital inspection the report suggested screens should be fixed to certain skylights to keep the flies out. Parson thanked the authorities concerned somewhat tersely but rejected the recommendation because the flies would only come in at the front entrance if the back were secured.

He was constantly hounding the offices of the colonial secretary and the mayor on the subject of the appallingly insanitary state of the Green Point Common and the open ground surrounding the hospital. Citizens tended to use these areas as a repository for all manner of refuse, including the carcasses of dead animals. This practice created a breeding-ground for pestilence and produced foul disease-bearing odours that inevitably wafted into the wards and the resident surgeon's spacious quarters on the ground floor of the hospital. The matron, Sister Mary Agatha, was billeted in the northern section of the ground floor which also housed the hospital apothecary, the clerk and the steward. So grand was the scale of the building that there still remained sufficient space for a surgery, an outpatients' room, an accident ward, a visitors' room, and the hospital kitchen.

A lift system operated between the kitchen and the wards on the first floor. Another, to the left of the baronial main staircase, elevated non-ambulatory patients from hallway to hospital bed. Electric lights (particularly important in the operating theatre) were installed in November 1886.

When an operation was to be performed, two nurses with their sleeves rolled up stood at the ready beside trolleys which were draped with white cloths and bore all manner of alarming instruments and receptacles. More elaborate contraptions and flasks were to be seen on the shelves of a large glass-fronted cabinet. The smell of carbolic would mingle with the clean aroma of Wright's coal-tar soap as Dr Parson washed and dried his hands. Then the acrid smell of chloroform wafted from the mask slipped over the patient's nose and mouth.

By the 1890s anaesthetics were routine, and, on the whole, safer. The transfusion of blood was to remain highly dangerous until after the turn of the century when the Austrian pathologist, Karl Landsteiner, demonstrated the A.B.O. system of blood grouping. Before that, surgeons would administer saline to counteract the effect of extreme blood loss. Strychnine was sometimes used as a stimulant in cases of severe shock.

The German scientist, Wilhelm Roentgen, discovered X-rays in 1895 and the use of this invaluable diagnostic aid quickly became common. At least nine X-ray machines were used by medical personnel during the Anglo-Boer War. Wounds of the soft tissues had long been successfully treated and now the new technology reduced the number of amputations previously necessitated by fractures. Injuries involving bone damage were treated by debridement (similar to that used with soft-tissue injuries). The wound was then packed and covered with cotton wool before the injured limb was splinted. Bandages impregnated with plaster of Paris had been in use since the French introduced them in 1851.

But in spite of all these advances, there was still an overwhelming amount of faith in home remedies, patent medicines and so-called miracle cures. In 1909, the British Medical Association (B.M.A.) published a book called *Secret Remedies* giving the chemical analyses of many remedies together with the manufacturers' claims and the B.M.A.'s comments and their tacit warnings. For example, Stevens Consumption Cure was marketed in South Africa as Lungsava, 'the recipe for which is stated to have been long in use among the Kaffirs (*sic*) and Zulus'. Stevens himself gave his formula as '80 grains of Umckaloabo root and $13\frac{1}{13}$ grains of Chijitse to every ounce . . .', secret ingredients that defied explanation of their efficacy. The B.M.A. found the potion to contain rectified spirit of wine, glycerine and a touch of karameria (an astringent) with a cost value of onepence-ha'penny for a five-shilling bottle.

Beecham's Pills, advertised as 'worth a guinea a box' fared even worse; they consisted of aloe, ginger and soap, a cost value of about half a farthing for a box retailing at 14 pennies. Zambuk and Cuticura (ointment and

The reassuring bastion of the New Somerset Hospital was known to nurses as the 'haunted castle'.

soap) were among remedies examined along with the Teetolia Treatment, Dipsocure, Antidipso and other cures for alcoholism, cancer and gout among others.

Home remedies were even more popular than these dubious preparations and certainly cheaper. The two little Liesching girls were saved from the clutches of whooping cough by being rubbed back and front with honey at regular intervals. Buckfat plasters were applied to their chests in between. Sir Alfred Milner used a belladonna plaster on his chest for an 'agitated' heart.

Hildagonda Duckitt included these remedies in her diary:

❛I know of several instances where children seemed to be just wasting away at the ages of two and three, and have been strengthened and restored by a soup made by boiling down a whole tortoise after chopping off its head, scrubbing it well, and boiling it until the parts separate . . . The legs of the tortoise after it is boiled and the liver (which is a special delicacy), after removing the gall-bag, eaten with lemon, pepper and salt, is much appreciated by invalids when they can take nothing else (of course it is an acquired taste).❜

Her cure for toothache:

❛Mix cocaine 60 grains, 1 teaspoonful tincture of opium, and bottle. A tiny piece of cotton wool steeped in this and put in the cavity of the aching tooth will give instant relief. All such powerful application should be kept locked up and measured out by some person, not the patient.

'For jaundice, the yellow flowers of the wild hemp, known at the Cape as "dacha", *Cannabis sativa* (the leaves of which plant used to be dried and smoked by the natives) made into a tea and taken three times a day is most effective.❜

The genteel but very practical and hard-working Miss Duckitt was made of the same resilient stuff as the new breed of nurses who had taken up the challenge issued by Florence Nightingale. The work was hard and the hours long but there were few other careers open to respectable women. Although some die-hards held early Victorian views on the subject of young women who tended Men in their Beds at Night, the real physical danger was the second major case against the job. In 1882 no fewer than 4 000 souls in Cape Town alone had perished in a smallpox epidemic and nurses had been in the thick of the horror. At the turn of the century, a number of nurses paid the ultimate sacrifice by tending the dying when bubonic plague broke out in Cape Town.

At the New Somerset in the 1890s, Matron Sister Mary Agatha was largely responsible for setting the tone among her lay staff. The thrust of her jaw was emphasised by the billowing starched wimple strapped severely round her face. Her black habit flew around her heels as she swept through the wards. But nonetheless, some of the emancipated young women who had taken up nursing for the independence it offered them did not subscribe wholeheartedly to her doctrine of selfless dedication.

Not every female had the makings of a Doctor Jane Waterston, the Cape's only woman doctor at the time, a flinty Scot who had first served the colony in 1868 as headmistress of the girls' school at Lovedale Mission near Alice in the eastern region of the colony. She returned home to qualify first as a nurse and then as a doctor and re-entered the missionary service in Nyasaland. By 1883 her health was failing so she settled in Cape Town, where, in no time at all, she had established a flourishing practice, and 'made her mark as a leader in public spirited service and devotion to duty'. Dr Jane was Visitor to the Robben Island Infirmary and the Old Somerset Hospital. She worked tirelessly with the poor and trained midwives at the free dispensary and clinic she had set up for slum dwellers.

But dedicated or not, an increasing number of young ladies applied to train as nurses. When the New Somerset opened in 1862, it mustered only two female and five male nurses, all untrained. In 1877 Sister Helen Bowden – a Nightingale-trained member of the All Saints Anglican Sisterhood – revolutionised staffing and sanitary conditions before ill-health forced her home to retirement in 1882. Sister Mary Agatha, of the same order, continued the good work when she became matron in 1885, immediately instituting a school where nurses could be trained according to the Nightingale system and then sent out to other hospitals to spread the word.

The Florence Nightingale of the colony, Sister Henrietta Stockdale, was a close friend of Matron's. As matron of the Carnarvon Hospital in Kimberley, Sister Henrietta had started the first training course for nurses in the subcontinent. Her lectures ranged from the subject of technical skills to higher matters – ethics, integrity, moral values and professional conduct. It was largely thanks to her efforts that nursing was transformed in the colony from an ill-rewarded and poorly regarded last resort for drudges, to a respected profession. Hospitals all over the colony were in the capable hands of her graduates. She believed that the future of nursing was secular, although of course each and every one of Sister Henrietta's protégées nurtured a sense of calling and dedication, for, in the words of Florence Nightingale, a nurse 'must look upon her vocation with reverence, for the Divine Flame of Life is often entrusted to her hands'.

Sister Henrietta and Sister Mary Agatha conferred regularly, and the training course at the New Somerset benefited from the programme tried and tested in Kimberley. Together the two campaigned for the registration of trained nurses, and their efforts were rewarded by the Nurses' and Midwives' Registration Clause in the Medical and Pharmacy Act of 1891.

But Sister Henrietta was idolised by younger colleagues for her personal qualities as much as for her professional achievements. She came from an excellent family and her father had given her a classical education. She had a powerful intellect which, combined with considerable charm, enabled her to win the confidence and respect of the leading figures in the colony. Her understanding was such that her projections were often astonishingly accurate – her belief that the future of nursing was secular was a case in point.

Except for a short sabbatical, her friend and colleague held the reins as matron at the New Somerset until after the turn of the century. Then, in 1901, the Mother Superior wrote to the Bishop explaining why the nuns were about to withdraw from the hospital altogether.

Thanks to rapid advances in medical procedures, convalescence had become a pleasant business.

❛Our community has worked at the hospital for 24 years. During that time we have had four sisters successively acting as matron and five acting as ward sisters. I think the influence we were able to exert over both nurses and patients was much greater in the past than it is now … A lighter and less serious spirit has gradually found its way into hospital work; it has become a fashionable way of earning one's livelihood, whereas in years gone by this was not at all the case, but generally speaking was only taken up by those who wished to do something for the love of God and to help others …

'The Superior of the Community has written to the Managing Committee resigning the charge of the hospital and withdrawing the sisters at the end of January 1902 …❜

Faith and Life's Milestones

The population of Cape Town had grown to such an extent by the last three decades of the nineteenth century that the luxury of greater social religious and political division could be indulged in.

The Anglican Church was a case in point. After the second British occupation of the Cape, members of this originally small congregation had initially held services at the Castle. They then gratefully accepted houseroom from the Groote Kerk at the top of the Heerengracht (later Adderley Street).

At that time the Cape was included in the see of the Bishop of Calcutta and, when he visited in 1827, the desirability of building an Anglican church was agreed upon. The colonial government donated a piece of land at the lower end of the Garden, the first of a series of similar moves which became the cause of great acrimony amongst the other churches. St George's Day in 1830 was appropriately chosen for the laying of the foundation stone and Eerste Berg Dwars Straat was renamed St George's Street at the same time.

The new church was in the Greek Revival style and based upon the design of St Pancras' in London. Until close to the end of the century its tall spire lent a graceful note to the city's profile. But alas, this focal point was not universally admired.

The cathedral - it had been promoted to that status in 1848 upon the arrival of Bishop Robert Gray – was regarded by late Victorian taste as too closely resembling a pagan temple to serve as a house of God. The Bishop's lady, Sophy, was a prolific church designer herself, and all her creations, however small and humble, were in the 'correct' Gothic style. On the corner of Burg Street and Greenmarket Square, Charles Freeman's restrainedly beautiful standard Gothic Wesleyan church served, in some sticklers' eyes, as a reproach to the 'temple' at the top of St George's Street.

Before the end of the century, it had been decided that the old cathedral would be demolished and a new Gothic edifice designed by Herbert Baker's firm would rise in its place. No question of retaining any part of the 'temple' was entertained. It was all to go – classical spire, portico, the lot.

Left St George's Cathedral on the corner of Wale and Queen Victoria streets was based on St Pancras' in London.
Right The handsome mosque on the corner of Castle and Chiappini streets had been established in 1850, and it was extended and embellished as the century drew on.

Anglicanism, as the 'official' religion of the dominant class had attracted the ire of other churchgoers. In 1854, Saul Solomon, member of the new Cape Parliament for Cape Town, introduced the so-called Voluntary Bill in terms of which every church should be made responsible for raising its own funds.

Until then, select Anglican and Dutch Reformed churches had benefited from a government subsidy. This naturally did not strike non-conformist Christians, Jewish people and Muslims as an equitable arrangement. Solomon was a Congregationalist and he was supported by other influential members of the Union Chapel, including Ralph Arderne, the member for Somerset.

In 1856 a memorandum was sent to the Queen in connection with the grant of land at the lower end of the Garden to the Anglican Church. Now it was learned that yet another piece of the Garden had been granted by the governor, on his own responsibility, to the Anglicans.

The memorialists based their objection on the fact that 'it is of importance to the citizens of Cape Town that these Gardens, the ornament of Cape Town and almost the only place of recreation for the people, should not be reduced in their extent ... and that under no circumstances ought the alienation of any portion of them to take place except with the consent of the colonial legislature'.

They pointed out that 'the section of Christians to whose religious Superior' the grant had been made already had 'considerable portions of those Gardens for their exclusive use ... while applications for sites in the same locality by other religious denominations had been steadfastly ... and most righteously refused'. The Queen received this communication sympathetically; the matter was referred to the House of Assembly who did not approve the appropriation of the land.

But it was not until 1875 that the Voluntary Bill was finally passed, and the two dominant churches had to stand, as it were, on their own feet financially.

Meanwhile, the Anglican community was also rocked by internicene controversy. The squabbles went all the way via the local Supreme Court to the Privy Council, whose ruling was hailed as a victory by both sides. In-fighting was only resolved when the 'evangelicals' hived off from the Church of the Province, and, in 1870, formed the Church of England in South Africa.

Other causes of religious acrimony were numerous. Among many

Muslims carrying a coffin to the Mowbray cemetery – this was an important part of the religious ritual which they observed in the burial of their dead.

examples were the differences between Russian and English Jews on the subject of the highly profitable kosher meat contracts.

All the numerous Christian churches ran mission operations aimed at reclaiming lost souls and drawing non-Christians to the light. Among the most zealous was Henrietta Schreiner, a tower of fundamentalist strength and the physical opposite of her authoress sister Olive. Henrietta kept up a running battle against the demon drink. Olive's husband, Samuel Cron Cronwright, was filled with admiration and wrote: 'She really loved the outcast – she did not pretend to. A person swarming with vermin, reeking foully with dirt, perhaps drunk, would be brought to the home for inebriates which she ran, called Highlands in Cape Town. She would put her arms around him, beam ecstatically in his face, call him brother and welcome him with all the love in that great mother heart. She would put him into a mud bath which was one of her cures. She would give him unfermented fruit juice. She would wash him, clean him up, put clean clothes on him, help him with his work and generally be as bright and apparently happy as she could be, though I doubt not her heart was almost breaking at the misery and sin which she was in contact with.'

Another angel of mercy, Canon Lightfoot, who started Bree Street's St Paul's congregation, used the prevailing appetite for education, even among people in the most desperate of circumstances, to attract possible converts to the church. Church schoolrooms provided an acceptable outlet for the energies of genteel ladies many of whom still regarded working for money as unacceptable.

The Muslim community did not overtly object to Christian attempts to convert its members, but there was strong objection to the closure of traditional cemeteries above the so-called Malay Quarter on the slopes of the Lion's Rump. An attempt to force them to use the new cemeteries at Maitland gave rise to the 'Malay Riots'.

One would have thought that the Christian Victorian with his very evident obsession with death, might have sympathised with the Malay's passionate adherence to his traditional religious burial practices, instead of treating them simply as a symptom of intransigence. Cape Town's Christian cemeteries boasted some of the most elaborate and ostentatious memorials that could be imagined. The route to the cemetery in Mowbray was the most profitable for buses and cabs which ferried a stream of mourners to and fro every day of the week. Maitland, which was even further away, proved proportionally more profitable.

Darwin and thinkers of his ilk had shaken up old religious securities and in the new secularised world the power of man and science were deeply revered. But death was one area where neither man nor science held sway. Up until the end of the century epidemics ran amok through the com-

The pulpit of the Groote Kerk, a masterwork by Anton Anreith installed in the present building's predecessor in 1789. The original clock tower was incorporated in the new building which was dedicated in 1841.

munity without warning or respect of persons. If even the royal family was not exempt – the Queen's beloved consort had been claimed by typhoid in 1861 – who was safe? So one ritualised death, announcing it with superbly printed mourning cards and dressing it up in sable crêpe and plumes … perhaps in an unconscious attempt to propitiate it.

An echo of the same sentiments was to be found in the contemporary obsession with correct mourning wear. The fashion rules applying to these clothes were complicated and strictly adhered to. They constituted a major sub-section of the clothing industry and had been the foundation of several city businesses, including Stuttafords. Queen Victoria had gone into mourning in 1861 when her regent died, and she remained in mourning for the rest of her life, so the fashion for widows' weeds was set by the highest of possible arbiters, known to the irreverent as the 'Widow of Windsor'.

A proper widow's costume ranged in price from three-and-a-half to four guineas. Nun's veiling, cashmere, and crêpe (none of which revealed even the suspicion of a shine) were the preferred fabrics. Children's mourning costumes followed suit. Much attention was devoted to correct accessories. The mourning umbrella might be covered with grosgrain or linen. Lace-edged or dotted net veiling was de rigueur for face and head or, with a dun plume or two, as suitable decoration for a widow's headgear. Jewellery too was specialised. Restraint was the watchword: one might wear a string of fine jet beads with a miniature portrait of the departed or a locket containing a twist of hair. The mourning ring would be set with dark stones such as garnets and jet and might have a concealed compartment for a twist or a plait of hair worked into the band. Linked hands symbolising loyalty over death's great divide were an often-used decorative motif.

Mrs Marie Koopmans-De Wet and Mrs Sophia Jamison (benefactress of the South African College) were two of several notable city personages whose wardrobes contained nothing but mourning wear in respect for lost partners. Other dowagers opted for a version of mourning dress because its dignity indicated a serious moral temperament. Black gave one an importance and an identity.

Little Kathleen Liesching never missed the awesome ritual of her grandmother's preparation for church: 'She . . . [was] a stately figure in her dress of black brocaded satin with its boned bodice and full . . . skirt. With this she wore a small sequinned bonnet trimmed with lace and tiny white ostrich feathers . . . tied beneath her chin with black velvet ribbons. The bow at her throat hid the great gold brooch encircling a glass-enclosed plait of Grandfather's hair tied by a minute bow of faded blue ribbon. In her gloved hands she carried her Bible with its brass clasp and gilt-edged leaves. In her capacious pocket was slipped her purse with the linen handkerchief which I had been allowed to sprinkle with eau-de-cologne.'

Malay burial rituals had always been a part of traditional Muslim religious practice and were not peculiar to this period. Failure to give due cognizance to their importance had caused trouble during the smallpox epidemic when the Malays refused to bring out their dead because religious law insisted that the corpse must be carried to the cemetery by particular members of the community for burial. This was the law which was affected by the cemetery closures which had been discussed since mid-century.

As the city spread and grew and periodic epidemics swept through the community, cemeteries became crowded and presented a health hazard. Bodies not buried deep enough were dug up by Cape Town's enormous population of stray dogs or were washed out by winter rains. Others were deposited in poorly constructed above-ground vaults whose air vents allowed noxious gases to escape. Consequently a large piece of ground in Maitland was set aside for a new cemetery and an inter-denominational committee was set up to ensure fair treatment for all groups. In spite of the fact that Malays constituted a large fraction of the population there was not one Muslim on the committee. Further, they argued that their traditional graveyards were not overcrowded and that their custom of digging a grave six feet deep ensured that Malay cemeteries were not insanitary. The Maitland cemetery was too far to walk carrying a coffin and so they requested permission to extend the Tana Baru graveyard a little way up the Lion's Rump. But the authorities reiterated their emphatic 'no'.

In spite of internal ideological divisions, the Malay committee united on this issue under the leadership of Abdol Burns, a refined and educated man who enjoyed the respect of the entire Cape community. He led diplomatic deputations to nearly every single influential Cape executive but in vain.

So the evening of Friday, 15 January saw the Cape Muslims without a burial ground. Their existing cemeteries had been officially closed that day by government decree. There was nowhere legal to bury the corpse of anyone who died over the weekend. And, sure enough, on Sunday a child did die – the offspring of Amaldien Rhode, one of the fishermen who lived at Burke Cottages in Woodstock. That afternoon at two o'clock, a funeral procession 3 000 strong walked along Sir Lowry Road, down Darling and up Shortmarket streets on their way to the Tana Baru cemetery at the top of Longmarket Street. The procession broke up after the burial but marchers regrouped to stone the 12 policemen who were on hand to take the names of the offenders. The officers fled for their lives, some badly injured.

On the Monday the Corps of Volunteers was called out to maintain law and order. By Thursday morning nearly a dozen leading Malays, including the great Abdol Burns, had been arrested. They were all sentenced to two months' hard labour and Burns had to pay a £10 fine as well. As a compromise, the community was allowed to purchase the old Brick and Tile Company land at Observatory for a cemetery.

Although funerals tended to be more impressive displays of pomp and ceremony than weddings for most of the Cape's religious groups, weddings were often far from workaday affairs. Very special nuptial outfits were to be had – including white satin wedding corsets embroidered with orange blossom – and veils were commonly worn but many brides were not married in white. The wedding breakfast often seemed to be the most important part of the day's programme which was why a wedding could involve considerable expense.

Romance was very much in vogue and marriages among well-to-do Capetonians were often made in Heaven . . . with the shrewdly orchestrated benefit of family alliances thrown in. Such was the wedding of Florence Arderne and the barrister Sidney Twentyman in 1878. No one questioned that it was a love match – the flighty Flo had been falling in love by her own confession since she was a 15-year-old schoolgirl. And everyone lauded the fact that their union would also draw closer two important Cape families.

The couple had become engaged at a dance and the wedding date was set for four months later. Florence was the favourite daughter of patriarch Ralph Arderne, and every member of this enormously extended family was engaged in preparations for the festivities which had been the talk of the town – or the fashionable part of town, at any rate.

The *Cape Argus* rhapsodised about the ceremony which took place at seven in the evening by which time preparations were 'a marvel of completeness . . . the carriageway from the [Arderne] house to the church was covered with matting and carpets were spread from the hall door to the two large marquees fitted up as a supper room. The interior and the exterior of the house were entirely altered, the former being fitted up as dancing, card and retiring rooms and the latter, by means of platforms and flags, changed into a cool promenade'.

Apart from the guests, the immediate vicinity of the church was crowded by 'an immense concourse of people who had come as spectators from Cape Town and Wynberg'.

'The bride wore a costume of white Cashmere soie, covered with Honiton point lace' made in England especially for her. There were seven bridesmaids, seven groomsmen and six flower girls and pageboys. The bridesmaids wore outfits of white gauze de Cyprus supplied by Stuttafords.

When the happy couple emerged from the church, they were met by a procession of the band of the Connaught Rangers and the men of the Wynberg Company of the Rifle Volunteers in which Twentyman was a lieutenant. 'Each man of the company held a lighted torch . . . The band played Mendelssohn's Wedding March, and escorted by the torchbearing Volunteers the procession walked to the residence of the bride's father.

'The crowd by this time in Mr Arderne's ground was immense and it was calculated that between two and three thousand persons were present. Meanwhile the tents fitted up as a supper room were open to the inspection of the public and some idea may be formed of the nature of the sight when we mention that the tables were laid, regardless of expense, for 250 persons.

Saint Mary's Roman Catholic Cathedral on Stal Plein was erected in mid-century on a piece of land known as Tanner's Square and bought from Baron von Ludwig.

'In closing this notice we may say that no marriage ever took place in this colony under happier auspices. The families of the bride and bridegroom have been settled in Cape Town for very many years and each possesses troops of friends not only in this city but all over the Colony.'

The young Mr and Mrs Twentyman travelled next day to Bredasdorp for their honeymoon. Members of polite society would tend to spend as much as a month away on a holiday of this kind. Kalk Bay and Hout's Bay were popular spots as were some of the nearby country inns like Rathfelder's.

But the romantic image of shared bliss, propagated by Victorian St Valentine and wedding cards, belied the increasingly political nature of church membership and the discrimination among members of each denomination. The Dutch Reformed Church provided separate facilities for members of its congregation who were not white. In the English church, where traditionally members of the upper classes sat at the front, it now became accepted that dark-skinned people automatically joined those at the back.

Bed & Board

The problems of finding suitable accommodation increased with Cape Town's growing population.

Families were large: between six and ten children were the norm with a grandparent and a single uncle, aunt or cousin often increasing the head-count. But only prosperous people could afford to buy and run a household of decent size. If one could put up collateral or security, several financial institutions in the city offered loans against first mortgages on private houses. The alternative was to pay an exorbitant rent. In 1899, for example, a comfortable double-storey villa on Sir George Grey Street in the Gardens was available for rental at £27 a month. Admittedly it had ample grounds − a front garden and a piece of ground at the rear large enough for keeping poultry and other small stock − but an annual rental of £324 was steep, nonetheless. The medical superintendent of the New Somerset Hospital, for example, was paid £300 a year for a live-in post with rations for three people and stabling for his horse.

Speculative builders and landlords looking for new investments were increasingly buying up the farmlands surrounding Cape Town and putting up rows of houses but these were small, shoddily built and did not have enough ground to allow even for a vegetable garden. For the many Capetonians barely managing to keep body and soul together, these little homes might have seemed like castles but, ideally, a housekeeper needed a vegetable patch, a couple of fruit trees and a poultry run.

Single people experienced different but equally serious difficulties. Well aware of the plight of college students, in 1885, Charles Lewis, Professor of Classics and History (and initially Mathematics) at the South African College, proposed the formation of an old boys' union whereby the Alma Mater could benefit materially from the love she had inspired in her alumni. The idea was taken up enthusiastically, most notably by the Dutch Reformed Synod sitting in Cape Town at the time. Many of the dominees present were South African College old boys and heartily in favour of the union. Its first project was to hire Mayville, a spacious property on Breda Street, and convert the place into College House, a residence for male students. The cost of living there was £45 a year and by the mid-1890s the premises had been bought and extended to offer bed and board to 40 men.

No residential facilities were available for female students so out-of-towners had to find their own lodgings. The lucky ones had relatives prepared to put them up. Otherwise, one might ask the church to put one in touch with a suitable family. Hope Mill, a spacious house virtually at the top of Government Avenue, was an example of the type of establishment where young lady boarders were taken in. The house had been acquired by two English spinsters, Miss Jones and Miss Small, with the object of setting up an experimental private school. Boarders put the unused space to use and supplemented the ladies' income.

Young men in town on their own might take lodgings in a boarding-house too. The more exclusive (and expensive) offered the resident his own sitting-room and dressing-room as well as a bedroom. Ablution facilities were inevitably shared.

Visitors to the city who intended to make a lengthy stay might also seek accommodation in a boarding-house, hotel tariffs ranging, as they did, from six to 12 shillings a day. At least there were some hotels to choose from now.

Above *Even in high-quality accommodation, ablution facilities were often rudimentary.*
Right *The run-down boarding house in Commercial Street where Anreith, Schütte and Thibault were said to have met for social evenings earlier in the century.*

The London Hotel with its offending stoep harked back to an earlier era.

But despite the 'blazing heat and choking dust' of town, the new Grand Hotel on the corner of Strand and Adderley streets was admired as a marvel of luxury and drew the *crème de la crème* . . . that is, until the Mount Nelson rather cast it in the shade at the end of the century. Shops occupied the ground floor of the Grand and the main entrance was on the Strand Street façade. The first floor offered a dining-room, Moorish bar and a billiard-room with two of Thurston's finest tables lighted by electroliers (the modern version of chandeliers). There were special lavatories for visitors to the dining- and billiard-rooms. The dining-room ceiling was 16 feet 6 inches high and its main decorative feature was a mahogany-coloured dado of lincrusta Walton work with salmon and gold wallpaper. The furniture was of walnut upholstered with crimson plush. Diners sat at separate tables, each table being lit by an individual electric light with wires connected via the floor. The kitchen was on the top floor and connected to the dining-room by a lift. The drawing-room was decorated in old gold and brown with velvet upholstery. A grand piano stood on the velvet-pile Axminster carpet. The fireplace had a carved walnut mantlepiece with electro-brasswork and porcelain tiles of Italian design. Some of the pictures on the walls were so splendidly framed, the eye tended to rest on the frame rather than the study within it. The first floor balcony promenade with its luxuriant hanging baskets of ferns was a popular meeting place for the fashionable set. On a practical note, there were adequate servants' quarters and the fire precautions and sanitary arrangements were of the most up to date.

In spite of all this grandeur, very important visitors were still invited to stay at Government House. For example, in 1890, Sir Henry Loch (governor at the time) and his wife invited Baron de Rothschild to stay there as soon as they heard he had arrived, but he had already been invited to put up at Groote Schuur by Cecil Rhodes.

When the Leightons visited in 1889, they were not so fortunate:

❛. . . we found ourselves housed in Cogill's Hotel, Wynberg. We had written beforehand for room – bedroom, dressing-room, maid's room, sitting-room. We were shown into a large room with three beds in it – a bedroom in an annex was offered to the maid. The bath and lavatory arrangements were very deficient, and the same remark applies to most South African Hotels. It is with much difficulty that a dressing-room can be procured at any South African Hotel. A sitting-room was out of the question. To visitors who have many acquaintances the discomfort of having no sitting-room is great. It is not pleasant to receive your visitors on the "stoep" or verandah, or in the public room. When our friends called, the servants saved themselves the trouble of inquiring whether we were at home, by always saying that we were out.

The Royal on Plein Street boasted, in the late 1890s, telephonic communications with the government offices and all the principal establishments in town. The Masonic was specially convenient – facing the Parade, close to the railway station and on the tram route to and from the Docks. A 'family and commercial hotel', it offered private sitting- and dining-rooms, oysters daily, wine and billiards. The old St George's Hotel on the corner of St George's and Church streets, was a double-storey Georgian-style structure with shuttered windows. Its dining-room was noted for a *plafond* painted by Antonio Chiappini, a founder member of the Commercial Exchange back in the 1820s.

The International Bon Accord up near Mill Street was like a little oasis, yet only 10 minutes' walk from the main attractions – Government House and Avenue, the Houses of Parliament, the library, the museum and the Good Hope Hall. It had its own cabstand and trams passed every five minutes. The hotel grounds were so generous that cows could be kept there for the supply of fresh milk. The special attraction for visitors was the trellis promenade – 'seated under this airy archway the visitor may well fancy himself or herself miles away from the city, for here the air is bright and bracing and the dust and smells that so often permeate the town thorough-fares are altogether unknown'.

'The hotel was full, as indeed all the hotels in Cape Town were, and great was the discomfort to which some of our fellow-passengers were put. Lord and Lady Seaton were hunting about on the day of landing until eleven o'clock at night for a bed.'

Not a very pleasant task considering the poor street lighting of the time.

'General Stuart C.B. and his wife spent their fortnight in South Africa in a dirty and dusty pothouse at Kalk Bay. Mr Donkin M.P., his wife and daughter and his relatives, the two Misses Trotter with their brother and Mr Harrison and Mr Pennington doubled up in amazingly narrow quarters at the Diep River Hotel; so on the whole we felt we ought to have congratulated ourselves on the accommodation we had secured.'

Later, when they were on a tour of the western (or 'Dutch') part arranged for them by Mrs Marie Koopmans-De Wet, they stayed with the Kriels who had made arrangements for the reception of visitors at their farmhouse. Mrs Kriel showed them to one room with one double bed in it and one set of washing things.

'After a little explanation another room was found of the same size but with two beds in it and a third "shakedown". This was intended for a family due to arrive the next day.'

It was decided that Leighton should occupy one room and his wife the other and that they should stay for only one night instead of two.

'Dinner was at 12.30. Mr Kriel sat at the top of the table and repeated, sitting, a rather long grace in Dutch. The meal consisted of a piece of beef and a piece of mutton, we could not identify the joints, but the meat was good – potatoes and beetroot, and a baked custard pudding – one glass of Cape sherry was poured out and a tumbler of water – grapes and figs. At 3 o'clock we had a cup of tea and a bun, at 7 o'clock, rissoles and scrambled eggs, tea, bread and butter, fig and gooseberry jam.'

The Leightons would not have been able to comment on the threepenny lodging houses patronised by those unfortunates at the bottom end of the social scale. To get the full horror of the picture, an establishment of this type was best visited late when business was in full swing because business here began when the canteens closed. The drinker who had retained enough sense to hang on to a tickey, groped his way to the lodging house where his money would buy him a corner on the floor. His clothes would have to keep him warm and he would have to lie pretty straight so as not to encroach upon somebody else's threepennyworth. The boss of this establishment was mounted upon a small narrow bed, from which he enjoyed a good view of the customers. Once the rooms were full, men were placed head to foot along the passages. For further overflow there was always the yard, no matter that it stank: seeking refuge there for the night at least kept one safe from being arrested as a vagrant and put to work at the harbour.

The Clifton Hotel offered an ideal setting for relaxing out-of-town holidays overlooking the Atlantic.

THE CAPE HOUSEKEEPER

The day began very early for the middle-class Cape housekeeper who wished to maintain genteel standards in the face of a soaring cost of living, the scarcity of vital household requisites and the difficulty of finding and keeping good servants.

In working-class areas, housing was woefully cramped. Ideally, a housekeeper needed elbowroom – a home spacious enough to shelter an extended family and a garden large enough to accommodate a vegetable patch, a couple of fruit trees and a poultry run to provide both meat and eggs. Steam incubators had been introduced at the Cape which was ironic as eggs were well-nigh impossible to buy. 'The cook's despair in South Africa is the absence of eggs' noted an advertisement for Bird's concentrated egg, custard and blancmange powders which promised to fill the gap. Powdered or condensed milk, also costly imports, were indispensable standbys for those who had larders and the money to stock them. Fresh milk curdled alarmingly quickly in the Cape summer. There were dairy farms on the lower slopes of Table Mountain and as close to town as Woodstock and Mowbray but a couple of cows of your own were regarded as essential by those fortunate enough to be able to accommodate them. Obviously stabling for a horse and a shed in which to keep a Cape cart were necessities for genteel people.

Domestic pets were also high on the list of priorities for the Victorian household. Cape Town's poorer areas were cursed with an appallingly high population of stray dogs but in upper-class suburbs even watchdogs were petted and spoilt. The Society for the Prevention of Cruelty to Animals was founded in 1879 and kennel club figures demonstrated that household breeds (particularly the ubiquitous fox terrier) far outnumbered sporting dogs. These spry little canines were always game for a rat-hunt but were not proof against other invited guests which included puffadders, cobras and boomslangs who also came after the vermin. If the worst came to the worst, one could call in the professional exterminator who employed ferrets and usually a mongoose or two in his service.

Poverty among the lower classes and inadequate lighting and policing of the wealthier outlying suburbs created an epidemic of crime and this

Left *The Criterion stove with its built-in water boiler cost £5/10/-.*
Right *Rondebosch laundrywomen collected from their clients and did the washing in the pond on the Common.*

132

was where Rover earned his bones. Presumably, the Kenilworth resident who wrote to the *Cape Times* in March 1899 did not own a dog. He told of three incidents in his area. In the first, a domestic servant was attacked and stabbed in her room by an interloper; not long afterwards another servant was murderously assaulted on the Main Road between Claremont and Kenilworth; finally, his own house was broken into and 'violence attempted on his daughter'.

For Mr Thomas Edkins Fuller, M.L.A., a mastiff was the answer: he even suggested that this noble hound was a more appropriate representative of the British spirit than either a lion or a unicorn. During a panegyric delivered on the subject at a literary soirée, he said that the mastiff was 'a very embodiment of Teutonic strength and calm [until] her blood was up [when] every hair stood on end like a thousand tiny bayonets ... My house is somewhat isolated and lonely, but no burglar or fowl-stealer or pantry-robber ever troubled me after the mastiffs mounted guard, although before they arrived we had more than one successful raid on the poultry-yard, and occasional attempts to break into the house'. Fuller, needless to say, kept a fox terrier to alert his mastiffs when danger threatened.

Once space for family and livestock had been taken care of, there was staff to be considered. While a very rich man's household would ideally include a butler, a housekeeper, two or three maids, a coachman and a groundsman, many a colonial housekeeper had to make do with one maid and a groundsman-cum-groom. Or just one general factotum. The problem seemed to be finding the right person.

The recruiting and training of servants from among the indigenous population was held to be difficult but it was certainly not impossible. At Herbert Baker's Muizenberg house, Sandhills, a black manservant known as Alfred cooked, waited at table, made the beds and cleaned the house with superb efficiency. Some of the older Dutch families had maintained satisfactory master/servant relationships dating back to the days of slavery. Mrs Koopmans-De Wet always kept a little black page to open the door of a visitor's carriage and present the calling card to his mistress. This small retainer was dressed in a smart velvet suit and, for thrift's sake, as soon as a page outgrew the suit he was replaced with a smaller boy. She boasted playfully that conditions in her service were so good that these pages grew at an unbelievable rate. Suitable replacements were not in short supply.

Importing servants from 'home' (i.e. England) was a costly and short-term solution. The minute they arrived, their white skins automatically placed them above brown-skinned Capetonians and presented opportunities that would have been denied them in England. A treasure-chest of minerals had opened up north and Lady Luck bestowed her favours regardless of class.

Many Britons, right up to the turn of the century, felt that there was no real substitute for white servants from England, in spite of the difficulties and the fact that as early as the 1870s they had to be paid 50 shillings a month with board and lodging. Others had discovered the pleasures of employing refined and gently spoken immigrants from St Helena – they were in great demand and short supply.

Doyenne of the domestic arts and author of the only book on housekeeping in South Africa, Hildagonda ('Hilda') Duckitt, suggested that as trained servants were neither plentiful nor good one should

> ❛get a young white or coloured girl and train her. I have found training a girl, if you can get one out of a nice home, very satisfactory, paying, if she is capable, £1 a month for the first six months and increasing to £1/10/- or £1/15/-; ours makes very nice bread and simple puddings. Men are paid by the week and women by the month ... Many English ladies who keep an English nurse say they get on very well with a coloured cook, and perhaps a young girl as a housemaid. I find the best way to train them is just to devote some time when you first get them, and give them an object-lesson in cooking and housework, letting them do things under your supervision – for instance I would have cutlets and soup several days running, till they know exactly how to do it, and so on; take a cookery book, if you don't know much yourself, and teach practically, not by description ...❜

And if anyone understood the practicalities of housekeeping at the Cape, it was Miss Duckitt. She was born on her father's farm, Groote Post near Darling, in February 1840. In 1804, the Dutch had decided that Groote Post should be dedicated to the production of breeding-stock from a small parcel of Spanish wool-sheep which had been acquired from Europe by Colonel Robert Gordon during V.O.C. days. When the British once again resumed control in 1806, the work was continued. William Duckitt, Hilda's grandfather, had been sent to the Cape in 1800 (during the first British occupation) to establish model farms and improve colonial agricultural practices and livestock. He functioned as secretary of the board that ran Groote Post until 1815 when Lord Charles Somerset took the place over for his own horses and for shooting. In 1836 Groote Post was put on the market and Frederick, William's son, bought it.

Hilda was the sixth of the ten children Frederick and his wife, Hildagonda Johanna Versfeld, reared at Groote Post. Hilda and some of her siblings were educated at home by a governess. At 20, she was engaged to Lieutenant William Brown and waited faithfully for him for seven years though she seldom saw him during that time. After he broke the engagement shortly before they were due to be married, she bravely threw herself into the pleasant and busy life of a housekeeper and sometimes a manager on a prosperous farm. The life she recorded in her diary there was in essence very similar to the life of a housekeeper in one of Cape Town's rural suburbs, the main differences being in the number of servants, the size of the vegetable garden, and so on. When Hilda herself moved to the suburbs, she simply tailored down her old routines.

On the farm, her day began at 5 a.m. For her crisp cotton day-dresses, she favoured a fresh shade of lavender that enhanced her clear complexion and brown hair and eyes. Fresh as a flower though fierce in her energies, she would repair to the meat room, envelop herself in a voluminous apron and dispense rations to the dozens of souls who found means of livelihood on the farm. To feed the small community, a sheep was slaughtered every day and a bullock once a week.

Then there was milk to be separated and, every few days, butter to be churned. The poultry had to be seen to and eggs collected. Rooms were turned out and polished in rotation. Monday was washday: the large iron pot where water was heated over an open fire was situated conveniently close to a natural spring.

It took a cartload of *renoster* bush to heat up the ancient range set in a recess under the chimney in the kitchen. This was undertaken twice a week when Abraham, the East African cook who'd been rescued from a slave dhow, baked all the bread required on the farm, together with a supply of sponge and tea cakes and turnovers for picnics.

After every harvest of fruit or vegetables, Hilda meticulously laid up a store of jams, preserves, and pickles. She devised some recipes herself, garnered others from her extensive reading and wide network of friends and relatives.

In March, when the grapes were ripe, Hilda made wine, grape jam and *mosbolletjies* – buns in which the fermented juice of steen grapes was used instead of yeast made of raisins in the common way at the time. The traditional Duckitt method for making raisins involved dipping small baskets of selected grapes into a pot of boiling lye made of the soda-rich ashes of the Gouna scrub. The mixture had to be so strong that an egg would float on it. After a few minutes' immersion, the now-cracked grapes were drained and laid out to dry for a fortnight or so on a conveniently flat roof.

Once her housekeeping and catering responsibilities had been met, the good housekeeper would still have time and energy for needlework. Hildagonda Duckitt, needless to say, was an accomplished dressmaker, copying special gowns for herself, her sisters, or her nieces without recourse to the paper patterns which had proved such a boon to less skilled women. As a special treat, some years Hilda sent her own flower sketches to England to be printed on her summer muslins which cost sixpence a yard.

A variety of fish, game, meat and fresh produce was to be had from this Longmarket Street shop.

As a matter of course, she wrote two or three letters every day. A busy woman couldn't always be out visiting and writing was the only way one could keep in touch with friends and family even in adjacent suburbs. At one time, Hilda acted as governess to two of her nieces and she would always try to make time after Sunday service to instruct the servants and labourers in the catechism.

Hilda's mother had been a devoted gardener and Hilda inherited her passion for plants.

'Love is the best compost for flowers,' Hilda was wont to say.

Under her care, the grounds surrounding the farmhouse developed into the earthly paradise that a well-tended garden symbolised. Bright drifts of mignonette, stocks, poppies and cornflowers breathed their sweet fra-

Hawkers plied their trade up and down suburban streets and lanes.

grances against tumbling hedges of blue plumbago and pink French roses, introduced to the colony by the Huguenots. Banks of scarlet and pink geraniums nodded at their reflections in the mirrored surface of the large pond. Beyond the fertile vegetable garden lay the orchards, and, further still, a grove of poplars with a riotous undergrowth of arum lilies, nasturtiums and a variety of indigenous gladiolus.

When there was a house party at the farm, Hilda would send the younger women and girls out to gather wild and garden flowers. The centre of attraction in the dining-room was always provided by a magnificent basket of flowers hanging over the table. Wall sconces overflowing with blooms would complete the effect.

Gardening brought Hilda great joy and she took special interest in indigenous plants, collecting and distributing the seeds of *Nemesia strumosa* which became tremendously popular in England. She initiated the export of chincherinchees by sending parcels of these resilient wildflowers to her friends Mary and Catherine Frere (the wife and daughter of the governor, Sir Henry Bartle Frere), once they had returned to London. When her brother, Jacob (who had inherited the farm), married in 1888, Hilda and her younger sister, Bessie (with the aid of small inheritances from their father), moved to Plumstead where they worked for the church and she completed the manuscript of her book *Hilda's 'Where is it?' of Cape Recipes*. Designed for South African housekeepers and including recipes from all the racial groups at the Cape, it was published in London in 1891.

Two years later the sisters moved to Nemesia Cottage where Hilda once again made history by establishing an indigenous flower garden. After the outbreak of the second Anglo-Boer War in 1899 they moved again, this time to St Lucia at Waterloo Green, Wynberg, the more effectively to aid with the care of the sick and wounded. Hilda's second book, *The Diary of a Cape Housekeeper*, was published in 1902.

She advised brides, immigrants and established household managers alike, not to despair in the face of Cape Town's 'servant problem' and a cost of living higher than that in England for 'the climate is beautiful and makes up for much'. Some may not have agreed with her for during the summer when winds whipped up horrific clouds of dust, grime and grit, many cleaning chores were no sooner completed than they needed doing all over again.

Before sweeping a very dusty room, the housewife was advised to sprinkle the floor with clean damp tea-leaves. 'Proceed then to sweep, not in an excitable manner, throwing the dust up into the air, but by keeping the broom steadily on the floor rather draw than push the dust along.' The bedstead might be brass or wood but in either case had to be polished and its steel springs dusted. The thin firm mattress or palette needed a weekly airing. The featherbed was to be shaken out every day and aired in the sun frequently. Sheets and blankets needed regular laundering and the quilt or comforter had to be shaken thoroughly and aired.

A range-type stove, like the popular Dover, had to be cleaned every day when it was quite cold. The best way, advised one household manual, was to 'spread a mat or clean sack in front of it and then wearing old gloves, sweep it down with a hair broom kept for that purpose. Then with a round black lead brush, cover the whole carefully with black lead that had been dissolved in a little water in a bowl. Before the lead dries, polish it vigorously with another brush'.

Gleaming glassware and windows were a particular pride and kept at their sparkling best by regular cleaning with a weak solution of water and washing soda. Some of the handsomest lamps were made of glass and they, too, had to be cleaned daily, their wicks trimmed and their bowls filled with paraffin.

Keeping knives and forks shiny was a battle never entirely won (the new stainless steel cutlery was still a rarity). As soon as it was removed from the table, cutlery had to be washed, without wetting the handles, then rubbed on a leather-covered knifeboard impregnated with polishing powder. Plain deal boards spread with bathbrick powder were also used sometimes but the harsher abrasive caused rapid wear and the sound of its use set most people's teeth on edge. Cleaned pieces were then dried and smeared over with either a special rust-protector or a mixture of oil and whiting to prevent tarnishing.

The next most daunting challenge was keeping a cemented stoep white. Sweeping and scrubbing were followed by a coat of English hearthstone powder, painstakingly smoothed on so that it dried in the pattern of fine-grained wood, not in round smears. An alternative was sifted white wood-ash mixed with a little water and drawn over the cement with a flannel in the same way. If the process were carefully carried out, the stoep dried beautifully white and clean, the only disadvantage being that the surface trod off more easily into the house than the hearthstone did.

Almost every week, a new gadget promised to lighten the housekeeper's burden. A patent cream separator speeded up the business of making butter. The first 'washing-machine' had been advertised mid-century. It was made of wood and had a roller to which clothes were tied. When one turned the handle, the clothes revolved round the roller in such a way as to give a continuous 'rubbing and beating motion'. Nannucci had opened steam laundries in Plein and Long streets, but until the turn of the century, laundry work at the Cape was largely done by women in the city's municipal wash-houses or in suburban rivers and ponds. On fine days the slopes of Devil's Peak, the lower slopes of Table Mountain and also Platteklip Gorge were bright with household linen bleaching in the sun.

The laundrywomen called personally on all their customers to collect soiled linen and deliver it back dry and clean: a great convenience to the housekeeper. As Hilda Duckitt remarked

6at Wynberg, and the other Cape Town suburbs, every requisite is brought to the door ... Firewood [too] ... and a very expensive item it is! I find coke and wood the most economical fuel ... I would advise having two good paraffin stoves ... These if lit at six-thirty give a can of hot water for baths; then the maid puts on another kettle, and makes the porridge in a pot placed on an "Asbestos Sheet" to prevent burning ... The maid then tidies the dining-room, lays the table, and prepares breakfast — coffee, bacon, and so on. Then we have prayers and breakfast ... Excellent toast can be made on a Beatrice stove by adjusting the flame and putting the slice of bread on the top, where you would place your saucepan or kettle. Give the stove a careful wiping beforehand, and the most dainty person would not detect any taste of paraffin, and a slice of toast can be made in a few minutes without the bother of lighting a fire ... Next the butcher comes for orders, and often a cart calls bringing vegetables, or the Damara women living at Constantia bring baskets of greens to your kitchen door.9

Red meat was a scandalous price — going for as much as tenpence a pound — so in spite of his noisy horn, the man with a fish cart was often a welcome caller. The local waters yielded a wide variety but discerning housewives preferred either stockfish or roman. Snoek 'a big coarse but nourishing fish' formed an important part of the diet of poorer Capetonians and large quantities were pickled and sent to Mauritius. At the height of the season a large snoek would cost a tickey.

Dinner, the main meal of the day, was commonly served at midday and, thanks to improved public transport, more city workers were able to come home at this time. A substantial tea would be served in the early evening and then a light supper before bed. The prudent housekeeper set terrier and mastiff on guard before the last lamps were extinguished.

Plumbing was the new status symbol and patent sanitary ware was fancifully embellished. Essential details — like an|S-bend on a lavatory pan — took a little longer to perfect.

Shops and Shopping

The new department stores revolutionised shopping for virtually every non-perishable item a consumer could desire in the last three decades of the nineteenth century. Up until then, individual tradesmen, specialist suppliers, and mail-order houses had met some of the community's needs. Cape Town boasted hundreds of small stores but it was the larger department stores like Stuttafords and Garlicks (both with premises on Adderley Street) that attracted personal visitors – including ladies. The often tedious journey from the suburbs and the noise, heat and bustle of town were worth enduring for the pleasures of viewing merchandise before making a purchase. A day's shopping became an outing, a social occasion.

A lady would not care to take refreshment in a public tearoom unescorted but the major stores as well as the City Club showed singular delicacy of feeling by providing special rooms where ladies could rest and refresh themselves during one of these sorties. Lavatories and washbasins were provided as well as a sitting-room where tea and a gentle gossip could be enjoyed. During the season, baskets of grapes were placed on shop counters with an open invitation to nibble.

The new-style shopping was not the exclusive preserve of ladies: gentlemen, too, found the offerings of large menswear departments a welcome alternative to the old bespoke tailor and specialist gents' outfitter. Stuttafords' eminent patrons included Lord Roberts and Colonel Baden-Powell. On at least one occasion, though, the hero of the siege of Ladysmith did not plan a purchase: he was mobbed by a horde of well-wishers in Adderley Street and had to take refuge in the store, much to the delight of the young lady attendants. (Men were commonly engaged as sales attendants until the outbreak of the Anglo-Boer War when women filled the gaps created by men who had enlisted.)

A healthy rivalry was maintained by Stuttafords and Garlicks, which was situated lower down Adderley Street. Stuttafords boasted a portable staircase of generous dimensions which was raised and lowered mechanically; Garlicks made sure they were the first to have the new hydraulic elevators installed to bear their customers up to one of the three aboveground sales floors and workrooms. They also had a smoke-detecting sprinkler system installed to fireproof the premises.

Samson Rickard Stuttaford, founder of Garlicks' competition, was born in 1833 to humble Cornish parents. After serving a hard apprenticeship as a London shop assistant, he emigrated to the Cape and by 1857 had opened a draper's shop in Harrington Street. By 1870 he was able to raise £10 000 to buy the old Colonial Bank site at the corner of Adderley and Hout streets. Samson's brother, William Foot, had joined him and in 1872 William Thorne came aboard the company. A buying office was opened in London to which Samson repaired as director, leaving Thorne as chairman of the South African company which now owned the block from Shortmarket to Hout streets as well as prosperous branches on the gold and diamond fields. Stuttafords' trade in diamonds (only of the highest caratage and quality) had been hived off into a subsidiary company.

Staff members from Cape Town made regular forays into the outlying

---

Above *The 'Medora' long-waisted corset was shaped with real whalebone for a perfect fit and offered in black or dove shades for 9/11.*
Right *Flowersellers opposite Stuttafords added bright splashes of colour to Adderley Street.*

districts, both to visit agents and to trade in negotiable commodities. In a letter to an agent written in 1872, Mr Thorne wrote: 'Our Mr [William Foot] Stuttaford is out on a trip through Swellendam and Mossel Bay and will probably run up via Prince Albert to Beaufort West and back via Worcester. The silks you sent us last week we cannot match in Cape Town. The American spider we will enquire about. I think they can be imported at much less than the £100 quoted by you. We have some broughams ordered to arrive next month and we will enquire at home what they can be got at and try to send you a drawing. Goods left Cape Town by Tuesday's wagon.'

Of the outlying regions, Mossel Bay particularly became an important trading centre and there was much trafficking in sealskins from the coast and in ostrich feathers. The feathers from wild birds were worth more because they were supposed to keep their curl better in winter. In 1881 the export of ostrich feathers was valued at £883 000.

Mindful of the wider market of the colony, retail merchants went to endless trouble with their catalogues to ensure that every whim of the long-distance customer should be satisfied. There was no finer example of the art of mail-order selling than Stuttafords' 1897 'price list' – a handsome 630-page cloth-bound volume with the firm's coat of arms embossed upon it in gold and red. And lest this expensive surface should give an incorrect impression, the cover bore the promise: 'We have only one price, all goods are marked in plain figures.' But all goods were certainly not plain.

The thin, high-quality pages profusely illustrated with lithographs showing every detail of the merchandise on offer invited days – no, weeks – of delightful immersion. Each of the 13 pages in the index bore three columns of items in fine print – nearly 2 500 entries in all. It included everything from horse-drawn carriages to knitting yarn. Customers included the Free State Army (they wanted Prussian-style uniforms made up to their own design). There were special sections for furniture, lamps, games, corsets, cutlery, birdcages, bicycles, buckles, bedsteads, coal scuttles, novels, sunshades, gloves, fans, racquets and clubs, fishing tackle, hats . . .

Fashion, thanks to the advent of ready-made clothing, was now also accessible to the emerging middle class. In the *Cape Argus* of 7 January 1889, Wilson Miller and Gilmore of Atherstone House in Adderley Street announced they had unpacked a shipment of white piqué costumes – the 'Newlands' with an open coat and skirt for 18/6, the 'Worcester' with a double-breasted reefer coat and skirt for 23/6 – as well as a grand selection of shirt blouses from 3/6.

There was no question that this innovation would put the city's few fashionable dressmakers out of business, let alone the made-to-order services offered by department stores. The thrifty and diligent Cape housekeeper, Hildagonda Duckitt, sent her own wildflower designs off to England for custom-printed muslins but she was her own dressmaker. There was a variety of sewing machines on the market including a child's model – girls learnt to sew from the age of six or seven. A treadle machine in a stand cost about £5 while a more modest table model with a hand wheel fetched £2/15/-. In spite of these somewhat daunting prices, business was so brisk that the American Singer Company opened its own shop in Adderley Street. Hire-purchase sales agreements were available there from 1890. Paper dress patterns could be ordered from weekly English magazines like *Home Notes* for between thruppence and fivepence each. Local newspapers carried sketches of the latest fashions from Europe and copies of the new American fashion magazines were available for the privileged.

Colonial women at the Cape did not, however, follow the American example and cut their stays. The corset was woman's most indispensable fashion garment. 'However costly or elaborate a costume or ballgown may be, it cannot produce the desired effect unless worn over a well-shaped corset,' pronounced a Cape advertiser in the 1890s. 'No article has risen in the estimation of well-dressed women during the last decade to such an extent as the corset.' The advertiser had constructed his product after 'studying every phase of colonial taste and needs and every advantage which science and comfort could suggest'.

The voluptuous doe-eyed creatures modelling corsets, bodices and camisoles attracted many a surreptitious male glance, but business was business and the price list did not beat about the bush. There was a corset to fit every figure and every situation. There were children's corsets and men's stays. Tropical corsets had ventilating net between the stays. For horsewomen, there were shorter corsets. The 'Invigorator' ('heavily boned and handsomely embroidered') featured a harness that pulled drooping shoulders back and improved posture. For accouchement or ladies tending to 'embonpoint' the effects of the corset could be enhanced by an additional 'abdominal belt' which, with the aid of elastic inserts, buckled fulcrum straps, whaleboning and laces, held the stomach firm.

In the Stuttafords' price list other delicate items for the personal toilette, like washable sanitary towels, were described and illustrated. Knickers and drawers were shown discreetly folded so that the lace frilling or embroidery at the knee was the focus of attention.

Eiderdowns – Russian down, vegetable down and flock quilts – were offered in profusion. At the top of the range, a down quilt measuring six by five feet topped with figured velvet with a plain silk border and a silk-frilled reverse was listed at 105/-. Customers who cared to call personally at Stuttafords' premises in Adderley Street could choose their household textiles in a special 'dark room' equipped with electric lights to give an accurate impression of the way colours would appear in the evening.

Anyone who aspired to polite society understood the importance of a home that spoke of prosperity and good taste. Their price list proved that Stuttafords understood this too: and the most tasteful of domestic accoutrements were illustrated in its pages. There were extending brackets for candles and a ravishing assortment of paraffin lamps from sumptuously ornate hanging models to table lamps with coloured etched glass pedestals. Fancy glassware was all the rage – frilly, fluted flower and undersea shapes were used for fanciful coloured lampshades, vases and tablewear.

Fresh produce was one of the few lines of merchandise in which the titans, Stuttafords and Garlicks, competed with neither each other nor any other traders. Imported delicacies like tinned butter, preserved and condensed milk, cheeses and ham were a speciality, but perishables were left to the open market.

The common populace could bargain for fish and meat, fruit and vegetables and green fodder at one of Cape Town's several markets, which the genteel tended to avoid. Although Frank de Jong was prompted by patriotism to publish his guide *Cape Town and its Surroundings* in 1894, he made no attempt to mince matters where the markets were concerned. 'The markets of Cape Town are nothing like one would expect to find in the capital of South Africa,' he wrote. 'Perishable table produce and meat are sold in the Municipal Market on Caledon Square, a covered-structure, usually extremely dirty, and always uninviting. Fish is sold in a series of dilapidated tumble-down sheds at the bottom of Adderley-street. This place . . . is a standing, or rather a tumbling down reproach to the city.'

Suburban chatelaines were still able to purchase almost everything they needed in the way of fresh produce at the kitchen door. Butchers, dairymen and firewood merchants also called on households in the 'better-class' areas.

There were a number of itinerant pedlars among the immigrants from Russia and eastern Europe and they serviced suburbs as well as country districts. The *smous* usually had timepieces, thimbles, bootlaces, silks and framed mottoes among the exotic gewgaws in his cart. A similar variety of colourful and often poor-quality knicknacks was offered by stall-holders and barrow-men who frequented the Adderley Street end of the Grand Parade. During regular auction sales in the same area anything from job lots of fabric to discarded bedsteads from the New Somerset Hospital came under the hammer.

The shops in the Peninsula's suburban villages closed one afternoon a week and kept their doors open late on Saturday nights. In the *Wynberg Times* of 9 April 1892, the scene was described in Paul Pry's 'Suburban Notes':

❝Claremont streets assume a very busy appearance on Saturday nights. The shops are literally thronged with people, whilst the main road is a gay promenade, being lit up from end to end by the lights from the numerous shops. The bright colour of the dresses and head-gear of the Malay "moetjes" adding considerably to the brilliancy of the scene, and making the whole appear more like an Eastern bazaar than a colonial village. In one place may be a couple making purchases for Sunday's dinner and publicly questioning each other's family matters. At another, a group of young girls chatting gaily whilst admiring the bonnets and fal-lals in a window, which has enough pretty things in it to make a hundred girls happy and still will have enough for a "clearance sale". Passing on and through the knots of young men smoking and chatting, you may meet a couple of coloured minstrels; one with a banjo and another with a concertina or flute.❞

There was no shortage of buyers, sellers, or merchandise. Ready cash was the problem, aggravated by Cape Town's cyclical depressions and crippling cost of living. But though the Cape community had evolved far beyond village status, shops and shopping still conveyed the same highly sociable and celebratory spirit that characterises market-days and trading-posts.

The two largest department stores, Stuttafords and Garlicks, vied with each other for clientele and offered a variety of services including mail order and deliveries.

THE VICTORIAN CHILD

Childhood in late Victorian Cape Town meant different things to different children ... Elsie and John Kipling skipping barefoot about the gardens at Groote Schuur, chasing butterflies with their pet lion cub ... Little Jim No-name, undernourished and underclad, playing paraffin-tin cricket in a slum alley ... the children's home inmate, guilty of sins he had not committed, his head shorn to discourage lice.

For the offspring of the Calvinist extreme and children institutionalised 'for their own good', life was a continuum of discipline and drudgery. 'Spare the rod and spoil the child' was the maxim of the fierce benefactors who regarded children as small adults from whom original sin was to be ruthlessly expunged so they might become useful cogs in the wheel of Empire.

Luckier children enjoyed increasing freedom of affection, behaviour and dress. Instead of being constricted by scaled-down adult garments, they wore looser clothes specially designed for them and their perceived needs for lots of fresh air and exercise. Little boys and girls were dressed alike until the boys could run about and were 'breeched'. Given the very high infant mortality rate, reaching this age was something of an achievement.

Parents who took pleasure in their offspring indulged youthful high spirits and natural curiosity. For a father like the unofficial poet laureate, Rudyard Kipling, children were a joy and inspiration. A fellow guest at the Mount Nelson Hotel was struck by Kipling's absorption with his toddlers: 'He carries them about and wheels the perambulator about the grounds and sets all the ways of the high and mighty at defiance.' In their first summer at The Woolsack, Rhodes' guest house on the Groote Schuur Estate, Elsie and John Kipling spent much of the time out of doors, running over to play with the Struben children at their house, Strubenheim. There were long summer evenings of hide-and-seek in the garden which was a paradise of old oak trees with cannas, arums, roses, violets, fig and oleander, myrtle and plumbago. The lion cub, Sullivan, was best of all at hiding. He'd been adopted by the Kiplings when his mother, an inmate in the Rhodes zoo, had rejected him. Some of the animals in the menagerie were allowed to roam free within the bounds of the estate – much to the children's delight. These included kangaroos, zebras, kudu, emus and a lama.

Left *Master Albert George learns to ride on an upholstered chair.*
Right *While the dominee reads the newspaper,*
little orphan girls face an uncertain future from the steps
of the old Weeshuis (*orphanage*).

Exotic animals delighted all Victorian Cape Town. One was free to visit Groote Schuur at all times, but special treats were often on hand at the regular local agricultural shows. At the Observatory Show in 1889, for example, elephant rides were offered. The *Cape Argus* carried a photograph of four solemn Indian pachyderms and a calf, the adults each loaded with three or four passengers. At another show there were camel rides – smelly, but ever such fun.

And it would be no wonder if children privileged to have such encounters preferred Mr Kipling's *Jungle Books* and the *Just So Stories* to *Alice in Wonderland*. On the frequent crossings he made between England and Cape Town, Kipling whiled away many a sunny day with the youngest of his fellow passengers, sitting cross-legged on the deck, entertaining an enthralled barefoot audience with wonderful tales. Three-year-old Master Baker (son of Rhodes' architect, Herbert Baker) spent much of his first voyage on the poet's knee.

While some parents were able to keep their children with them by travelling with nursemaids and governesses in the great traffickings to and fro on the business of Britannia, other well-heeled parents left their children with relations. Some were bundled off to England; some were sent from India to the more favourable climate of Cape Town; some to board with family members; some to boarding schools. Within the colony itself, young children were passed about to a certain extent.

The financial straits in which their parents found themselves in 1890, were part of the reason why four-year-old Ruby and three-year-old Kathleen Liesching were sent away from the home farm at Potberg to Cape Town to live with their grandmother, Dinah Liesching, and a maiden aunt, Bessie. The dowager was showing no signs of recovering from the loss of her husband and it was felt that the children would cheer her up. The initial plan was to send only one, but the girls were so distraught at being parted that they were eventually both dispatched.

The children began their formal education at Mrs Perceval's Kindergarten at the top of Long Street. Much of the first two years was spent stitching, with thick needles and coarse thread, the outlines of apples and pears which had been traced on to special cards. Grandmama, who understood the value of learning, was horrified when she discovered that her young charges were not being schooled in their letters. They were promptly moved to Mrs Langham Dale's Infant School. (Professor Langham Dale was the colony's leading educationist.) Here progress was more satisfactory for by the time the little girls graduated to St Cyprian's, a private Anglican school founded in 1871, they could give quite a good account of themselves. They were sent to an English church school by their Dutch grandmother, whose husband had been of German descent, because she wanted them to speak proper English. Englishness was a most desirable attribute and 'the standard of London was held absolute in all matters of personal decorum, dress or entertainment'.

Sister Theodora, the principal of St Cyprian's, placed great importance on manners and morals. The school was proud of its honour system – regarded as part of the English heritage. For example, while their classmistress was out the children were expected to exercise self-control and not speak a word. A lapse could earn the miscreant a sentence like spending an entire Saturday morning learning *The Slave's Dream* by heart.

Public occasions were known to be of salutary educational value and staunchly Victorian Grandmother Liesching made sure her granddaughters attended every public event of any moment in the city. Together with other good, dutiful little girls dressed in white, they waved miniature flags and sang the national anthem in the grounds of Government House or beside one memorial or another and received commemorative mugs and medals and listened to speeches on national occasions.

These events were not reserved for children of any particular class. As long as they had learned how to stand still and not fidget and were neatly dressed, all children were expected to present themselves.

Archdeacon Lightfoot's biographer records a special occasion in the progress of the missionary's zealously nurtured infant school at St Paul's.

'The eve of Jubilee Day – apart from its regal significance – must have been a proud day for Archdeacon Lightfoot as he with his Mission School vari-coloured children, numbering 260, with their teachers marched to Government House grounds where, with other schools, they were inspected by His Excellency Sir Hercules Robinson . . . There was a muster of six thousand children in all. "God save the Queen" was sung with more than usual feeling and meaning. As the strains died away, eager glances were cast in the direction of Government House. . .'

When the Governor stepped on to the lawn at 11 o'clock exactly, 'Dr Dale, Superintendent-General of Education, said, "May it please Your Excellency: the school-children of this City are glad to have Your Excellency's permission to present themselves before you this happy day. They wish to show their love and esteem for the Queen. To meet the Governor face to face is a high privilege, and the event will long live in their memories. There are (*sic*) thousand children of various races, whose home-tongues are English, Dutch, German, Arabic and Kafir (*sic*) – they are *one* in the feeling of reverence for the Queen."

'The Governor in his reply expressed his pleasure at their being present, and in the course of his speech bade the boys remember that the Governors, Judge, Ministers, members of Parliament, Doctors and Lawyers of the future were now all boys of the same age as themselves; that those whom he saw before him must prepare to take their share in working out the destinies of the Colony. Addressing the girls, His Excellency said their mission in life was nobler than the boys, that it was for them in their respective little worlds to rule by love and not by fear, and above all not to show their rule. He cited Her Majesty as a pattern for them to imitate. Finally he called upon them to sing "God Save the Queen". After singing the National Anthem . . . they saluted the Governor and marched away to their several destinations.'

Singing 'God Save the Queen' twice in such a short space of time was nothing unusual: the anthem was by far the most popular and often-heard tune of the day.

When, in 1870, the Duke of Edinburgh opened the Alfred Dock, named in his honour, thousands of children of all creeds, ranks and colours stationed on either side struck up 'God Save the Queen'. In 1890 when the railway line was extended to Simon's Bay the little people once again rolled out in force to sing and were rewarded by the special treat of a free train ride to Kalk Bay and back.

The Liesching girls were taken to hear Lord Kitchener address a crowd in Greenmarket Square during the darkest days of the Anglo-Boer War. They saw the Duke and Duchess of Cornwall and York who visited Cape Town in 1901 on their way home from Australia. They paid their respects to the memory of Cecil Rhodes when his remains lay in state in the House of Assembly.

For Ruby and Kathleen, the tedium of these occasions was compensated for by leisurely rambles in the nearby public gardens, shopping trips to Adderley Street with Aunt Bessie, or forays to 'Old Rachel's', a small sweet shop in Long Street owned by a bird-like woman from St Helena. The air in this little emporium of pleasures was heavy with the fragrance of aniseed, peppermint and the aroma given off by a heap of brick-red burnt almonds under a muslin cloth. There were glass jars of brandy balls, 'so treacle dark as to be almost black'. There were duminy klontjies and striped sugar sticks, some brown and buff, others pink and white. Rachel's bull's-eyes melted on the tongue. 'Rows and rows of tamaletjies, each in its white paper shell with the corners neatly pinched, each richly encrusted with almonds' were displayed on a shelf in the window. Alas, this 'fount of sweetness' dried up during 1901 when Old Rachel died in the bubonic plague epidemic.

But of all Kathleen's favourite treats, being allowed to sleep with her grandmother was the best. 'Had I had my own way I would have enjoyed this privilege nightly; but Granny firmly believed that an old person drew life from a child during sleep, and she would not allow it.'

On Sunday afternoons the two large family Bibles, one in English and

In conservative households where the liberating influence of Kate Greenaway fashions for small fry were not approved, children were dressed as scaled-down adults.

one in Dutch, would be brought out of Granny's vast press and the little girls were allowed to turn the pages and study the old wood-block engravings or trace the record of births, deaths and marriages written in copperplate on the flyleaves by Lieschings and De Beers.

A precious china doll would also be taken out at a special time like this to be reverently stroked and cradled and then put back in a safe place. Very special dolls had jointed kid bodies and hand-painted faces. If one had up to 25 shillings to spend there were dolls that walked (albeit falteringly), cried and shut their eyes to sleep. In the 1890s, Cleghorns advertised a clockwork walking jumbo for 2/6. Sturdier toys like golliwogs, toy bears, rag dolls and their new washable India-rubber sisters shared everyday games – play was now regarded as a natural and permissible aid to development, but the Victorian child who was rough or careless with toys was certainly not indulged.

To satisfy youthful energies, the well-stocked middle-class nursery would have a rocking horse, tricycles (or even a tricycle horse), a toy cart 145 and a toy perambulator for wheeling the inhabitants of the toy cupboard about. Skipping ropes, parlour quoits, a humming top and a set of ninepins would all provide most welcome diversions. Decorating and furnishing a doll's house was an absorbing project for girls, while little boys held military reviews with their regiments of lead soldiers or intrepidly drove toy railway lines across the carpet.

Nimble fingers whiled away many happy and instructional hours cutting and folding paper shapes and creatures. And, with luck, Christmas would bring noisy paper crackers, cardboard cut-out-and-fold model buildings, a paper doll set with fashionable outfits, and at least one jigsaw puzzle. A decent Victorian compendium of games would include ludo, tiddlywinks and halma – popular with members of all generations and a blessing on rainy days or during convalescence.

For children born into poverty, the street was nursery and playground and they made toys of whatever they could find: an iron hoop, an ox vertebra, a broken plank for a cricket bat, a length of sash cord long enough to skip with. Variations of lively skipping songs proliferated. But ditties like

> *Johnny Morgan played the organ,*
> *Jimmy played the drum,*
> *His sister played the tambourine,*
> *Till father smacked her bum*
> *and*
> *Julius Caesar,*
> *The Roman Geezer,*
> *Squashed his wife*
> *With a lemon squeezer*

were far too 'vulgar' for tolerance in a genteel household.

Purity of mind and heart and physical health ideally went hand in hand, but alas, in the often rude air of the Cape all the known illnesses of childhood flourished, and some exotic variations as well. The urban mother, if she had money, could avail herself of hundreds of patent medicines.

Country mothers and nursemaids relied on home remedies for the treatment of sick charges. Buckfat plasters would be applied to the chest of a child with whooping cough. Rubbing with honey, back and front at regular intervals, was also believed to be beneficial. A diphtheria patient should be dosed with sulphuric acid (four drops in three-quarters of a tumbler of water) which encouraged coughing and vomiting, thereby removing the harmful membrane. A poultice of mashed raw onions applied to the soles of the feet was recommended in cases of malaria, typhoid and scarlet fever.

In the metropolis one could have a doctor call round. When Grandmother Liesching decided the time had come to do something about eight-year-old Kathleen's infected tonsils, the doctor was summoned. Kathleen was sat up upon an easy chair near a window, her head resting on a favoured velvet cushion with a silk frill. The doctor approached from behind and held a chloroform mask over her face. When she regained consciousness, her tonsils were still intact and another attempt had to be made upon them. This time the ordeal was repeated in Aunt Bessie's bedroom. There was a different doctor who brought a nurse with him. Kathleen was bathed, dressed in her nightgown, presented with a new picture book and invited to lie down on the table which had been pulled over to the window. The doctor placed a flannel bag over Kathleen's nose and dropped chloroform on to it. The memory of the searing aroma of the fumes lingered long after her throat had healed.

For mites who had to make their way in the world without the aid of a Granny or an Aunt Bessie with some kind of income, there was a children's ward at the New Somerset Hospital, or, more likely, an early death. Children's homes like All Saints' Home in Kloof Nek Road had a prison for the confinement of small transgressors and a mortuary for those who succumbed to one of the scores of ailments of childhood. Croup, diphtheria, measles and tuberculosis were among the most common killers.

Like St Michael's and all too few other similar institutions, All Saints' took in abandoned or orphaned children of every age from infancy to early teens. Many poorer white families were immigrants and lacked the support of an extended family so if the father (almost invariably the breadwinner) died or absconded the mother had little choice but to give up her children for care.

All Saints', which had originally been known as St George's, had been opened as a penitentiary by Bishop Gray in 1868. It was run by eight English women selected by His Lordship for the task. They had not taken vows but they were known as the Mission Sisters and were also responsible for St Michael's which was described as a home for 'parentless Boys and Girls (or for such children whom it might be considered were better away from their unhappy homes and miserable surroundings of evil influences) . . . the children were taught "not to covet nor desire other men's goods, but to learn to labour truly to get their own living, and to do their duty in that state of life unto which it should please God to call them"'. The development of a creative imagination or any notion of self-worth were most definitely not on the curriculum.

The aim at these institutions was to discipline the children in order to overcome bad 'inherited tendencies', to teach them to be obedient and diligent and turn them out as useful God-fearing servants who could contribute to society. Scrubbing furniture, floors, passages, workrooms, schoolrooms, stairways and balconies seemed to constitute a major part of the daily programme and, according to Sister Superior, the children did it most willingly; they liked it; and it was obviously good for them for most of them were healthy. The soap bill, she boasted, was as high as £7 a month.

The children rose at six, dressed in simple working clothes with large coarse aprons, and, barefoot, set about their chores of bed-making, sweeping and dusting before they fell to scrubbing. Some girls were engaged in laundry work for a couple of hours each morning and again from three to five. The boys worked outside in the poultry run, the stable and cow byre and in the vegetable garden. There were also carpentry and cobbling workshops. Girls of 10 upwards had extra sewing classes three times a week when they learnt to mend. The recreation period between tea at five and bedtime at eight-thirty p.m. was commonly spent knitting.

The boys were usually apprenticed out at 13 and girls could leave the school after the fourth standard and go into service as housemaids, nursemaids or sewing maids. Unfortunately they could not be taught to cook because the food prepared at the home each day was 'of the simplest description'.

Some citizens claimed the sisters spoiled the children but at All Saints' they believed that a happy child was a good child and the idea was not to take them 'out of the world in monastic sorrow' but to keep them 'from its evil in a shepherded place'. There were problems, of course. Delinquent parents sometimes re-appeared to claim their abandoned offspring once they had been trained to earn a living. Some of the girls were impertinent, which home staff believed was evidence of a lack of moral backbone. The boys tended to be untruthful and babyish, crying too easily, in the view of their keepers.

'They are simply not as manly as English lads,' said Sister Superior. Colonial children were not taught to 'bear the yoke of obedience and discipline in youth'; they were 'allowed to run wild, in the mistaken idea that lawlessness meant freedom'.

So while the Kipling crowd went on imaginative adventures with Mowgli and Kim, other children learnt from Struwwelpeter that life was an unforgiving business: if you played with matches you would be burnt to a heap of cinders and if you sucked your thumb, the red-legged scissor man would snip it off.

From the ages of five or six, young Capetonians from poorer homes had to earn their keep.

EDUCATION AND CHARACTER

In the last half of Victoria's reign, education came under the spotlight throughout the Empire. In Britain, the reform of the universities of Oxford and Cambridge, particularly the abolition of the religious tests, allowed a new breed of leader to emerge, independent of the declining aristocracy and the rising plutocracy. His progress depended on a trained intellect rather than on social patronage or fashionable friends.

In the less rigidly class-conscious colonial society of the Cape where the aspirations of members of all classes stirred the common experience of life like a hot berg wind, education was one of the most effective and attainable routes upwards. Numbers of lower class and poor men, women and children (mainly black) crowded into the night school run by Canon Lightfoot as part of his missionary effort. For the more privileged classes, educating one's children was as tangible a stage in material self-improvement as building a bigger house with bigger grounds further out of town.

Schools were no longer simply centres for the mass education of slave children or a means to coax pagans into the influence of missionaries. Good tutors in a sufficient variety of subjects were hard to come by and excessively expensive in the colony so the scions of genteelly progressive families now went off to the new schools in groups. Preferably they went to public schools – those funded by public as opposed to government money.

Schooling was not compulsory and school boards were not organised. As one school inspector pointed out, a proper system could only be set up once there were adequate schools, properly staffed.

Of all the people striving to rectify this situation, Professor Langham Dale was the most eminent and the most successful. The superintendent general of education for 33 years, he was knighted in 1889 for his contribution which included the grading of pupils into standards according to their levels of learning, an increase in opportunities for higher education, a uniform exam system for student teachers and pupils, an extension of the inspectorate and the grading of schools – A for non-sectarian public schools, B for mission schools and C for black schools.

Left The Lioness Gate on Government Avenue,
designed by Anreith as an entrance to the zoo, now led to the
South African College campus.
Right Schools were no longer a haphazard affair,
more teachers were trained and standards were introduced with
proper examinations to maintain them.

148

The *Cape Town Guide* of 1897 lists no fewer than 42 schools – though admittedly they varied considerably in size and quality. A dozen or so of these were established by specific churches. St Aloysius (Marist Brothers) in St John's Street was one example. At least eight of the city's private establishments were run by spinsters. The sort of dedicated woman who might have been a governess in earlier times was now running her own school (usually for young ladies) at home.

At the other end of the scale were the colleges which took a large number of pupils and offered them education right up to the level of a university degree. Of these, the college in Zonnebloem (which accepted pupils of all races) probably provided the most varied curriculum. Founded by Bishop Robert Gray in 1858, it offered the usual arts and classics subjects for matriculation and university examinations, but the major emphasis was on industrial training – boarders (and day scholars if they wished) spent two hours a day in the workshops. Females were taught marketable housekeeping skills and, eventually, typewriting.

The task of educating the lower classes was normally relegated to the church. The Dock District School at No. 59 Breakwater Cottages and the Roggebaai Church School in Dock Road were just two examples of several similarly worthy establishments.

The introduction of electric lighting meant that night schools could be opened for children and adults who had to earn a living during the day.

The Normal College for teacher training, established by the Dutch Reformed Church in 1842, had a girls' department and model school for day pupils attached. A new teacher training college was established in the newly named Queen Victoria Street as part of the jubilee celebrations.

The Diocesan College near the Camp Ground in Rondebosch was fed by the Diocesan Preparatory School. The College offered preparation for matriculation, the intermediate and B.A. examinations. Here, as at the Cape's other colleges, all matriculated students had first to complete an 'intermediate' year before choosing either science or classics. This intermediate year included the study of Greek, Latin, English and Dutch Literature, Physics, Arithmetic, Algebra, Geometry and Trigonometry. Only truly remarkable students like Jan Smuts did both science and classics concurrently. In 1891 he had come second in both sets of examinations at the Victoria College in Stellenbosch, a feat which won him the Ebden Scholarship. (It was worth £100 a year for three years and enabled a South African candidate to study at Cambridge University.) In 1896 Smuts was one of the candidates for a law lectureship at the South African College but he was passed over in favour of old boy, Advocate A.J. McGregor.

The South African College also produced its share of political notables. Hjalmar Reitz, son of President Reitz, started work on his degree in 1893

but he was not the first presidential type on the campus. President Brand had been a professor at the college when he was offered the premiership of the Orange Free State in 1863.

Of all the distinguished educationists to be found in Cape Town, the South African College scientist Paul Daniel Hahn was probably one of the best known. He was born while his missionary parents were at the Rhenish station at Bethany in Great Namaqualand and his guttural and emphatic consonants had been formed at this remote outpost and fixed during his boyhood. When he was three, the family moved back to Germany, so throughout his education English remained a second language.

'Oom Daantjie', as he was affectionately referred to, taught chemistry in all its branches – organic, inorganic, agricultural and analytical – as well as mineralogy, metallurgy and physics. But he also took a keen personal interest in the moral and academic advancement of every student, thus earning himself another sobriquet: 'Father of the College.' With the professors William Ritchie and Charles Lewis, he formed the triumvirate that ruled the establishment.

His tall square figure, always formally coated and top-hatted, was as much part of the South African College landscape as the old Lioness Gate that dated back to the days when the grounds had housed a zoo.

Through the gate to the left, the classics building with its colonnaded courtyard lay in dappled sunshine. 'Hahn's Palace', as envious colleagues dubbed the new chemistry laboratory, stood in solitary splendour down to the right of the oak grove. By 1897 a physical laboratory had been erected on the site of the nearby tennis court. At the far end of the ground, a low white structure housed the South African College School to which, in 1874, the pre-matric scholars had been diverted.

It was a far cry indeed from the early days when the College opened in rooms kindly loaned by the orphanage in Long Street. The 115 students had ranged from very young preparatory scholars upwards and the fledgling institution suffered a chronic shortage of teaching staff and funds.

By September 1875, when Hahn returned to the colony he had left some 24 years earlier, the College had put down roots. He and his new wife, Marie (they had been married in Germany in July), set up home in York House, lower Orange Street, where they were to rear three sons and three daughters. On his 27th birthday, 5 January 1876, Hahn was appointed professor of chemistry. The post carried an emolument of £200 per annum, which by the '90s had increased to upwards of £500. The previous incumbent, Robert Noble, had been professor of physical science and English, but upon his death two separate chairs were created. Hahn automatically became a member of the College senate and convocation elected him to the council. He was also elected to the first council of the University of the Cape of Good

Hope, an examining body created by the University Consolidation Act of 1873. The University took over and extended the work of the old Board of Examiners, maintaining uniform standards of educational qualification in the colony, and eventually promoting the craze for examinations which was to reach epidemic proportions by the turn of the century.

The ultimate purpose of true education was, of course, not to pass examinations but, in the words of Rev. A.P. Bender, to 'prompt and lead mankind to the most comprehensive, most exalted, and most generous humanity'. Sport was, of course, to be paramount to the education of civilised people – it was character-building, and it made healthy bodies for healthy minds.

Like the proverbial ball of fire, Hahn wasted no time in raising funds for a proper chemistry laboratory. Thanks to the charm and magnetism of his personality and his formidable powers of persuasion, he had soon amassed an amount in excess of £6 000.

The fairy godmother of the College, Mrs Sophia Barbara Elizabeth Jamison, had contributed the bulk of this sum. The history of her benefaction to the cause of learning dated back to 1872 when she had presented a scholarship fund of £5 000 to the Board of Examiners. In 1875 she gave the same amount as an endowment for a chair of physics and chemistry. The opening of the new chemical laboratory in June 1881 was yet another monument to her generosity.

Hahn's energies and concerns extended far beyond the needs of his own department. In 1893, for example, the indefatigable chemist took up a suggestion from his colleague, Professor Lewis, and together they visited Kimberley and Johannesburg to drum up funds for the erection of physical laboratories. At both centres they met with hearty support and were particularly gratified at Mr Rhodes' donation of £300. Within a fortnight they had swelled the existing fund to a handsome £5 500.

By 1893, thanks to the efforts of the likes of Dr Hahn, the South African College had a proper constitution and a governing council. In 1874, scholars in all but the three pre-matric classes had been diverted into the South African College School under Dr John Shaw who had previously been headmaster of the school at Colesberg. He ran the South African College School until his death in 1890.

'The sun never caught me in bed,' was one of Dr Hahn's favourite sayings. 'You are here to learn punctuality and a little chemistry. Ja.' With his splendidly Teutonic whiskers bristling, he would lock his laboratory door on the last stroke of the bell and start his lecture, quorum or no. On at least one occasion only one student made the deadline, but completely undeterred, the eminent scientist removed the velvet skullcap he wore indoors, closed his eyes and recited the prayer with which he always began

In the comparatively lax atmosphere of a sunny colonial seaport town, children from rich and poor families alike, enjoyed far more freedom than their early Victorian counterparts.

the day's teaching. He then replaced his cap, delivered his carefully prepared lecture and demonstrated the six experiments that were a feature of every class meeting – all for the benefit of a solitary student.

The Father of the College might be kind but indulgent he was not. There was an iron hand in that velvet glove. Students who failed to achieve the 50 per cent mark in the 20-questions quiz he conducted at the end of each term were invited for a private interview. The professor would enumerate the consequences of academic delinquency with such grace, elegance and courtesy that the miscreant felt honour-bound to mend his ways.

Hahn's good favour was a most desirable commodity. Apart from the friendship and support he offered students, there was the opportunity of travelling with him. During vacations, the savant was wont to visit the hinterland with an entourage of select students. On expeditions, he would collect experimental material and dispense wisdom on a variety of scientific subjects to farmers and disciples alike. A significant contributor to the progress of science and education, Dr Hahn was named Royal Prussian Professor by his fatherland and recognised as lecturer-at-large by the universities of St Andrews, Glasgow and Edinburgh. This meant that colonial students who wished to become doctors could gain credit for their scientific studies under Hahn before they proceeded to one of the great Scottish medical schools.

> *Some students are girls, South African Pearls,*
> *And ladies of high degree;*
> *They blend sweetness with light,*
> *Mingle meekness with might,*
> *And add grace to the grave QED,*

went the new verse of the College anthem.

It was largely through Daniel Hahn that women had been admitted to the South African College. Professor Peter MacOwan had conducted extra-collegiate botanical classes for ladies at the Lodge in the Gardens, but Hahn went one step further.

For some years he had assisted the Good Hope Seminary with classes in chemistry and metallurgy and so impressed was he by the scientific aptitude he had encountered there, that he introduced the idea of teaching these young ladies at the South African College so that they could benefit from the facilities available in his well-equipped modern laboratory. After due hithering and thithering between senate and council, it was decided that ladies could be admitted for a one-year trial to Professor Hahn's classes. It was believed that physical weakness would militate against females with ambitions beyond the fulfilment of their naturally ordered functions.

In August 1886 four students from the Good Hope Seminary joined Hahn's gentlemen among whom they more than held their own. In fact, two of their number took first and second place, but as they were not doing a full course of subjects at the South African College, they were not eligible for class prizes and these went to the men who had actually come third and fourth.

When Dr Hahn reported that 'no ill consequences had resulted from the experiment', council approved the admission of lady students to all departments. In honour of Queen Victoria's Jubilee, the College became a fully co-educational establishment on 29 August 1887. Mrs James Rose Innes and Mrs J. W. Sauer were among the ladies who took immediate advantage of the opportunity. Many of the earliest female students left again after matriculation or the intermediate year. Miss Isabel Stephens

Getting ready for Girton? An increasing number of girls and young women were excelling in schoolroom and college.

was among several young women who had blazed the trail. She gained first class honours in the matric examination in 1888, won the Governor's Prize (one of the college's 'blue ribbons') in Intermediate in 1889 and the next year carried off the gold medal for literature. In 1891 she came first in the B.A. exams and was awarded a munificent university scholarship of £50 a year for two years.

Miss Stephens was by no means the first colonial lady to gain academic distinction. The University had never barred females from sitting its examination and before local colleges modernised their admission policies, Professor Lewis' sister, Agnes Eileen, became the first locally produced female Bachelor of Arts. She had been born during the great storm of 1865, an ominous portent indeed. Agnes had studied at home with the aid of her brother, Charles, then completed four more years at Newnham College, Cambridge. She passed all her examinations but the British university did not grant degrees to women at that time.

This kind of prejudice prevailed in less progressive communities for some time. When the news got about the small country town of Swellendam that one of its daughters, Miemie Rothmann, had been awarded a Queen's Scholarship and a Webb Scholarship and was to study for a degree at the South African College, the community was a-flutter. Subscribers to the local library might have read of 'blue stockings' in the *Illustrated London News*, the *Queen*, and the *Ladies' Newspaper*, but there was still a good deal of headshaking. Miemie was to be fitted out for this great adventure with the equivalent of a trousseau and one local storekeeper, George Ravenscroft, said to her mother, 'Tante Annie, I suppose you are educating your daughters so they can catch husbands?'

'On the contrary,' snapped the offended matron. 'I am educating them so they can do without them if they wish to.' Annie Rothmann had no time for the new masculine women but the man's unfortunate remark had awakened the dormant suffragette in her.

The Queen's Scholarship was for £24 a year for three years and, in the 1890s, covered only the cost of tuition. The scholarships had evolved from a form of government sponsorship first negotiated in 1823. Earlier that year, a historic meeting had been held in the Groote Kerk at the top of what was then the Heerengracht. Those present had resolved to form the South African College, funding it by the sale of shares, each shareholder being entitled to a seat on the College council. The plan had proved impossibly optimistic and without government aid it would have come to an untimely end. This assistance came in the form of sponsorship for a certain number of students, initially known as free scholars, latterly as Queen's Scholars.

Further financial aid was allowed from the Prize Negro Fund – an accumulation of the fees paid by employers who wished to indenture freed slaves. This money had been used for the College's first building, which housed the classics department during the 1890s.

The architect's drawing for a suitable home for the University of the Cape of Good Hope promised an imposing new Cape Town landmark in Queen Victoria Street.

TEAM SPIRIT

ing Willow reigns, it has been said, wherever Englishmen gather together. But the cricket craze that gripped the Cape Colony observed no boundaries of race or class (though everyone played in his own separate group). The appeal of this most theatrical, subtle and eccentric of team sports reached from the upper echelons of the dominant classes right across the social spectrum into the dingiest of slums. Paraffin-tin wickets were set up in reeking cobbled alleys with just as much enthusiasm as officers and gentlemen leaped to the commanding thwack of leather on willow-wood.

Other sporting activities naturally occupied the time in between cricket matches, but while he boxed or watched a sparring contest, while he sculled in Table Bay, while he socialised his way through a game of mixed doubles on the tennis court, the typical Capetonian would very likely be talking about, or at least thinking about, cricket.

As early as 1809 a cricket match was played by the officers of the artillery against officers of the colony. Cricket was being played by pupils at the Diocesan School for Boys in the early 1850s and, shortly afterwards, by the 'men' of the South African College.

The Western Province Cricket Club was one of the first to be formed. On 11 October 1864, the *Cape Argus* announced: 'A cricket match will be played at Wynberg tomorrow between two teams of the newly-formed Western Province Cricket Club. One eleven will be composed of residents of Cape Town and Wynberg, and the other of those in Claremont, Rondebosch and Diocesan College. Wickets will be pitched at 10 a.m.'

The business of finding and creating teams to play against became a game in itself. Apart from the match of the year, Mother Country versus Colonial Born, popular contests included those between Married and Single, Handsome and Ugly (the two teams in this case being nominated by the ladies), Diocesan College and the officers of H.M.S. *Rattlesnake*. As new clubs opened at Cape Town, the Gardens, Green Point, Woodstock and Claremont, opportunities for competition among white teams were happily increased — an unwritten social code forced brown-skinned sportsmen to form their own teams. The opportunities were eagerly taken up by

Left *Sport was character building and found ardent supporters among Capetonians of all classes and creeds.*
Right *In spite of almost weekly changes in rules and philosophies, football in all its forms provided great sport when the weather wasn't right for cricket.*

Though the colony boasted some formidable female tennis players, their long skirts tended towards unfair division of labour in mixed doubles matches.

military men, civil servants, schoolmasters, clerics, businessmen, farmers and at least one architect – the tall and athletic Herbert Baker was a keen player who retired from the game only when he was advised that the harsh African sun was taxing his precious eyesight. Other prominent supporters of the game included Henry Cloete and H. M. Arderne – he gave the land known as Arderne's Field to the Claremont Cricket Club in 1897.

The Western Province Club first played on a field rented from Sir Richard Southey at Plumstead for £50. Those early games were very much social occasions. Governor Sir Henry Barkly was the club president and he, the admiral, the generals and the 'upper ten of the city' seldom failed to roll up in their carriages with liveried grooms and hangers-on, moustaches and top hats gleaming. A military band added to the atmosphere. On the occasion of the opening of the Newlands ground, for example, the band of the Royal Inniskilling Fusiliers rendered extracts from *The Mikado*. And sometimes an impromptu sideshow added spice to the day's sport.

There was a considerable to-do when it got about that Canon Ogilvie, captaining one side, had challenged the opposing Captain van Renen to race 100 yards on the field before the game commenced. Both were to be in cricket kit and padded up. Van Renen had also to carry a bat. The canon was to receive a 50 yards' start and, instead of a bat, would carry one of his team members, also padded up and carrying a bat instead of a whip. Supporters measured off the course. Betting was keen. Van Renen, a huge man and a popular draw-card at any match because of his terrific hitting, was the favourite. But the doughty canon raced to a clear victory without his jockey once having to use the bat on him.

In 1887 Western Province acquired lot 27 of Mariendahl farm which encompassed huge tracts of land adjacent to the Newlands station on both sides of the line. (One player was reputed to have hit a six right on to the platform.) Mariendahl had been owned by Jacob Letterstedt, a brewer, who had bequeathed it to his daughter, the Vicomtesse de Montmort. The Rugby Union decided to lease their ground on the upside of the line from the Vicomtesse in 1888. It was not until 1890 that the paperwork was complete, the ground cleared and the first match played there.

When the cricketers first acquired the ground, it included a pond and a vlei large enough for boating. Drainage was arranged some years later via a barter deal with the railways and this made space for tennis courts.

Tennis is said to have been introduced to the Empire by Major Wharton Clopton Wingfield in 1874. The Western Province Lawn Tennis Association was formed in 1878 and the inaugural South African tennis champion tournament was held in Port Elizabeth in 1891. Tennis was much favoured by both sexes and the ball was lobbed about with degrees of seriousness ranging from the intently athletic to the unashamedly social.

The subject of women on the cricket pitch was one of controversy. *Lantern* reported on behalf of the scandalised: 'Twenty years ago a woman's place was at home studying the comfort of the sterner sex . . . [She] whose main duty it was to be gentle and kind and pure . . . now [seeks to] emulate man . . . Horsiness and fastness seem to be the tendency, a halloo, old chappie, have a brandy and soda sort of style . . . if they must play cricket, let them by all means do so, but let it be cricket, not tomfoolery in which a few silly male mortals make idiots of themselves by acting contrary to what nature has taught them. How fathers and husbands can allow their daughters and wives to make such public exhibitions of themselves is surprising, especially as many of these would be most strenuous detractors of ballet girls.' Local cartoonists illustrated with positively Hogarthian emphasis the idea that these cricket-playing Corinthians had made an unwomanly display of their charms by shedding their stays before taking up the bat.

In December 1888 a historic event occurred, exercising ineradicable influence on colonial cricket: an English team under the management of

Major Wharton visited South Africa, playing matches before huge crowds of spectators throughout the country. As an extra match 'for the benefit of the professionals', a team of the Malay community's talented cricketers were pitted against the second team, not Wharton's. Touring teams regularly played against teams of more than 11 players.

Sir Donald Currie of the Castle shipping line donated a splendid trophy, known as the Currie Cup, to be presented by the visitors to the centre which did best against them. The honours went to Kimberley who donated the Currie Cup as a floating trophy for an annual inter-provincial cricket tournament.

A suitably exciting curtain-raiser to this first international competition was provided by matches between various Cape Town teams and Kimberley's Stray Klips in 1887 and 1888. The visitors from the diamond fields recovered from the rigours of the eight-day trans-Karoo journey with conspicuous success, trouncing the home team. The match of the tour was Stray Klips against United Metropolitan Clubs and what a match it was! Many members of the fair sex even sported Kimberley colours.

'The crowd stood up and shouted and cheered without intermission. The frantic banging of sticks, the howls and stamping and dancing must have been seen to be believed. Never before have I seen such extraordinary, such furious excitement so long sustained,' reported one of the throng.

That superb batsman P.J. van Renen slammed fast and tricky balls with ferocious accuracy and the scoreboard jumped by tens. The heady scent of victory drove the crowd even closer to hysteria. Van Renen had to lie down from sheer exhaustion more than once but, encouraged by cries of 'Get up, Jack! Time's short!', he would rise, strike another ball over the trees to deafening applause and then lie down again.

An exceptional bowler and mad-keen cricketer, P.H. de Villiers, who had come to the Cape with the Klips, remained to play for Western Province for several years, eventually returning to the north in 1892. This meant he missed the match played at Newlands against a visiting British side in 1895. The whole town was out in force. Even the banks had closed.

At a particularly tense moment in the game, a telegram boy came flying in with news from the North: Mr Jameson's infamous raiding party had crossed the border into the Transvaal. The rest of the afternoon was punctuated by more telegrams . . . and cheers for the excellent performance on the pitch.

Being a burgher, when war broke out De Villiers fought until he was captured — wearing distinctly battle-stained cricket togs. Banished to a prison camp in Ceylon, De Villiers lost no time in recruiting 70 fellow-Boers for a sports club. They improvised a matting wicket and a local Currie Cup contest — Transvaal prisoners against those from the Orange Free

State. The Colombo Cricket Club got wind of the match and challenged the prisoners to a contest on the club's fine turf wicket. Rules and red tape were diplomatically waived with only one condition: no controversial subjects were to be raised. The prisoners certainly won the day even if they lost the match – they were rewarded for their performance with a hearty ovation and afterwards entertained like heroes.

But for a freak coincidence, another great cricketer, Napier ('Nap') van Ryneveld, might also have landed up in Ceylon. Nap was languishing in the prisoner of war camp on Green Point Common when he was summoned by some British cricketing pals to make up a team. When he was returned to camp, he discovered that he had missed the transport ship bound for Ceylon and was consigned to St Helena instead.

Cricket was played at the Cape throughout spring and summer and deep into the winter – a match on the Queen's Birthday in June was a regular event on the calendar. Only when winter set in did football hold sway. For cricket die-hards football was simply a stopgap for those dreary weeks when local wickets were too sticky to permit play. But the less than fanatic 'flannelled fool' was happy to play 'muddied oaf' between seasons.

A type of football was no doubt played at the Cape during the first British occupation, but the first published commentary on a game appeared in the *Cape Argus* in 1862. The occasion was a five-and-a-half hour contest between civilians and a team from the 11th Regiment on Green Point Common which was decided in two sessions, the first on 23 August and the second on 5 September. One of the civilians did not show up so the teams appeared 15 against 14. Adrian van der Byl kicked off at 3 p.m. exactly. John X. Merriman (who was later to become a Cabinet minister when representative government was introduced) was one of the staunchest members of the civilian team. All that was 'bravest and fairest' in the colony turned up to watch, the *beau monde* of course led by the Governor and Lady Wodehouse. The goals were 150 yards apart and the game lasted 105 minutes, whereupon the wind changed, giving the military team an unsporting advantage so they declared a draw, neither side having scored.

The *Cape Argus* reported: 'The Eton, Rugby, Winchester Marlborough and other schools [of football were] played with the activity of youth and the wisdom of experience. Over and over again did the combatants roll in their brave charges; over and over again did the unerring drop kick of the goal keepers save the game as those terrible rushing outsiders swept past the crowd … but no ungenerous hurt was received, and no advantage beyond that of superior weight was taken …'

When the game was taken up again on 5 September the wind obliged by remaining constant so they were able to get in a good three-and-a-quarter hours' play before sunset. The military team won by two goals. As late as

1866 Rugby School's Laws of Football stated that a game should not last more than five days, three if no goal had been obtained by either side.

On 13 September 1862 the *Cape Argus* reported that the Diocesan College ('Bishops') had challenged a combined military and civilian team and defeated them by three goals to one on the cricket ground at Rondebosch. Football had been introduced at Bishops the year before by the new headmaster, Canon George Ogilvie, known as 'Gog' because those were the most emphatic letters in his signature.

Ogilvie was born in Wiltshire in 1826, the only son of a gentleman. He attended Winchester College until ill-health forced him to leave – but not before he had acquired a love for the special football that Wykehamists had developed to suit conditions on the college field known as Meads. This game differed radically from the football evolved, for example, to suit conditions at Rugby School's field, The Close. Continuing ill-health dogged Ogilvie's undergraduate days at Wadham College, Oxford. But by 1852 he had been ordained deacon and made vice-principal of Bradfield College where yet another set of rules governed football. After being ordained priest in 1855 he set out in search of a healthier climate, sojourning briefly in Buenos Aires as head of a grammar school, before coming to Cape Town to take over St George's, the school attached to the Cathedral irreverently known as 'the old pagoda'. He was made a canon in 1861, the year he moved over to Bishops, taking 40 boys from the overcrowded St George's with him. He retired from Bishops in 1885 and the following year, his 60th, he married Miss Ellen Anderson, daughter of William Anderson of Erinville. He served as vice-chancellor of the University of the Cape of Good Hope for two years from 1895. For photographs, the canon affected a patriarchal solemnity; biblical beard, beetling brows and craggy features portraying the devout and philosophical Ogilvie but giving little intimation of Gog, the man of action. He played football until he was 54 and shone, as we have seen, on the cricket pitch. He was fond of quoits, archery and chess. He was very partial to games of chance but not even the all-night card games he shared with select cronies could affect the magnificent voice he raised in prayer each morning.

'Gogball', the game created for Bishops by its new principal, had elements drawn from the codes of Winchester, Oxford and Bradfield but in effect it was a different type of football. It was played with a large round ball and, unlike the Rugby version of the game, the goal posts did not have a crossbar. Handling the ball was not permitted unless a player caught it after it had been touched by an opposition player and before it hit the ground. This was known as a fair catch and meant one could either run with the ball or claim a free kick. Although Gog defended his game as less dangerous than the Rugby code, which increased in popularity steadily, 'Gogball' was a pretty hazardous affair. The game began with a scrummage (known as a 'hot') in which all players took part and which could last the duration of the game as heeling from the hot was not allowed. A maul was the other legalised free-for-all which took place when possession of the ball was physically disputed right in the goal – known as the 'worm' and formed at Winchester by laying down two scholars' gowns. If the ball went over the goal line it was known as a 'shit'. Shouldering opposition players was permitted as was hacking – kicking between the knee and ankle. Admittedly hacking (part of the Rugby game) did have its protocol: you were not to hold your victim while you kicked him and he was not supposed to flinch or back off even if you were wearing navvies (metal-capped boots). The practice was in line with muscular Christianity and at times the referee would shout 'Alleluia!' to signal the start of a bout of hacking. The Gog-style line-out when the ball was rolled between the lines of opposing players, offered marvellous opportunities for hacking. But by 1878 'Gog's Game' had been superseded by Rugby Union which was promoted by William Milton (later Sir William of Rhodesian fame). Both games were played for some time before Rugby Union became standard.

Rugby was taken up in the country districts with a gusto that made it clear that cricket was not to be South Africa's national game. As roads improved and transport became more sophisticated, the hithering and thithering between country and towns increased apace. Malmesbury first played Paarl in 1881. In the match, victorious Malmesbury played to the Rugby Laws and Paarl to the Association Laws which, by 1894, boasted four clubs. In 1882 a special train took the Worcester team and a 'tremendous crowd of enthusiasts' to play the Hex River Valley at De Doorns. In 1884 Worcester went by mule wagon to play Montagu at Robertson. A public holiday was proclaimed and when the ball was punctured at half time and a replacement could not be found, they played on with the deflated pouch.

A Cape inter-town tournament was organised in 1884 and Grahamstown was the scene of a similar gathering in 1885. In 1888 Kimberley sent a touring team to Cape Town. But the lack of uniformity of rules reduced all these three get-togethers to acrimonious squabbles. It was clear that the only way round these problems was to appoint a body to standardise rules and co-ordinate tours. In 1889, the South African Rugby Football Board was founded in Kimberley, thanks to the special efforts of Percy Ross Frames of Kimberley and Bill Bisset of Cape Town, both legal men. Ross Frames became first president of the Board. At the organisation's meeting in 1895, regional teams registered their team colours. Most wore long-sleeved striped pullovers without collars or welts and striped or plain stockings into which long pants were tucked. Bishops got its colours from sailors' jerseys, SACS from the only colours available, and Villagers sported red

socks because the cheapest socks were white and the cheapest dye red.

The first English rugby team had toured South Africa in 1891. Cecil Rhodes guaranteed the tour; the moving spirits were T. B. Herold and the Richards brothers. A total of 19 matches was played, the tourists winning them all and having only three goals scored against them. Only one try was scored – by Hasie Versfeld of Cape Town Clubs in the very first match of the tour, at Newlands. Once again, Donald Currie of the Castle shipping line came up trumps, giving the captain of the English team a 'Currie Cup' to present to the team which performed best against them.

Love of one sport breeds a love of all and loyalties were happily divided between the less important team sports like hockey and individual sports like tennis, croquet, shooting and archery. But it was the great contests between teams of rugby and cricket players that captured the imagination and offered a fervent metaphor of human striving.

The cups presented for cricket and rugby by shipping magnate Sir Donald Currie.

THE GREAT OUTDOORS

The scenic splendours and glorious weather at the Cape offered endless opportunities to the privileged classes who had leisure, energy and the funds to indulge in outdoor activities. A trek up Table Mountain was an absolute must: you sent your picnic basket ahead with hired porters and, choosing a moonlit night, made a 3 a.m. 'Alpine start' and arrived halfway up Platteklip Gorge in time for breakfast at sunrise.

The next most important expedition was a trip to Cape Point which involved hiring ox-wagons and spending at least one night out in the open. The following description appeared in a newspaper in the 1890s:

'We arrived at Simon's Town on the 7.30 p.m. train, each of our party of five equipped with cushion, blanket and provisions. Our two wagons, each with 12 oxen, awaited us and we walked up Red Hill on foot before climbing into the wagons and setting off on the bumping track over boulders and tree stumps. Our Hottentot guides kept their teams on the move with flicks from their long whips. Someone had brought along a banjo which was the perfect accompaniment as we sang solos and choruses. Ghost and spirit stories were told and then the moon rose adding romance to the scene. By 11 p.m. we had travelled about eight miles so we halted and supped. By now all shyness and reserve had melted. The ladies climbed on to the wagons to sleep, the gentlemen curled up underneath. At 1 a.m. we inspanned and set off again. We reached Cape Point at 6 a.m. and had breakfast as we admired the sunrise. It was a steep and windy ascent to the lighthouse but worth it. The keeper explained all to us. We then clambered down to the beach to view an extensive but low cave. Revelling in the glorious scenery and "God's pure oxygen" we rested and lunched until 1 p.m. whereupon we set out again, most of the party walking now, gathering firewood to heat the tea, picking bouquets of heath and wild flowers. We took our tea break at Smiths Winkle Valley and reached Simon's Town again at 8 p.m. in comfortable time for the 9.20 train back to the city.'

Cycling, which had become a craze almost as soon as the first 'pedestrian accelerators' had disembarked at Cape Town in 1860, continued in

Left Climbing the chains on Lion's Head was a tricky manoeuvre, even without a long skirt and petticoats.
Right Maintaining a degree of sartorial decorum was a challenge in the tugging winds and glorious sunshine of the Cape.

popularity. The pneumatic tyre was only patented in 1888 but the Cape Town Bicycle Club was formed in 1880 and the City Cycling Club in 1891. A cycle track was built at Green Point – hence the name 'Cycle Track' for the adjacent station on the Cape Town to Sea Point railway line. Long-distance cyclists who might travel as far as Port Elizabeth were among the aristocrats of outdoor athletes. Nearer home, cycles were used for sunny afternoon recreation, for picnic outings and for festive parades. Taking part in a ride-past of cycles decorated with paper flowers or Chinese lanterns exercised the creative ingenuity of riders, and cycle gymkhanas provided a novel challenge to their skills. Tent-pegging from a two-wheeler was not for the novice. At these 'do's' a light element was provided by competitions for the best four- and five-in-hand, where a 'team' of four or five lady riders in matching gowns and hats were 'driven' by a single male rider who 'held them in' with bridles of satin ribbon. The duties of outrider were usually performed by a small boy cyclist in a kilt. Formation riding of this kind demanded some practice and a good deal of concentration.

Early female cyclists had quickly adopted the American 'Gibson Girl' look, an immediate success even with those who were ambulatory. Typified by the combination of white shirt blouse, dark skirt and boater, it was in tune with the local climate and the sporting spirit of many colonial women. From 1870 to the end of the century the new range of sporting activities open to women exerted a powerful influence on styles of dress. Crinoline frames simply would not do for local beauties who enjoyed mountaineering and cycling as much as they did a Government House ball. Riding had always been popular, but tennis, hockey, cricket and cycling were better choices for women of modest income.

By the 1890s, keen cyclists had adopted a fashion first suggested by America's Amelia Bloomer in 1850. A pair of baggy knickerbockers topped by a loose tunic just above knee-length helped rather than hindered the athlete. Divided skirts were also a boon to golfers. Tennis players adopted slightly shorter skirts and special longer knickers.

But let the emerging middle classes do and wear what they would, the upper classes still pursued their age-old pastimes. The Cape Hunt was under no threat to the bicycle brigade. While she was a guest at Government House in September 1899, Lady Edward Cecil enjoyed an excellent run which she described in a letter to her sister in England:

❛. . . Last Saturday I went out hunting and had an adventurous time. We left Cape Town station at six-thirty in the morning and went by rail with the horses and the hounds for an hour and a half to Klapmutz. The meet was in a most divinely beautiful place and we started off gaily, but owing to the fact that I was put on a horse which had never carried a lady before I was at once run away with through the field – and horror – over the hounds.

'The Master – one of the A.D.C.s – caught my bridle or I should be running still. After that I was put on a quieter pony and we started again. We found almost immediately and galloped over the hounds. There is no turf in this country – nothing but scrub almost as high as gorse through which you have to ride and trust to your horse not to get into the holes you can't see, of which there are masses, or bogs which no one can get out of.

'In the first five minutes in a field of fourteen three were down in various holes. They vanished like tricks, horses and all into things like sandpits – and I was in a bog and thought my last hour had come, but I got out all right without having to dismount, and after that was reckless and galloped over rocks and watercourses into bogs and "washaways" with the courage of despair.

'The hounds ran for four hours by which time my horse couldn't lift its head or its feet, so I did not see the kill, and had to crawl back to the station where I found the whole of the field – the only people who had lasted being the two A.D.C.s, the Master and the Whip . . . they each had two horses. It was a great day and we got back to Cape Town at six thirty in the evening having been out twelve hours. I am still stiff, tho' this is Wednesday.❜

The first hounds had been imported by Lord Charles Somerset for pleasure rather than serious vermin control, and the Cape jackal was pressed to do duty as fox. In 1822 a subscription pack, largely patronised by the English, hunted the Flats. Many were the tales of the prowess of 'Anglo-Indians' among the dunes of False Bay. The pack was periodically rejuvenated by the importation of fresh blood from England and by 1834 there were two packs, one run by Mr Blair who had left the Army to become Collector of Customs, and the other run by Mr van Reenen.

The Cape Hunt Club was founded in 1843 with a house at Durbanville where many a festive dinner was held prior to a stirring day in the field. During the 1850s, a favourite meeting-place was Ratherfelder's Inn at Diep River, the stirrup-cup being downed at the Fox and Hounds.

Like hunting, shooting in the classic tradition had to be somewhat adapted to Cape conditions, but where there's a will, there's a way.

Little regard had been paid to the closed seasons for game before Anders Ohlsson, as member of the Legislative Assembly, introduced the Game Bill in 1886. In terms of the new legislation, certain birds' eggs were protected and special permission had to be obtained from the governor before classified animals could be shot. Among those listed were elephant, bontebok, hippopotamus, gnu, buffalo and hartebeest. In the same year, the Western Districts Game Protection Association was formed with Ohlsson as vice-president and chairman. Its aim was 'to promote the interests of sportsmen . . . and to prevent the . . . destruction of game'.

The unpopularity of these restrictions in some quarters no doubt aggravated the furore in 1892 when it was discovered that the colonial secretary, J. W. Sauer, had granted Ohlsson the hunting rights on Robben Island without putting them out to tender. Ohlsson paid £25 a year for the rights on condition that he introduced partridges, pheasants, guineafowl and springbok to the island and managed them professionally. He was also to establish a small wattle plantation at one end and to restore an old building as a shooting lodge. The action was defended on the grounds that if open permission were granted to all comers (which had been the case for 30 years) the entire game population of the island would soon be exterminated.

Fishing was not included in the arrangement and up-and-coming anglers continued to ride out to Robben Island on the supply boat for a couple of hours' sport on still, sunny days.

Ohlsson was also responsible for the large-scale introduction of trout to local waters. He had set up an extensive trout-breeding experiment in the garden of Montebello, his Newlands house. The ova, imported from Scotland, were of three types: Loch Leran, Rainbow and Brown trout. The idea was to acclimatise and then release them and Ohlsson claimed that the Montebello fish were reaching a weight of five to seven pounds within two years. As a result of this success, the government hatchery was established at Jonkershoek and principal streams in the colony were stocked.

For other Capetonians, the combination of water and blue skies meant swimming and bathing. The seaside inspired endless enthusiasm in people of every class. Woodstock beach was within reach of many of the poorer working-class people. The water was cold but it was a safe distance from the refuse thrown into the sea at the fish harbour and the Shambles at the foot of Adderley Street. There were one or two bathing houses to let.

Muizenberg's universal popularity as a seaside resort was explained with the warmest approval by the author of the 1897 *Cape Town Guide*:

> ❛The beaches [are] alive with gaily dressed ladies and romping children – balmy even when other suburbs are damp and chill. It is situated on the downs of False Bay with its expansive beach safe at all times for bathing, with a unique geographical situation with its balmy breezes laden with the life-giving ozone of the South Pacific (*sic*) and with its scenery the most beautiful of the coastline [it] has well-deserved the appellation of the Cape Riviera.❜

The water at this wonderful spot was warmer than at Woodstock. There were bathing houses at intervals along the extensive beach but most were for the use of residents at the houses, boarding-houses and hotels that abounded here. For the convenience of strangers, two bathing screens had been erected in the water – one for women and one for men.

Bathing dresses presented a challenge to women who were modest and fashion-conscious at the same time. The most satisfactory models consisted of a commodious, short-sleeved overdress and a pair of pantaloons reaching to mid-calf. Grey serge or flannel were the best fabrics – they were not revealing even when wet. The Rutherfoord sisters made their own bathing dresses out of old blankets for a holiday at Kalk Bay. The correlation between the weight of these garments and the frequency with which inexperienced female bathers drowned was not commonly pointed out.

People who felt more secure swimming or bathing in a pool could indulge in this healthy exercise at a number of places. Separate times were allocated to males and females. Dressing boxes were available and one could hire a towel and bathing suit for sixpence and, in the interests of public cleanliness, the water in these pools was changed regularly. There was one at Claremont; the Sea Point open-air pool was filled with salt water while Observatory boasted a pool 60 feet long with a deep end measuring nine feet and a spray machine to chase the dirt to one end.

The four-in-hand was a popular novelty event at Cape cycle gymkhanas.
The gentleman holding the reins and the four 'fillies' setting the pace were sometimes
escorted by a brace of six-year-olds in full Highland costume.

THE TRANSPORT REVOLUTION

In spite of the approaching rumble of mechanised locomotion, the horse at the Cape in the 1890s was still the chief means of transport – as much a necessity as a bicycle had become in England. There was no shortage of bicycles to be seen about the colony, but when the south-easter blew, four hoofs were far more effective than two wheels. In nineteenth-century Cape Town 'one needed a horse and it had to be one that you could lead about and that wouldn't play tricks . . . He had to be able to amble, riding a beast with this pace you could travel all day without fatigue'.

For two centuries, willing quadrupeds, often disabled by age, ill-health, exhaustion and inadequate diet, had done sterling service for the colony. For if a horse did not, what else would drag often overloaded and unroadworthy vehicles over the appalling wind and rain-eroded tracks that passed for roads in the Peninsula and across the isthmus of sand that separated Cape Town from Stellenbosch, Paarl and points east and north?

When the railway finally reached the colony in the 1860s there were surely no equine complaints among the hubbub of objections raised by carriers afraid of losing profitable monopolies on routes that criss-crossed the south-western Cape Colony. But it was to be several decades before the horse was relieved altogether of his duties as a draft animal. Before retiring from public life, he had first to haul in the precursors of the 'horseless carriages' which were to set a graceless new pace to life at the Cape, propelling colonials into a changed world from which there was no turning back.

The earlier carts and wagons fitted with primitive benches which had passed for public transport had given way to the diligence (a type of stage coach) and the horse-drawn omnibus – a French invention from earlier in the century. Rail links, improved roads and regular services between town and Sea Point to the west and Wynberg to the south had revolutionised life in the Cape. Families who had migrated to salubrious suburbia for the hottest, unhealthiest months could now contemplate making permanent homes away from the dust and pestilence of town. Previously, a breadwinner domiciled in Wynberg would have to ride to town every day and somehow find the wherewithal to meet the exorbitant cost of stabling his horse near his office for the day.

The solution was just a train or an omnibus ticket away. Not that the conveyances that assisted this development were exactly transports of delight. Maximum profits for minimum outlay seem to have been the premise upon which many an operator's business principles were based.

The ideal bus was brightly painted and varnished with a secure stairway leading to the upstairs seats. Inside (reserved for ladies and non-smokers) all was plush comfort with windows that opened and shut. (Joseph Upjohn, wooing select clientele, even offered popular newspapers and magazines for entertainment during the journey.) It would have been almost impossible to maintain a vehicle in anything like good trim on the shocking roads, so most bus operators did not try. Overloading and speeding compounded the natural hazards of south-easter and rutted routes.

A disillusioned commuter described the Cape Town to Wynberg run for the *Cape Argus*:

Above *Cape Town's steep and rutted roads were not ideally suited
to the horse-drawn omnibus.*
Right *The iron and glass roof of the Cape Town railway
station was in the best Victorian tradition.*

'The omnibus is ready to start. Ten pairs of legs are dangling over its sides, and 12 human biffins are jammed closely within its inner regions. Four miserable scarecrows, complimentarily called horses … in harness even more dilapidated than their own unfortunate carcasses … make a heavy lunge forward … and the omnibus turns … and faces the South Easter … the omnibus has reached the toll, and the [wind] is pitching into it in all its fury. Gentlemen who are doubtful as to the adhesive properties of their wide-awakes are holding on to them in desperation; while the wind struggles against them, and roars at them … determined to get the heads off as well as the hats, if he can … at right angles with … Devil's Peak … all is rendered invisible by a dense cloud of sand and dust … At last [we reach] Wynberg and descend … Our eyes are lined with sand and dust, our nostrils are stopped up with the same compound our mouth is all gritty … our clothes are of one uniform tint of yellow-brown … '

No wonder those who could, preferred to travel by train. The London-based Cape Town Railway and Dock Company put in a line to Kuils River which was opened on 23 February 1862, two years after the arrival of the eight British-made locomotives. By May the rails had reached Stellenbosch and by November, Wellington. The engines achieved ferocious speeds, often in excess of 30 miles an hour. On one occasion, with Governor Sir Philip Wodehouse on board, 60 miles an hour was clocked between D'Urban Road and Salt River. None of the party suffered ill effects in spite of a theory that travelling at even half that speed could cause brain damage.

The privately financed Wynberg line opened on 19 December 1864 and, along with the Wellington line, was taken over by the government in 1873. The temporary wood-and-iron railway terminus on Adderley Street was replaced in 1875 by an imposing stone-faced brick station building with a great steel-framed arch protecting the platforms from the weather. The line was pushed right through to Muizenberg in 1882 and to Simon's Town in 1890. The Cape Town and Suburban Railway Company completed a project initiated by the failed Green & Sea Point Company and from 1892 one could travel by train from Cape Town to Sea Point for ninepence return. These developments were greeted with howls of protest from carriers who feared inroads on their business and puritan clerics who believed that

The horseless carriage was hailed severally as the craze of the century and a dangerous rich man's plaything destined never to get anywhere.

operating trains on Sundays would spread throughout the land 'a flood of immorality, dissipation, and recklessness'.

Horse-drawn rail transport, introduced by the Green Point Tramway Company in 1863, had met with instant success. And it had proved cheaper to lay down rails than repair and maintain the road surfaces. Each car was designed to carry a total of 54 passengers (including roof passengers) but sometimes during rush hours as many as 90 squeezed aboard. This was a load the four horses could not move uphill so it was customary for gentlemen to jump down and walk up steep inclines.

The tram might have been a vast improvement on the old omnibus (which, of course, continued to do service in places not reached by rails) but it was not without its hazards. A tram could become de-railed and capsize at the cost of life and limb. Reduced visibility at night or in the frequent dust storms whipped up by the south-easter heightened the risk of being knocked down. At night tramcars were lit inside by a pair of oil-lamps mounted on the bulkheads, one fore and one aft. But this light proved inadequate warning and more than one drunkard staggering along the unlit thoroughfare between Adderley Street and Woodstock gasped his last under the wheels of the tram. It was not until 1885 that outside lights were compulsory.

Speed was only to become a problem in the 1890s when Dobbin's load was permanently lightened by the phenomenal electric tramway. Henry Butters of the Thomson-Houston Electric Company of New York had arrived in Cape Town in July 1894 with the intention of taking over the entire Cape tramway system, electrifying it and extending it. The potential of this grand scheme attracted major investors from the goldfields and on 6 August 1896 Cape Town was out in best bib and tucker for the first public run of the new electric tramways. Bunting decorated the curlicued wrought-iron crossbars on the electric poles down the middle of Adderley Street and the three ceremonial cars were liberally dressed in Union Jacks and the American flag. Strong men wept; grandmothers crossed themselves. The new Sea Point railway, which had posed such a terrible threat to the old Green Point horse tramway, was promptly bankrupted.

Concurrently with all this, the railway line was steadily spreading its network outwards, eastwards and northwards, driven by the ever-increasing impetus of the mining industry. When Charles Cooper visited in 1895, he solicited local opinion on the benefits of a government-run railway and was assured that no government in its right mind would make and own railways, if it could get them made by private enterprise. 'The Cape Government had made theirs that the country might be developed, and because private enterprise would not undertake the task . . . Two objections were made – the one, that Government ownership led to great pressure by traders for undue reduction of rates; the other, that it led to great pressure by the workers for undue increase of pay. The Cape government, in spite of these and other financial hazards were making a handsome return on their investment.'

Difficulties encountered in running the operation of the service included swarms of locusts settling on the line in the Karoo, completely blocking them. Compensation claims for animals killed by locomotives were also a constant concern. Eventually set rates were fixed. The pay-out for a dead ostrich, for example, was £6.

In spite of its depredations, the arrival of the 'iron horse' was the experience of a lifetime for many country folk, though most, of course, did not demonstrate their wonderment quite as extravagantly as diarist Iris Vaughan's young sister: 'Florence never saw a train [before]. She and the pointer dog Bell fell over backwards with fright. It was a new sort of train with a passage and a washbasin. At five o'clock men climbed on the roof and pushed the lamps in the holes to light [the train].' Iris' previous rail journey had been in a 'dog-box' carriage with no access to other carriages. There were no lavatory facilities aboard – one had to wait until the train stopped at a station and then make a dash for it, along with all the other passengers.

The Cape Government Railway with its handsome green-liveried locomotives may have steamed its way into the heart of the colony – and beyond – but, in spite of gloomy predictions, there was still plenty of work for the droves of hansom cab operators who plied their trade about the streets of Cape Town. Rail transport stole the bus trade but it could not compete with quick and cheap door-to-door service of driver, horse and cab. And, as for that new-fangled contraption, the horseless carriage, it was far too expensive and complicated ever to become a serious threat to the cabbie's livelihood, no matter that it did not need tracks and was designed for transporting small parties. Colonials had not been privileged to view some of the more inventive prototypes – including a French runabout that was strongly reminiscent of a tricycle locomotive and had to have a full-time stoker aboard – hence the origin of the term chauffeur.

A Benz, the first motor carriage in South Africa, went on display in Pretoria early in 1897. On payment of half a crown one could view the invention in Berea Park. 'Even the ox wagon will be propelled by this machinery in time,' stated the billboard poster. It was destined to become 'the craze of the century' because it bade farewell to all the problems of animal-drawn transport: rinderpest, horse sickness, expensive forage, broken harness, lazy grooms and runaway horses. On top of this, the motor carriage could be left unattended in the street without a groom to hold its head. Even President Kruger was fascinated, but when he was offered a ride, he

*Durban Road, Wynberg, where one could still dally
at the leisurely pace of yesteryear.*

declined with a smile, saying that the conveyance might frighten the dogs and, if they barked, it would surely bolt. The Johannesburg to Cape Town journey was completed by motor carriage that same year in 10 days.

Yankee Jenkins, manager of Garlicks Cycle Supply Department, was the first Capetonian to propose the import of one of these marvellous vehicles. The idea appealed to John Garlick and, through the firm's London office, a vehicle known as the Royal Enfield Quad was ordered from the famous firearm manufacturers. It arrived in 1898 – a spidery vehicle with a tubular frame and the famous De Dion single-cylinder air-cooled engine. It was either on or off, there were no gears. The driver's seat (positioned above the engine) and the wheels were almost identical to those of a bicycle and one steered with handlebars. A wicker passenger chair was mounted between the front wheels. Starting up was no simple matter: it usually involved pushing and, once the engine was turning over, it was advisable to keep going until a breakdown or the end of one's journey necessitated a halt. If one was caught up in traffic or wanted to pause on one's journey, it was advisable to steer round and round in circles – anything to avoid switching off and having to start again.

After it had been put through its paces during various test-runs round the Common, the vehicle was sold to Alfred Hennessy for £110. He caused a sensation merely by driving it from his lodgings in Green Point to his place of business in town. On his first day, as he pushed off from in front of Garlicks store, he lost control and the vehicle ran amok among the gathered spectators.

Maintenance of the machine was neither a simple nor an inexpensive matter. The owners of both petrol- and steam-driven vehicles had to import their own fuel, shipped from America as deck cargo in four gallon tins at 37/6 for eight gallons. So 10 gallons of petrol would cost about five per cent of the purchase price of the Royal Enfield. Fortunately Hennessy was well-to-do and his enthusiasm was unquenchable. He believed his machine could assist the war effort and mounted a Maxim gun on the Royal Enfield. But, alas, when he attempted to demonstrate this combination to Lord Kitchener in the Castle courtyard, the 600-pound load of machine gun and ammunition proved too heavy.

The war of course saw the press-ganging back into service of the pensioned-off horse along with any other quadruped who might be capable of pulling a load. Horses were at a premium. Mules drew the ambulances that ferried wounded soldiers from the station to one of the many hospitals that had sprung up under canvas round the Peninsula. Oxen pulled farm wagons converted into communications balloon carriers. The contrast between the stolid bovines leaning into their yokes and the futurist form of a large helium balloon floating above its carrier made the subject of many a photograph. Steam engines on active service were armour-plated with sheets of bomb-deflecting metal which gave them a ferocious appearance. Locomotives too were camouflaged and dressed in protective 'battledress'. One particularly eye-catching tactic was the application of a full 'wig' of heavy chains which covered the whole engine, giving it the appearance of a giant metallic sealyham urgently in need of a trim.

Cycles too were among the first wheeled vehicles to volunteer for service. Their riders included Lionel Curtis, a New College Oxford man who after the war became one of Milner's 'Kindergarten' – the team of young administrators charged with the reconstruction of South Africa. While his corps of 18 were in camp at Green Point, they continually rode back and forth to the city bearing messages. Out in the field, military cyclists sometimes covered greater distances at greater speed on an ingenious contraption consisting of four cycles bolted together and fitted with wheels grooved to correspond to a railway track. Travelling along in this way was as smooth as flying compared to negotiating the open veld.

And the open veld in most cases would have been the only roadway for Mr Hennessy's Enfield had it not proved unfit for service. Undaunted by rejection, Hennessy set about organising the growing nucleus of fellow autocarists into a body to protect their rights against those who saw the car owner as 'a wealthy sportsman, liable to career about in an aggressive fashion, endangering other road users and livestock', not to mention numerous colonial livelihoods. In the unlikely event of this 'expensive and unreliable contrivance' ever amounting to more than a 'mere plaything' and becoming a useful form of transport, 'the demand for draft animals and fodder would fall off, to the ruination of farmers. Talk of road tolls, severe speed limits and heavy taxation was in the air' when Hennessy and seven fellow car owners met at Arderne's Buildings in October 1901 to form the Automobile Club of South Africa.

During the Anglo-Boer War, slow but reliable mule-drawn ambulances ferried wounded soldiers from the station to one of Cape Town's numerous military hospitals.

THE TURNING OF THE CENTURY

GOD BLESS OUR QUEEN

VIVAT REGINA

The new spirit that had first started to stir 51 years earlier when Cape Town defied the Home Government and refused to allow a consignment of convicts to land, had matured by the end of the century. Responsible government took its first faltering steps in 1872 but was now fully operational. Local industry had suggested the possibility of self-sufficiency. Serious talk of a common customs union pointed towards the ideal of closer political and economic unions with the other parts of South Africa.

But like a bloody ritual of passage, the Anglo-Boer War saw the century – and the old order – out. Miraculously, the feeble flame of conciliation was not extinguished by the horrors and the new century began with the new spirit burning more brightly than ever.

The fighting never reached Cape Town, though at times the invasion threatened by Jan Smuts was a real possibility, but the Mother City was terminus, refuge, prison camp, hospital and graveyard for the spectators, soldiers, refugees, prisoners and the wounded.

Ridiculous as it may seem, the spectators presented a very real problem. On 3 April 1900, Joseph Chamberlain, the British prime minister, sent this telegram to Sir Alfred Milner at Cape Town:

❛ . . . The Queen regrets to observe the large number of ladies now visiting and remaining in South Africa, often without imperative reasons, and strongly disapproves of the hysterical spirit which seems to have influenced some of them to go where they are not wanted. I consider their presence interferes with [the] work of civil and military officers, and they must largely occupy [the] best hotel accommodation required for wounded or invalid officers. Can you send [a] telegram with or without [the] concurrence of Roberts and General Commanding Cape Town representing that [the] number of lady visitors is now so considerable as to encroach materially on Hotel and Railway accommodation etc and otherwise impede business, and suggesting that some notice might be issued there calling attention to [the] inconvenience of this unusual number of ladies visiting [the] seat of war. This I would submit to the Queen and Her Majesty would instruct me to publish. ❜

Left *The Queen, the Empire and all things British were objects of adoration for jingoists.*
Right *Symbol of the old order, the Castle survived the worst excesses, though it was several times threatened with demolition.*

170

Milner duly complained as his sovereign had requested him to do and his telegram – with the same message as Chamberlain's but more discreetly worded – was published on 10 April 1900. Inevitably it caused a great cackle among critics of the beleaguered bachelor governor.

A very special acquaintance, Lady Edward Cecil who was later to become Lady Milner, concurred that some check was needed on the tourist traffic. 'But I confess I was relieved when Lady Gwendolen [Cecil] let me know, soon after this, that the Queen had asked kindly after me on 29 April, when my sister-in-law had been at Windsor. I was glad to be assured that I had not been included in the Queen's disapproval.'

The Cecils' South African tour of duty had been motivated in July 1899 at the War Office in London when Lord Edward, an officer in the Grenadier Guards, was briefed by Lord Wolseley. Rested after campaigning in Egypt with Kitchener, Cecil was to go to South Africa on the staff of Colonel Baden-Powell. In Cape Town they were to gather supplies and raise a corps of Irregulars with the object of garrisoning Mafeking and holding it in the event of war with the Boer Republics.

'We never knew why it was thought advisable to hold Mafeking,' Violet Cecil noted in her memoirs. 'In after days Lord Kitchener used to say that it was because the War Office believed that it was the nearest sea-port to Pretoria, but he was very likely prejudiced.'

The situation at the Cape was viewed in a very serious light by Lord Salisbury (Violet Cecil's father-in-law) for the Bloemfontein Conference had been held at the beginning of June and Milner had failed to get any concessions out of President Kruger. Nevertheless, Lord Salisbury suggested that Violet should accompany her husband, a suggestion she acted on eagerly, even though it meant leaving their toddler, George, with his grandparents at Hatfield.

The Cecils arrived in Cape Town on the *Dunottar Castle*, disembarking on Tuesday 25 July, the day after Black Monday when everyone in South Africa who knew anyone in England had telegraphed home to try to make the easy-going, comfortable, safe English aware of what was going on in the colony and neighbouring territories. The atmosphere of anxiety and crisis in the colonial capital was immediately evident to the newcomers.

Lady Edward Cecil met Lady Charles Bentinck shortly after her husband had gone up to the front and the two ladies were invited to stay at Groote Schuur while Cecil Rhodes went off to Kimberley on 11 October and spent the duration of the siege there. Both their husbands were at Mafeking which was cut off that very day. Since September, they had been seeing men off to the front.

Violet Cecil wrote later: 'The first of the regiments was the "Old and Bold" going off to the garrison at Kimberley. How many times since then has the scene been repeated, with the joking [troops] in high spirits and confident of their victorious destiny!

'"I'll bring you back a lock of Krooger's 'air," shouted one man to a pal who stood by the train waving to the crowded, excited men who were packed in the carriages.'

When, in November, the Army Corps arrived from England in massive numbers, the ladies of Cape Town grouped themselves under the banner 'Tommy's Welcome to the Cape'. It was an enormous commitment needing day and night attendance. Hundreds of ships came and went at all hours bringing troops from every corner of the Empire and carrying off the wounded homeward bound, and Boer prisoners into exile.

One February day no fewer than 128 ships were either docked or waiting in Table Bay. They created an unforgettable tableau: rigging etched against the white-hot sky, anchored ships rising and falling smoothly in a steely sea amid dancing diamonds of light.

Emily Hobhouse led a crusade to improve conditions in concentration camps, while her compatriots, Ladies Edward Cecil and Charles Bentinck devoted their energies to the refugees from the Transvaal. 'They had been thrust into trains and on to trucks with the double [aim] . . . of getting rid of any British who were in the Transvaal and of blocking the railway lines. The interior of the country had barely the resources to support its own sparse population, so these people had no choice but to make for the ports.'

At the threat of this invasion, a body of women workers was collected with Dr Jane Waterston as president, and Lady Edward and Lady Charles on the committee.

❛From the end of September and well into October the trains rumbled into Cape Town all day and all night. The people who fell out of them, quite exhausted, had to be fed, clothed, sheltered. They had for the most part travelled in open trucks for three or four days and nights. They were all shaken, hungry, furious at the way they had been treated. Most of the men of military age enlisted in the local irregular corps. But the women and children had to be helped and housed.

'This avalanche of human beings only lasted a few weeks, but it was tremendous while it lasted. We worked in shifts, day and night, meeting the trains. I have a vivid recollection of one poor woman who had been taken with labour pains before the train stopped and that I only got to hospital in a Cape hansom just before her baby arrived. It was a nervous journey for me as well as for her, for of all places to be confined in, a rickety cramped Cape hansom was the worst. The stamina of these British Johannesburgers was beyond all praise and their resourcefulness a perfect wonder . . . What this tremendous upset demonstrated in the sight

At ease in their tented camp on Green Point Common, members of Her Majesty's armed forces drink to victory and to sport.

of the whole world was the solidarity of the British people, wherever they were . . . From Australia, Canada, India, New Zealand and other parts of the Empire, offers came of help in men, money and material.❜

All overseas colonials were stationed at Maitland Camp. And this was where Australian George Witton of Breaker Morant's Bushveld Carbineers was posted after he had been injured in action but refused shipment home.

The Canadians impressed Witton most. 'There were miners from the Klondyke, hunters from the backwoods, troopers from the . . . Frontier Police, and included were some of the hardest cases that the land of the maple leaf ever produced . . . for downright and original profanity it

173

would hardly be possible to find their equal ... but for all this they were the men above all others for a tight place or a desperate enterprise and they rigidly adhered to the rule of never allowing their enemies to bother them a second time.'

The Empire had found itself, Lady Violet Cecil later recalled in her own memoirs.

But the letters she wrote at the time were less confident than the memoir which was written later. To her sister on 1 November, she confided: 'I have one sensation – anxiety. Personal anxiety for Nigs (Lord Edward, her husband), military anxiety for everywhere. Everyone has got a little more than they can carry, everyone is overworked, everyone is mortally anxious and ... nothing is any use but a certain grit and a power of holding on tight without making a fuss.'

Five mornings a week, the two friends took the 8.30 a.m. train at Rondebosch and spent the next hours in Cape Town assessing cases and distributing food and clothing provided by the Lord Mayor of London's Fund. They returned home in time for lunch at 1.30 p.m. before the afternoon's work began with the Rand Relief Committee or the Red Cross.

By mid-November, hospitals had become their main concern. They were badly found and indifferently staffed. 'Lady Charles and I had control of very large Red Cross Funds but we could not persuade the doctors and nurses to use what we gave them. The officers were, to some extent, looked after by their servants, but the men had no one but each other to depend on. All we could do was to get as many invalids as we could into Groote Schuur.' Every available corner in the great house was used, witness the fact that when Violet Cecil's new sister-in-law came out with her soldier husband she had to take lodgings in a nearby boarding house.

When the Lords Roberts and Kitchener arrived on 10 January, Violet Cecil,

who was closely acquainted with both of them, was among the official welcoming party. 'The only thing I wanted from the two generals was some improvement in the hospitals,' she wrote. 'I saw them both about this ... Lord Roberts said, "Is there any simple thing I can do quickly to improve them?" And I asked him to double the number of nurses, certain if he did this we should get some good ones. He sent a telegram at once and the nurses came and soon made a difference, but owing to the appallingly insanitary conditions they were placed in, many of them died of typhoid.'

There were thousands of prisoners of war in and around Cape Town – some held on a prison ship off Simon's Town, several thousand quartered on the racecourse at Green Point. There were overflowing military hospitals at Green Point, Woodstock, Rondebosch and Wynberg. When bubonic plague broke out in the city an extra hospital was created for the isolation of cases at Uitvlugt.

Death was never far away ... and then came the news that Queen Victoria, too, had died. The unthinkable had happened. Perhaps nothing, after all, was sacred.

But the century ends for Cape Town not with the passing of the Queen on 22 January 1901, but with an image of women tending the graves of their countrymen at Wynberg. The women are English-speaking and members of the League of Help and Remembrance, and the dead are Boer prisoners.

The women feel themselves to be English-speaking South Africans, rather than simply English. The initiative is civilian, not governmental or military. In Cape Town, the first steps towards the reconciliation of Boer and Britisher are taken.

The spirits of those brown herdsmen who migrated to Table Valley each year before Van Riebeeck arrived exerted a less obvious but just as insistent demand but, at the turn of the century, they remained unheeded.

Boer prisoners with the toys they made to help fill the empty days on the prison ship SS Armenian.

NOTES AND CREDITS

This list is informal but every effort has been made to ensure it is comprehensive. Any inadvertant omissions are regretted. The list is designed to aid the reader who wants more information and to credit sources not already mentioned in the text. Direct quotes as well as paraphrased passages and major sources of information and ideas are acknowledged here. In each case a name or key phrase has been used to identify the whole passage.

❖ Indicates further references in following pages

INTRODUCTION

PROFILE OF THE PENINSULA

THE CITY CENTRE

THE GRAND PARADE AND GARDEN

ON THE WATERFRONT

SUBURBS − A STRING OF COUNTRY VILLAGES

CAPE TOWN'S PEOPLE

THE VERY POOR

THE OLD RICH AND THE NEW

AT LEISURE

ARTS AND LETTERS

p 71 'The "incoherent" poetry in Rhodes' – Baker, op. cit.

p 71 David Gill – Forbes, op. cit.

p 71 'In my visits to the old farms' – Baker, op. cit.

p 71 The never-articulate Rhodes – ibid.

THE MOUNT NELSON

The story of the property – Bolsmann, *The Mount Nelson*

p 74 'The palatial Mount Nelson' – Unger, *With "Bobs" and Kruger*

p 74 The *Cape Times* report of the hotel opening paraphrased in Bolsmann, op. cit.

p 77 Princess Catherine Radziwill – Roberts, *Cecil Rhodes*

COMMERCE AND TRADE

The story of the Commercial Exchange and Chamber of Commerce – Immelman, *Men of Good Hope*

p 78 The Hout's Bay fishing industry – Van Sittert, 'Gebrei in die ambag'

p 81 The stock exchanges – Rosenthal, *On 'Change through the Years*

p 82 The bank crashes – Rosenthal, *Other Men's Millions*

p 83 'Indeed the national bank of South Africa' – Henry, *The First Hundred Years of the Standard Bank*

THE POLITICAL SCENE

General outline – Hattersley, *An Illustrated Social History of South Africa*

p 86 Stockenström – ibid.

p 86 Froude – quoted in Hattersley, ibid.

p 86 Ohlsson – Ryan, 'Anders Ohlsson'

p 87 Effendi – Ryan, ibid., and Davids, *The Mosques of Bo-Kaap*

p 88 Three factions – Leighton, *Notes on a Visit to South Africa*

p 89 The reactions of Miemie Rothmann – Rothmann, *Huisgenoot*, 19 January 1934

THE GOVERNMENT HOUSE SET

p 92 The reception for Henry Bartle Frere – anon. pamphlet

p 92 Government House ball – Cooper, *By Castle to the Cape*

p 94 'Gilded youth' – Curtis, *With Milner in South Africa*

p 94 Lady Robinson's manner – Leighton, *Notes on a Visit to South Africa*

p 94 ❖ Milner (unless otherwise stated) – O'Brien, *Milner*

p 94 The Cape Hunt – Milner, *My Picture Gallery*

p 95 A weekend at Sandhills – Baker, *Architecture and Personalities*

IN COUNCIL

The political ramifications - Bickford-Smith, 'Keeping your own council'

The development of Council's role – Laidler, *The Growth and Government of Cape Town*

p 96 The conservatives, dubbed the 'Dirty Party' – Bickford-Smith, op. cit.

p 98 'Sing a song of smallpox' – *Lantern*, 1 July 1881

p 98 Fifty gallons of water – Bickford-Smith, op. cit.

p 99 The Molteno reservoir story – Burman, *The Table Mountain Book*

p 100 'Cape Town first saw electric lights' – quoted from Carruthers, 'G. H. Swingler and the supply of electricity to Cape Town'

p 100 'Until 1895 Cape Town bought its supply' – ibid.

PRESS AND PERIODICAL

p 102 Local newspapers – Unger, *With "Bobs" and Kruger*

p 104 It was hardly surprising – Hattersley, *An Illustrated Social History of South Africa*

p 104 'A large number of girls' – Rosenthal, *160 Years of Cape Printing*

p 104 The meeting between Fuller and Solomon – *South African College Union Annual*

p 104 'The great days of the *Cape Times*' – Hattersley, op. cit.

p 104 Ohlsson's stout advertisement – *Lantern*, 9 February 1889

p 105 Edgar Wallace – Brock, Brock and Willis, *Historical Simon's Town*

p 106 'I saw an open carriage' – Unger, op. cit.

p 106 Conan Doyle volunteers – introduction to Doyle, *The Great Boer War*

p 106 Reaction to his death – introduction to Steevens, *From Cape Town to Ladysmith*

p 107 'A man distressed in his mind' – letter to *Lantern*, 12 January 1889

CLUBS AND PUBS

The history of the Civil Service Club – Botha, *The Civil Service Club*

The story of the City Club – Little, *History of the City Club*

p 108 'The charm of the Society House' – Rosenthal, *Tankards and Tradition*

THE WORKING WORLD

Working conditions at the hospital – Searll, *A History of the Development of Nursing in South Africa*

p 114 'The very babes' – *Lantern*, 19 Jan. 1889

p 114 Ohlsson – Ryan, 'Anders Ohlsson'

p 115 The native depot etc. – Saunders, 'Africans in Cape Town in the nineteenth century'

p 115 Mozambican workers in Cape Town – Harries, 'Mozbiekers: the immigration of an African community to the Western Cape'

HEALTH, HYGIENE AND HOSPITALS

p 118 'To some people the mere mention of hospital' – letter from 'a digger' to *Lantern*, 25 July 1891

p 120 The Liesching girls – McMagh, *A Dinner of Herbs*

p 120 Remedies – Duckitt, *Hilda's Diary of a Cape Housekeeper*

p 120 Jane Waterston – Burrows, *A History of Medicine in South Africa*

p 120 A nurse's vocation – Nightingale, quoted in the *South African Medical Journal*, 18 August 1962

FAITH AND LIFE'S MILESTONES

p 124 The Voluntary Bill – Hattersley, *An Illustrated Social History of South Africa*; Tredgold, *The Ardernes and their Garden*

p 125 Henrietta Schreiner – Cronwright-Schreiner, *The Life of Olive Schreiner*

p 126 Grandmother Liesching's preparation for church – McMagh, *A Dinner of Herbs*

p 126 Malay burial and the 'cemetery riots' – Davids, *The Story of Tana Baru* and *The Mosques of Bo-Kaap*

p 127 Florence Arderne's wedding – Tredgold, op. cit.

BED & BOARD

p 130 'We found ourselves housed in Cogill's hotel' and all else relating to the Leightons – Leighton, *Notes on a Visit to South Africa*

p 131 Threepenny lodging houses – Easton, *Four Questions of the day*

THE CAPE HOUSEKEEPER

p 134 Mr Fuller's mastiff – *South African College Union Annual*, 17 December 1891

p 134 ❖ Duckitt quotations – Duckitt, *Hilda's Diary of a Cape Housekeeper*

p 134 ❖ The Duckitt story – Kuttel, *Quadrilles and Konfyt*

SHOPS AND SHOPPING

Stuttafords' history and quotes – Gill, *The Story of Stuttafords*

p 140 'However costly or elaborate a costume' – the makers of the Specialité Corset advertising in Stuttafords' price list

THE VICTORIAN CHILD

p 144 ❖ The Liesching story – McMagh, *A Dinner of Herbs*

p 144 ❖ Lightfoot – Barnett-Clarke, *The life and times of Thomas Fothergill Lightfoot B.D.*

p 146 ❖ All Saints' Home – Thomas, *Stray Hours*

EDUCATION AND CHARACTER

p 151 The purpose of education – Bender, *South African College Magazine*, December 1902

p 152 ❖ A woman student – Rothmann, *My Beskeie Deel*

TEAM SPIRIT

The rugby story – Dobson, *Rugby in South Africa* and *Bishops Rugby*

p 157 Women on the cricket pitch – *Lantern*, 19 January 1889

THE GREAT OUTDOORS

p 160 'We arrived at Simon's Town' – *South African College Union Annual*

p 162 The Cape Hunt – Milner, *My Picture Gallery*

p 162 ❖ Ohlsson – Ryan, 'Anders Ohlsson'

THE TRANSPORT REVOLUTION

p 164 'One needed a horse' – Milner, *My Picture Gallery*

p 166 'The omnibus is ready to start' – *Cape Times*, quoted in Coates, *Track and Trackless*

p 167 A government-run railway – Cooper, *By Castle to the Cape*

p 167 'Florence never saw a train before' – Vaughan, *The Diary of Iris Vaughan*

p 167 ❖ All information on motor cars and motoring – Johnston, *Early Motoring in South Africa*

p 169 Military cyclists – Curtis, *With Milner in South Africa*

THE TURNING OF THE CENTURY

p 170 'The Queen regrets' – O'Brien, *Milner*

p 172 ❖ All quotes relating to Violet Cecil unless otherwise stated – Milner, *My Picture Gallery*

p 173 Maitland Camp – Witton, *Scapegoats of the Empire*

CHRONOLOGY

1860

The first train in South Africa operates between Durban and the Point
The Cape Point lighthouse is functional
Prince Alfred inaugurates work on the breakwater
Indian immigrants arrive in Natal
Telegraph lines link Cape Town and Simon's Town
Pretoria is declared the capital of the Transvaal Republic
The first cycle arrives at the Cape

1861

The Commercial Exchange becomes the Cape Town Chamber of Commerce
Canon Ogilvie becomes principal of Bishops
Football is played at Bishops

1862

Sir Philip Wodehouse is governor of the Cape Colony
The New Somerset Hospital is opened
Herbert Baker is born
First recorded football match in the colony takes place
The Civil Service Club opens
Steam incubators for eggs are introduced

1863

The railway line to Wellington is completed
A telegraph link with Grahamstown becomes functional

1864

The privately financed Cape Town to Wynberg railway line is operational
The noon gun is now fired electrically from the Observatory
Patent mincing machines are available to local butchers

1865

Abraham Lincoln is assassinated
Eighteen ships are wrecked in Table Bay
The Robben Island lighthouse is functional

1866

Cigarettes, a new invention, go on sale
Diamonds are discovered at Hopetown
End of the Basotho War

1867

Marist Brothers' School in Cape Town is founded
Kanaladorp or District Twelve is redesignated District Six by municipal act

1869

The Suez Canal is opened

1870

The harbour complex is opened
Sir Henry Barkly becomes governor of the Cape Colony
Diamonds are discovered at Du Toit's Pan
Gold is discovered in the Eastern Transvaal
Arc lighting is demonstrated in Cape Town

1871

Sophy Gray dies
St Cyprian's is founded
The South African Fine Arts Association is established

1872

Responsible government is established at the Cape
John Molteno becomes the colony's first prime minister
Bishop Robert Gray dies
A fountain is erected at the Good Hope Lodge to mark the centenary of Freemasonry in Cape Town

1873

Griqualand West becomes a crown colony
The University of the Cape of Good Hope is founded
Cape football gets its first written rules
The government assumes responsibility for telegraph lines
Fixed educational requirements are introduced for scholars up to Standard Four

1875

The foundation stone is laid for the new Houses of Parliament
Die Genootskap van Regte Afrikaners is founded in Paarl
A boom begins, lasting until 1882

1876

The telephone is invented
Die Afrikaanse Patriot newspaper is published in the Dutch patois to become known as Afrikaans
The Cape Times commences publication

1877

Britain annexes the Transvaal
Sir Henry Bartle Frere becomes governor of the Cape
Anthony Trollope visits the Cape
Lantern commences publication

1878

Frere dismisses Molteno's ministry

Sir Gordon Sprigg becomes prime minister of the Cape Colony
The ninth and last Frontier War ends
The first German settlers are sent to the Cape Flats
The telephone comes to South Africa
The telegraph link with Natal becomes functional

1879

Battles are fought at Isandlwana and Rorke's Drift
Griqualand West is annexed to the Cape Colony
Cetshwayo is incarcerated at the Castle and then at Oude Molen
The first cablegram reaches Cape Town via Aden – it is a message of congratulations and good wishes from Queen Victoria
The Society for the Prevention of Cruelty to Animals is formed

1880

The Afrikaner Bond is formed
Kruger and Joubert visit Cape Town to discuss independence for the South African Republic; they stay at the White House in Strand Street and are lionised by Cape Afrikaners
The Basotho War of the Gun is waged until 1881
The Empress Eugènie calls at Cape Town on her way to Natal to visit the site of the Prince Imperial's death
Cape Town boasts 11 private telephones
Boers meet at Paardekraal to unite in resisting British annexation
A glass-making company is opened at Woodstock

1881

The Battle of Majuba ends the first Anglo-Boer War
Diplomatic relations with the South African Republic are established at the Pretoria Convention which recognises Transvaal independence subject to British suzerainty
Sir Hercules Robinson becomes governor of the Cape Colony
Scanlen succeeds Sprigg as prime minister
Rhodes is elected MP for Barkly West
Valkenburg farm is purchased by the government with money left by The Hon. W. Porter for the establishment of reformatory facilities
Donald Currie is knighted for his services carrying news and dispatches, etc., for the British army

1882

Dutch, as well as English, is now permitted for debates and discussion in the Legislative Council and the House of Assembly
A smallpox epidemic sweeps through the Cape
A depression that is to last until 1889 sets in
Port Elizabeth gets the colony's first telephone exchange

1883

A Boer deputation travels to England with the purpose of amending the convention re suzerainty
The Standard Bank building in Adderley Street opens
A further party of Germans immigrates to the Cape Flats
Arc lights are installed at the Docks and railway station
The Western Province Rugby Football Union is founded
The Military wins a case against the Town Council and the beachfront butchers' Shambles (dating back to 1820) is declared a public nuisance

1884

The Cape Town telephone exchange is established
The Imperial authorities offer to sell the Castle to the colonial government for £83 340. The offer is declined by Sir Thomas Upington's ministry
Jane Waterston, believed to be South Africa's first woman doctor, opens a practice in Cape Town

1885

Bechuanaland becomes a protectorate
Stellaland becomes a Boer republic
The new Parliament buildings and the Volunteer Drill Hall are opened in Cape Town
Golf is introduced at the Cape by army officers
Horse racing is transferred from Green Point to Kenilworth
King Solomon's Mines by Henry Rider Haggard is published and is an overnight success

1886

The Witwatersrand goldfields are declared
Johannesburg is founded
Malay 'cemetery riots' split the Cape community
The South African Republic is the single biggest gold producer in the world and the gold law gives the government control of the goldfields

The first 'Coon Carnival' takes to the streets just after New Year
An Afrikaner Bond objection saves the Castle from demolition
The Western Province Coloured Rugby Union is formed
The International Rugby Board is formed
Rondebosch becomes a municipality
Coca Cola goes on sale

1887
Queen Victoria's Golden Jubilee is celebrated

1888
De Beers Consolidated Mines Limited is established
Dog tax is introduced

1889
Rhodes' B.S.A.C. is granted a charter for full control of Matabeleland and Mashonaland
A western undersea telegraph cable linking the Cape with Britain is installed
The Cape Town Stock and Share Exchange opens
A boom begins and will last until 1902
Langham Dale is knighted for his services to education
The S.A. Rugby Football Board is founded in Kimberley
The first interprovincial football tournament is held
A seismograph is installed at the Observatory

1890
Rhodes, with support from Bond members, is elected prime minister of the Cape Colony
The railway line reaches Simon's Town
Claremont becomes a municipality
The statue of Queen Victoria is unveiled in front of the Houses of Parliament
Newlands football ground is opened

1891
De Beers Consolidated achieves a monopoly of diamond mining
The Chamber of Commerce is incorporated by an Act of Parliament
The first tour of South Africa by a British football team is a resounding success
A new fire station on the site of the old Theatre Royal in Burg Street is opened
'The fountain' drinking trough is erected in Rondebosch

1892
The Coloured People's Association is formed
The new Cape Town railway station building is officially opened

Railway time for the Cape Colony is changed to that of meridian 22.5 east of Greenwich
Rail links the Cape and Johannesburg and the first train completes the trip in 2 days, 14 hours and 43 minutes
The first Cape Town-bound train leaves the Sea Point terminus in September; the one-way fare is ninepence
The South African Football Association is founded
The first Currie Cup football tournament takes place
The old Company's Garden and the Avenue are made over by the government to the municipality
The Commercial Exchange is demolished to make way for a new post office
The Association of Chambers of Commerce of South Africa is formed
Herbert Baker arrives in Cape Town on the *Norham*
The building that formerly housed the Cape House of Assembly is burnt down and rebuilt as the Good Hope Hall, opened in 1893

1893
Rhodes resigns the premiership over the Logan scandal and is reinstated the following day
War breaks out between the Chartered Company and the Matabele
The *Scot* creates a record of 14 days for the run from England to Cape Town
Herbert Baker starts to restore Groote Schuur

1894
Rail links Pretoria and Delagoa Bay
The W.P.R.F.U. purchases Newlands
Rustenburg School is founded
Olive Schreiner marries Samuel Cron Cronwright and he changes his name to Cronwright-Schreiner

1895
Joseph Chamberlain is British Colonial Secretary
Monopolies control the mines, the most important being Rhodes' Consolidated Goldfields
The Jameson Raid takes place between December 1895 and January 1896
Sir Hercules Robinson who was made a baronet in 1891 returns as governor of the Cape Colony and high commissioner for South Africa
The first municipal electricity supply (from

the Graaff Electric Light Station) is turned on with some streets illuminated
The first municipal electricity is used to light a banquet – held in honour of Sir Hercules Robinson at the Good Hope Hall
Rhodes buys Kirstenbosch for the nation
Kelvin Grove is remodelled as a country club by Baker
The Hotel Metropole opens in Long Street

1896
Rhodes resigns the premiership over the Jameson Raid
Rhodes and Jameson go to Britain for the inquiry
Sir Hercules Robinson is made Lord Rosmead
An epidemic wins this year the title 'The Year of the Rinderpest'
The first electric tramway from Adderley Street to Mowbray Hill is opened
Playing against a second British touring team, the South African football team wears green jerseys for the first time
The South African Coloured Rugby Football Board is founded
The Imperialist English South Africa League is founded
Groote Schuur is gutted by fire
Herbert Baker survives typhoid and commences rebuilding Groote Schuur
Mark Twain (alias Samuel Langhorne Clemens) visits Cape Town

1897
Queen Victoria's Diamond Jubilee is celebrated
Sir Alfred Milner succeeds Lord Rosmead as governor of the Cape Colony
The South African Republic and the Orange Free State enter a political alliance
Rondebosch Boys' High School is founded
The first car arrives, a Benz running on benzine
The new General Post Office on the site of the old Commercial Exchange is used for the first time

1898
The name Rhodesia is recognised by Britain
Rhodes and Kipling meet
The Grahamstown Exhibition opens and runs until 1899
A wild animal dealer offers tame zebra for £100 a head, young lions at £45 each and young hippo for £250 each.

1899
The Bloemfontein Conference: Cape Prime

Minister W. P. Schreiner and O.F.S. President Steyn arrange a fruitless meeting between Milner and Kruger
In May Milner telegraphs the British Government saying subjects are treated as helots on the Rand
The second Anglo-Boer War is declared in October
30 October is dubbed Mournful Monday and another low period for British interests in December is named Black Week
Sophia Jamison dies
A smallpox hospital is established at Rentzkie's Farm
Rhodes' gift, a statue of Jan van Riebeeck, is unveiled at the foot of Adderley Street
Rhodes introduces the European starling to the Cape

1900
Roberts and Kitchener arrive in January
The sieges of Mafeking (217 days), Ladysmith (120 days) and Kimberley (124 days) are relieved
Sprigg is elected prime minister for a second time in a reshuffle occasioned by the Cape Rebel issue
The foundation stone for the new City Hall on Darling Street is laid

1901
Queen Victoria dies
The buttress stone of the new St George's Cathedral is laid by the Duke of Cornwall and York
Nobel prizes are introduced
The hearing aid is invented

1902
The Anglo-Boer War ends; a peace treaty is signed at Vereeniging
Rhodes dies
Milner becomes the governor of the Transvaal and Orange Free State
The African Political Organisation is formed
Edison invents the battery

1903
The Wright brothers make aviation history
Rhodes Scholarships are offered

1904
President Kruger dies
Chinese labourers arrive to work on the mines

1905
The Cullinan Diamond is found
Einstein propounds his theory of relativity
Aspirins come on to the market.

BIBLIOGRAPHY

Abbreviation:
Studies — Studies in the History of Cape Town,
        6 vols., edited by Saunders, C. and
        others, University of Cape Town,
        1979-1988

ABRAHAMS, G., 'The archeological potential of
        central Cape Town', (University of Cape
        Town, unpublished honours thesis, 1984).
ABRAHAMS, I., *The Birth of a Community. The
        History of Western Province Jewry from the
        earliest times to the end of the South African
        War, 1902*, (Cape Town Hebrew
        Congregation, 1955).
ANDERSSON, C.J., *Notes of Travel in South
        Africa*, (London, Hurst & Blackett, 1875).
ANON., 'Sir Bartle Frere's reception and
        banquet', Cape of Good Hope, 1879 —
        pamphlet held by the South African Library.

BAKER, H., 'The origin of old Cape
        architecture', a chapter in *Old Colonial
        Houses of the Cape of Good Hope* illustrated
        and described by Alys Fane Trotter,
        (London, B.T. Batsford, 1900); *Cecil Rhodes,
        by his architect Herbert Baker*, (London,
        Oxford University Press, 1938); *Architecture
        and Personalities*, (London, Country Life,
        1944).

BARNETT-CLARKE, H.P., *The life and times of
        Thomas Fothergill Lightfoot B.D.*, (Cape
        Town, Darter Bros. & Co., 1908).
BEAN, L., and VAN HEYNINGEN, E. (eds.), *The
        Letters of Elizabeth Jane Waterston 1866-1905*,
        (Cape Town, The Van Riebeeck Society, 1983).
BENYON, J., *Proconsul and Paramountcy in
        South Africa*, (Pietermaritzburg, University
        of Natal Press, 1986).
BICKFORD-SMITH, V., 'Black labour at the
        docks at the beginning of the twentieth
        century', *Studies 2* (1980), 75-125;
        'Dangerous Cape Town: middle-class
        attitudes to poverty in Cape Town in the
        late nineteenth century', *Studies 3* (1981),
        29-65; 'Keeping your own council: the
        struggle between householders and
        merchants for control of the Cape Town
        Municipal Council in the last two decades
        of the nineteenth century', *Studies 5* (1983),
        189-207; 'Commerce, class and ethnicity in
        Cape Town, 1875-1902', unpublished PhD
        thesis submitted to the University of
        Cambridge, 1988.
BOLSMANN, E.H., *The Mount Nelson*, (Pretoria,
        HAUM, 1978).
BOTHA, C.G., *The Civil Service Club 1858-1938*,
        (Cape Town, privately published, 1939).
BRADLOW, F., and CAIRNS, M., *The Early Cape
        Muslims*, (Cape Town, Balkema, 1967).
BROCK, B.B., B.G., and WILLIS, H.C., *Historical
        Simon's Town*, (Cape Town, Balkema for the
        Simon's Town Historical Society, 1976).
BUNDY, C., 'Vagabond Hollanders and runaway
        Englishmen: white poverty in the Cape
        before poor whiteism', in *Putting a plough to
        ground: Accumulation and dispossession in
        rural South Africa 1850-1930*, edited by
        Beinart, W., Delius, P., and Trapido, S.,
        (Johannesburg, Ravan Press, 1986).
BURMAN, J., *Safe to the Sea*, (Cape Town,
        Human & Rousseau, 1962); *Great
        Shipwrecks off the coast of Southern Africa*,
        (Cape Town, Struik, 1967); *The Cape of
        Good Intent*, (Cape Town, Human &
        Rousseau, 1969); *The False Bay Story*, (Cape
        Town, Human & Rousseau, 1977); *Early
        Railways of the Cape*, (Cape Town, Human &
        Rousseau, 1984); *The Table Mountain Book*,
        (Cape Town, Human & Rousseau, 1991).
BURROWS, E.H., *A History of Medicine in South
        Africa*, (Cape Town, Balkema for the
        Medical Association of South Africa, 1958).
BURTON, A.R.E., *The Cape Colony Today*, (Cape
        Town, printed by Townsend, Taylor &
        Snashall, 1907).

CAMERON, T. (general ed.), *An Illustrated
        History of South Africa*, (Johannesburg,
        Jonathan Ball, 1986).
CAPE ARGUS
CAPE TIMES
CHISHOLM, L., 'The pedagogy of Porter: the
        origins of the reformatory in the Cape
        Colony 1882-1910', in *Journal of African
        History*, vol. 27, no. 3 (1986), 481-495.
CHURCHILL, LADY S.A. SPENCER-, *South
        African Memories*, (London, Edward Arnold,
        1909).
CHURCHILL, W., *London to Ladysmith via
        Pretoria*, (London, Longmans, Green, 1900).
COATES, P.R., *Track and Trackless: omnibuses
        and trams in the Western Cape*, (Cape Town,
        Struik, 1976).
COOPER, C.A., *By Castle to the Cape*, (London,
        printed by T. & A. Constable, 1895).
CRONWRIGHT-SCHREINER, S., *The Life of Olive
        Schreiner*, (London, Fisher Unwin, 1924).
CURTIS, L., *With Milner in South Africa*,
        (London, Basil Blackwell, 1951).

DAVENPORT, T.R.H., *The Afrikaner Bond
        1880-1911*, (Cape Town, Oxford University
        Press, 1966); *South Africa, a modern history*,
        2nd edition, (Johannesburg, Macmillan,
        1978); 'Olive Schreiner and politics', an
        unpublished lecture delivered at the
        Grahamstown Festival of the Arts, 1983.
DAVIDS, A., *The Mosques of Bo-Kaap: a social
        history of Islam at the Cape*, (Athlone, Cape,
        S.A. Institute of Arabic and Islamic
        Research, 1980); 'Politics and the Muslims
        of Cape Town: a historical survey', *Studies 4*
        (1981), 174-220; 'The revolt of the Malays:
        a study of the reaction of the Cape Muslims
        to the smallpox epidemics of nineteenth
        century Cape Town', *Studies 5* (1983), 46-78;
        The History of the Tana Baru, (Cape Town,
        Committee for the Preservation of the Tana
        Baru, 1985).
DE BEER, M., *The Lion Mountain*, (Cape Town,
        Balkema, 1987).
DE JONG, F., *Cape Town and its Surroundings,
        comprising an up-to-date description of the
        city and its business progress*, (Cape Town,
        J.W. Blinkhorn & Co., 1894; facsimile Cape
        Town, The South African Library, 1983).
DE KOCK, V., *The Fun They Had*, (Cape Town,
        Timmins, 1955).
DE VILLIERS, A., *Vrouegalery*, (Cape Town,
        Nasionale Boekhandel, 1962).
DE VILLIERS, S., *A Tale of Three Cities*, (Cape
        Town, Murray & Roberts, 1985).

*The ancient gateway to the
Castle of Good Hope.*

DICTIONARY OF SOUTH AFRICAN BIOGRAPHY, vol. 1, (Johannesburg, Nasionale Boekhandel, 1968); vol. 2, (Cape Town, Tafelberg, 1972); vol. 3, (Cape Town, Tafelberg, 1977); vol. 4, (Durban, Butterworth, 1981).

DIFFORD, I.D., *The History of South African Rugby Football*, (Wynberg, Cape, The Speciality Press, 1933).

DOBSON, P., *Rugby in South Africa, a history 1861-1988*, (Cape Town, The South African Rugby Board, 1989); *Bishops Rugby, a history*, (Cape Town, Don Nelson, 1990).

DOYLE, A. CONAN, *The Great Boer War*, (Cape Town, Struik, 1976).

DUCKITT, H. (selected by Kuttel, M.), *Hildagonda Duckitt's Book of Recipes*, (Cape Town, Balkema, 1966); *Hilda's Diary of a Cape Housekeeper*, (first published London, Chapman & Hall, 1902; facsimile Cape Town, Macmillan, 1978).

DU PLESSIS, I.D., and LUCKHOFF, C.A., *The Malay Quarter and its people*, (Cape Town, Balkema, 1953).

DURBACH, R., *Kipling's South Africa*, (Cape Town, Chameleon Press, 1988).

DU VAL, C., *With a Show through Southern Africa*, (London, Tinsley Bros., 1882).

EASTON, J., *Four Questions of the day*, (Cape Town, Juta, 1888).

EDWARDS, D., *Cape Town Guide*, (Cape Town, Edwards, 1894).

ELDRIDGE, R. (ed.), *Tennis: the South African Story*, (Johannesburg, Owen Williams, 1980).

ELLIOTT, A., *Architectural Beauty of the old Cape*, (Cape Town, Balkema, 1969).

ENGELBRECHT, C.L., *Money in South Africa*, (Cape Town, Tafelberg, 1987).

ERLMAN, V., 'A feeling of prejudice: Orpheus McAdoo and the Virginia Jubilee Singers in South Africa', *Journal of Southern African Studies*, vol. 14, no. 3, (1988), 331-50.

EYRE, F.G., *Diary 1879-1881*, (Cape Town, mss collection of the South African Library).

FORBES, G. (comp.), *David Gill, man and astronomer*, (London, Murray, 1916).

FRANSEN, H., and COOK, M., *The Old Houses of the Cape*, (Cape Town, Balkema, 1965).

FROUDE, J.A., *Short Studies on Great Subjects*, third series, (London, Longmans, Green, 1877).

GENERAL DIRECTORY AND GUIDE BOOK, (Cape Town, Saul Solomon and Co., 1882).

GEYSER, O., *Die Ou Hooggeregsgebou*, (Cape Town, Tafelberg, 1958).

GILL, F., *The Story of Stuttafords*, (Cape Town, The Firm, 1958); *Cape Trams, from horse to diesel*, (Cape Town, Fraser Gill and Associates, 1961).

GREIG, D., *Herbert Baker in South Africa*, (Cape Town, Purnell, 1970); *A Guide to Architecture in South Africa*, (Cape Town, Timmins, 1971).

GRUT, M., *The History of Ballet in South Africa*, (Cape Town, Human & Rousseau, 1981).

GUNNERS OF THE CAPE, (Cape Town, Cape Field Artillery Regimental History Committee, 1965).

HAGGARD, SIR H. RIDER, and HIGGINS, D.S. (ed.), *The Private Diaries of Sir Henry Rider Haggard*, (London, Cassell, 1980).

HANDBOOK OF CAPE TOWN AND SUBURBS, (Cape Town, *Cape Times*, 1905).

HANDY GUIDE TO CAPE TOWN AND SUBURBS, (Carmichael and Herman, Cape Town, 1902).

HARRIES, P., 'Mozbiekers: the immigration of an African community to the Western Cape 1876-1882', *Studies 1* (1979), 153-164.

HATTERSLEY, A.F., *An Illustrated Social History of South Africa*, (Cape Town, Balkema, 1969).

HEAP, P., *The Story of the Hottentots Holland*, (Somerset West, Cape, P. Heap, 1977).

HENRY, J.H., *The First Hundred Years of the Standard Bank*, (Oxford, Oxford University Press, 1963).

HERRMAN, L., *A History of the Jews in South Africa from the earliest times to 1895*, (London, Gollancz, 1930).

HIDDINGH, J., *Reminiscences of the late Michiel Hiddingh*, (Cape Town, *Cape Times*, 1928).

HINCHLIFF, P., *The Anglican Church in South Africa*, (London, Darton, Longman & Todd, 1963).

HISTORY OF THE BOARD OF GUARDIANS, 1859-1959, (Cape Town, Cape Jewish Board of Guardians, 1963).

HOBART HOUGHTON, D., and DAGUT, J., *Source Material on the South African Economy 1860-1970*, vol. 1 1860-1899, (Cape Town, Oxford University Press, 1972).

HODGKISS, D., *Woodstock Glass*, (Kalk Bay, Cape, Grafix, 1971).

HOLLAND, D.F., *Steam Locomotives of the S.A.R.*, vol. I 1859-1910, (Newton Abbott, Devon, David & Charles, 1971-72).

HOPKINS, H.C., *Die Moeder van ons Almal, geskiedenis van die gemeente Kaapstad, 1665-1965*, (Cape Town, N.G. Kerk Uitgewers en Boekhandel, 1965).

ILLUSTRATED GUIDE TO CAPE TOWN, (Cape Town, *Cape Argus*, 1890).

IMMELMAN, R.F.M., *Men of Good Hope, The Romantic Story of the Cape Town Chamber of Commerce 1804-1954*, (Cape Town, Chamber of Commerce, 1955).

JAFF, F., *They Came to South Africa*, (Cape Town, Timmins, 1963).

JAFFEE, J., *They Raced to Win 1797-1979: a history of racing in South Africa*, (Cape Town, Struik, 1980).

JOHNSTON, R.H., *Early Motoring in South Africa*, (Cape Town, Struik, 1975).

JORDAAN, B., *Splintered Crucifix*, (Cape Town, Struik, 1969).

JOURDAAN P., *Cecil Rhodes, his private life by his private secretary*, (Cape Town, Maskew Miller, 1910).

KEEN, A.F., 'The early history of Woodstock', unpublished manuscript, South African Library, 1977.

KILPIN, R., *The Old Cape House*, (Cape Town, Maskew Miller, 1918).

KNOX-JOHNSTON, R., *The Cape of Good Hope, a maritime history*, (London, Hodder & Stoughton, 1989).

KUTTEL, M., *Quadrilles and Konfyt: the life and journal of Hildagonda Duckitt*, (Cape Town, Maskew Miller, 1954).

LAIDLER, P.W., *Annals of the Cape Stage*, (Cape Town, William Bryce, 1926); *A Tavern of the Ocean*, (Cape Town, Maskew Miller, 1926); *The Growth and Government of Cape Town*, (Cape Town, Unievolkspers, 1939); and Gelfand, M., *South Africa, its medical history, 1652-1898*, (Cape Town, Struik, 1971).

LAING, R.D. (ed.), *The Royal Observatory of the Cape of Good Hope, 1820-1970*, (Cape Town, The Royal Observatory, 1970).

LAMOND, M.F., 'A consideration of the Cape Town elite at the end of the last century', unpublished honours thesis, University of Cape Town, 1985.

LANTERN

LEE, E., *To the Bitter End, a photographic history of the Boer War 1899-1902*, (Harmondsworth, Penguin, 1986).

LEIGHTON, S., and LEWIN ROBINSON, A.M. (ed.), *Notes on a Visit to South Africa*, (Cape Town, Balkema for The Friends of the South African Library, 1975).

LESLIE, A., *Jennie: the life of Lady Randolph Churchill*, (London, Hutchinson, 1969).

LEWSEN, P., 'The Cape liberal tradition: myth or reality?', *Institute of Commonwealth Studies collected seminar papers 1* (Oct 1969–April 1970), 72-88.

LINNEGAR, J., *SACS 150 Years: a history of the South African College School*, (Cape Town, SACS Committee, 1979).

LISTER, G., *Reminiscences of Georgina Lister*, (Johannesburg, Africana Museum, 1960).

LITTLE, A., *History of the City Club, Cape Town 1878-1938*, (Cape Town, privately published, 1938).

LITTLE, J.S., *South Africa: a sketchbook of men, manners and facts*, (London, Sonnenschein, 1884).

LOMBAARD, A., 'The smallpox epidemic of 1882 in Cape Town with some reference to the neighbouring suburbs', unpublished honours thesis, University of Cape Town, 1981.

LOOTS, I., and VERMAAK, M., *Pioneers of professional nursing in South Africa*, (Bloemfontein, De Villiers Uitgewery, 1975).

LOUW, J.H., *In the Shadow of Table Mountain, a history of the U.C.T. Medical School*, (Cape Town, Struik, 1969).

LOWNDES, E.E.K., *Every-Day Life in South Africa*, (London, S.W. Partridge & Co., 1900).

LUCKHOFF, C.A., *Table Mountain*, (Cape Town, Balkema, 1951).

MACKENZIE, B., *Salt River Doctor*, (Cape Town, Faircape Books, 1981).

MACSYMON, R.M., *Fairbridge Arderne & Lawton*, (Cape Town, Juta, 1990).

MARAIS, D., and RIEKERT, D., *Constitutional Development of South Africa*, (Johannesburg, Macmillan, 1981).

MARSHALL, J., and WILLOX, I., *The Victorian House*, (London, Sidgwick & Jackson, in association with the Channel Four Television Company, 1986).

MASSON, M., *Birds of Passage*, (London, Allen & Unwin, 1950).

MCMAGH, K., *A Dinner of Herbs*, (Cape Town, Purnell, 1968).

MELLISH, J.M., *A Basic History of Nursing*, (Durban, Butterworth, 1984).

MILNER, REV. J., and BRIERLY, O.W., *The Cruise of H.M.S. Galatea 1867-1868*, (London, W.H. Allen, 1869).

MILNER, VISCOUNTESS, *My Picture Gallery*, (London, John Murray, 1951).

MOLL, G., *Table Mountain, a natural wonder*, (Cape Town, The Wildlife Society of South Africa, 1987).

MURRAY, J. (ed.), *In Mid-Victorian Cape Town: Letters from Miss Rutherfoord*, (Cape Town, Balkema, 1953).

MURRAY, M., *Ships and South Africa*, (London, Oxford University Press, 1933); *Union Castle Chronicle*, (London, Longmans, Green, 1953); *Under Lion's Head*, (Cape Town, Balkema, 1964).

NOBLE J., *Descriptive handbook of the Cape Colony: its composition and resources*, (Cape Town, Juta, 1875).

O'BRIEN, T.H., *Milner*, (London, Constable, 1979).

ORPEN, N., *The Cape Town Highlanders 1885-1970*, (Cape Town, Cape Town Highlanders History Committee, 1970).

PAMA, C., *Vintage Cape Town*, (Cape Town, Tafelberg, 1973); *Wagon Road to Wynberg and Bowler's Cape Town*, (Cape Town, Tafelberg, 1977).

PARKER, A.C., *The Springboks 1891-1970*, (London, Cassell, 1970).

PARKER, G.A., *South African Sports*, (London, Low Marston, 1897).

PICARD, H.J., *Gentlemen's Walk*, (Cape Town, Struik, 1968); *Grand Parade*, (Cape Town, Struik, 1969); *Lords of Stalplein*, (Pretoria, HAUM, 1974); *Cape Epic*, (Howick, Natal, Khenty Press, 1977).

PICTON-SEYMOUR, D., *Victorian Buildings in South Africa*, (Cape Town, Balkema, 1977); *Historical Buildings in South Africa*, (Cape Town, Struikhof, 1989).

RABE, L., *Bit en Werk, Bete und Arbeite 1883-1983*, (Philippi, Cape, Eeufeeskomitee, 1983).

RANDALL, P., *Little England on the Veld: the English private school system in South Africa*, (Johannesburg, Ravan Press, 1982).

RENNIE, J., *The Buildings of Central Cape Town*, 2 vols., (Cape Town, Cape Provincial Institute of Architects, 1978).

RITCHIE, W., *The History of the South African College 1829-1918*, (Cape Town, Maskew Miller, 1918).

ROBERTS, B., *Cecil Rhodes: Flawed Colossus*, (London, Hamish Hamilton, 1987); *Those bloody women*, (London, John Murray, 1991).

ROSE INNES, J., *Sir James Rose Innes 1855-1942*, (Cape Town, Oxford University Press, 1949).

ROSENTHAL, E., *Other Men's Millions*, (Cape Town, Timmins, 1953); *The Story of Table Mountain*, (Cape Town, W.J. Flesch, 1956); *160 Years of Cape Printing*, (Cape Town, Association of Printing House Craftsmen and the Cape Chamber of Printing, 1960); *Tankards and Tradition*, (Cape Town, Timmins, 1961); *On 'Change through the years, a history of share dealing in South Africa*, (Cape Town, Flesch Financial Publications for the Johannesburg Stock Exchange, 1968); *The Best of Eric Rosenthal*, (Cape Town, Timmins, 1975); *Fish Horns and Hansom Cabs*, (Cape Town, A.D. Donker, 1977); *Milnerton*, (published by the Municipality, 1980).

ROTBERG, R.I., *The Founder*, (Johannesburg, Southern Books, 1988).

ROTHMANN, M.E. ('M.E.R.'), 'Vanslewe se universiteitsmeisies', in two parts, *Huisgenoot*, 12 and 19 January 1934; *My Beskeie Deel*, (Cape Town, Tafelberg, 1972); 'Die eerste universiteitsmeisies', from *U.C.T. at 150 — reflections*, edited by Lennox-Short, A., and Welsh, D., (Cape Town, David Philip, 1975).

RYAN, M., 'Anders Ohlsson brewer and politician 1881-1894', unpublished honours thesis, University of Cape Town, 1976.

SAUNDERS, C., 'The creation of Ndabeni: urban segregation and African resistance in Cape Town', *Studies 1* (1979), 165-193; 'Africans in Cape Town in the nineteenth century: an outline', *Studies 2* (1980), 15-41.

SAUNDERS, C., and others (eds.), *Studies in the History of Cape Town*, 6 vols., (Cape Town, University of Cape Town, 1979-1988).

SCHOFIELD, J., *The Malays of Cape Town*, (Cape Town, Africana Connoisseurs Press, 1963).

SCHREINER, O., *Thoughts on South Africa*, (Johannesburg, Africana Book Society, 1976).

SEARLL, C., *A History of the Development of Nursing in South Africa 1652-1960*, (Pretoria, South African Nursing Association, 1980).

SHAIN, M., *Jewry and Cape Society*, (Cape Town, Historical Publications Society, 1983).

SHELL, R., 'Rites and rebellion: Islamic conversion at the Cape, 1808 to 1915', *Studies 5* (1983), 1-45.

SIMONS, P.B., *Cape Dutch Houses, a concise guide*, (Cape Town, Struik, 1987).

SOLOMON, W.E.G., *Saul Solomon, the member for Cape Town*, (Cape Town, Oxford University Press, 1948).

SOUTH AFRICAN COLLEGE FANCY FAIR MEMORIAL PAPER

SOUTH AFRICAN COLLEGE FANCY FAIR PAPER

SOUTH AFRICAN COLLEGE MAGAZINE

SOUTH AFRICAN COLLEGE UNION ANNUAL

SOUTH AFRICAN MEDICAL JOURNAL, 18 August 1962, special edition to mark the centenary of the New Somerset Hospital.

STEEVENS, G.W., and BLACKBURN, V. (ed.), *From Cape Town to Ladysmith*, (Edinburgh, Blackwood, 1900).

STORRAR, P., *A Colossus of Roads: Thomas Bain*, (Cape Town, Murray and Roberts/Concor, 1984).

SUMMERS, R.F., *A History of the South African Museum 1825-1975*, (Cape Town, Balkema, 1975).

THOMAS, E.N., *Stray Hours: some children of our city*, (Cape Town, *Cape Times, 1898*).

THOMSON, D.H., *Not for School but for Life: the story of St Cyprian's*, (Cape Town, St Cyprian's Union, 1971).

TRAPIDO, S., 'The friends of the natives: merchants, peasants and the political and ideological structure of liberalism in the Cape 1854-1910', in *Economy and Society in Pre-industrial South Africa*, edited by Marks, S., and Atmore, A., (London, Longman, 1980), 247-274.

TREDGOLD, A., *Bay Between the Mountains*, (Cape Town, Human & Rousseau, 1985); *The Ardernes and their Garden*, (Cape Town, Arderne Book Trust, 1990).

TROLLOPE, A., and DAVIDSON, J.H. (ed.), *South Africa*, (Cape Town, Balkema, 1973).

UNGER, F.W., *With "Bobs" and Kruger*, (Cape Town, Struik, 1977).

VAN HEYNINGEN, C., 'Refugees and relief in Cape Town, 1899-1902', *Studies 3* (1980), 64-113; 'Prostitution and the Contagious Diseases Acts: the social evil in the Cape Colony 1868-1902', *Studies 5* (1984), 80-124.

VAN SITTERT, L., 'Gebrei in die ambag — farmers, fish and fishermen in the Hout Bay Valley 1880-1956', unpublished honours thesis, University of Cape Town, 1985.

VAUGHAN, I., *The diary of Iris Vaughan*, (Cape Town, Timmins, 1969).

WALKER, E.A., *The South African College and the University of Cape Town*, (Cape Town, University of Cape Town, 1929).

WALLACE, E., *Unofficial despatches of the Anglo-Boer War*, (Cape Town, Struik, 1975).

WALTON, J., *Homesteads and Villages of South Africa*, (Pretoria, Van Schaik, 1959); *The Josephine Mill and its Owners — the story of milling and brewing at the Cape of Good Hope*, (Cape Town, Historical Society of Cape Town, 1978).

WARNER, B.C., *Astronomers at the Royal Observatory*, (Cape Town, Balkema, 1979).

WEST, S.E.L., and LUKER, W.J., *A Century at Newlands, 1864-1964*, (Cape Town, Western Province Cricket Club, 1965).

WESTERN, J., *Outcast Cape Town*, (Cape Town, Human & Rousseau, 1981).

WHEATCROFT, G., *The Randlords*, (Johannesburg, Jonathan Ball, 1986).

WITTON, G.R., *Scapegoats of the Empire, the true story of Breaker Morant's Bushveldt Carbineers*, (London, Angus and Robertson, 1982).

WORSFOLD, W.B., *Lord Milner's Work in South Africa*, (London, John Murray, 1906).

The alleys of District Six were the only playground many young Capetonians knew.

INDEX

Note: The index is selective, concentrating on people, places and things in Cape Town. Page numbers in *italics* denote references in captions to illustrations.

A sentry guarded the Stal Plein entrance to Government House.

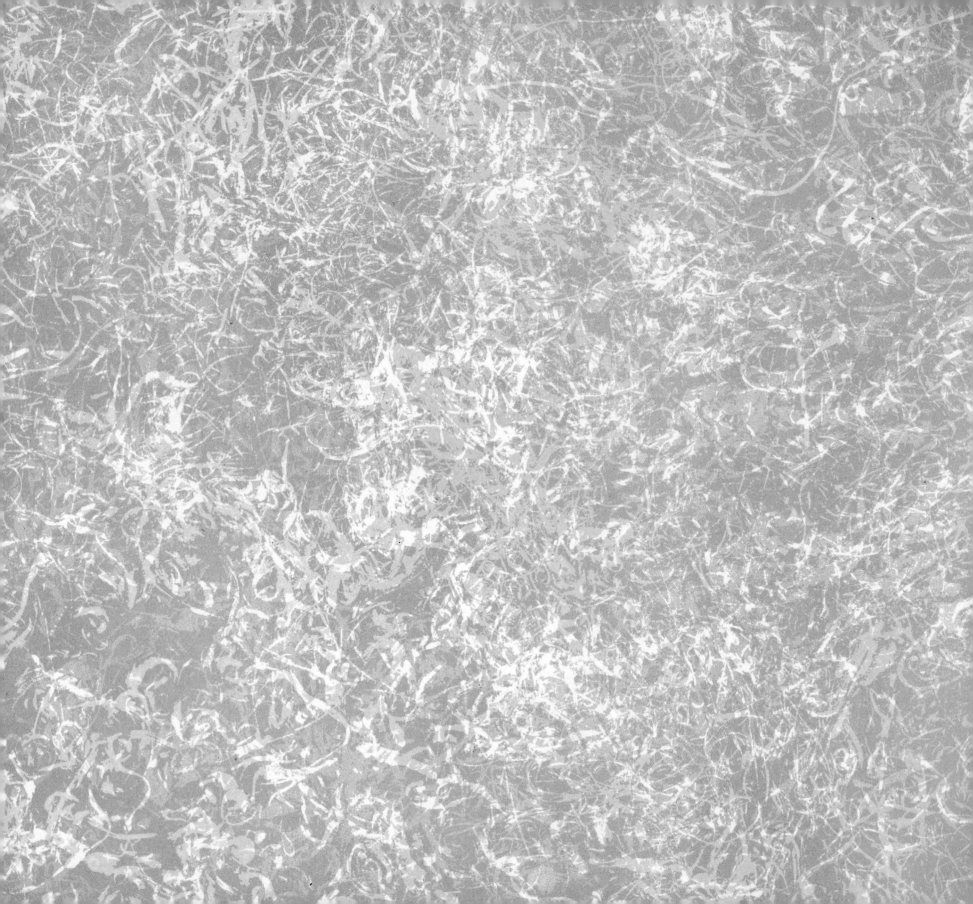